P9-CFU-584

Miss Manners'®
GUIDE TO A
SURPRISINGLY
DIGNIFIED
WEDDING

ALSO BY JUDITH MARTIN

No Vulgar Hotel: The Desire and Pursuit of Venice

Miss Manners' Guide to Excruciatingly Correct Behavior (Freshly Updated)

Star-Spangled Manners

Miss Manners' Guide to Domestic Tranquility

Miss Manners' Basic Training: The Right Thing to Say

Miss Manners' Basic Training: Eating

Miss Manners' Basic Training: Communication

Miss Manners on Weddings

Miss Manners Rescues Civilization

Miss Manners' Guide for the Turn-of-the-Millenium

Common Courtesy

Style and Substance

Gilbert: A Comedy of Manners

Miss Manners' Guide to Rearing Perfect Children

Miss Manners' Guide to Excruciatingly Correct Behavior

Miss Manners'®

GUIDE TO A
SURPRISINGLY
DIGNIFIED
WEDDING

Judith Martin

Jacobina Martin

W. W. NORTON & COMPANY · NEW YORK · LONDON

Copyright © 2010 by Judith Martin and Jacobina Martin
Copyright © 1995 by Judith Martin

Previous edition published under the titles
Miss Manners® on Weddings and *Miss Manners® on Painfully Proper Weddings*

All rights reserved
Printed in the United States of America

For information about permission to reproduce selections
from this book, write to Permissions,
W. W. Norton & Company, Inc.,
500 Fifth Avenue, New York, NY 10110

For information about special discounts for bulk purchases,
please contact W. W. Norton Special Sales at
specialsales@wwnorton.com or 800-233-4830

Manufacturing by RR Donnelley, Harrisonburg, VA
Book design by Dana Sloan
Production manager: Anna Oler

Library of Congress Cataloging-in-Publication Data

Martin, Judith, 1938–
Miss Manners'® guide to a surprisingly dignified wedding / Judith
Martin, Jacobina Martin.
p. cm.
Includes index.
ISBN 978-0-393-06914-3 (hardcover)
1. Wedding etiquette. 2. Weddings—Planning. I. Martin, Jacobina.
II. Title.
BJ2051.M368 2010
395.2'2—dc22

                                                      2009037620

W. W. Norton & Company, Inc.
500 Fifth Avenue, New York, N.Y. 10110
www.wwnorton.com

W. W. Norton & Company Ltd.
Castle House, 75/76 Wells Street, London W1T 3QT

1 2 3 4 5 6 7 8 9 0

For our husbands,

Robert and Ronald

Contents

Preface   XI

CHAPTER ONE   The General Principles   I

CHAPTER TWO   The Engagement   33

CHAPTER THREE   Three Terrible Ideas   66

CHAPTER FOUR   The Plans   99

CHAPTER FIVE   The Guest List   137

CHAPTER SIX   The Paper (and Electronic) Work   170

CHAPTER SEVEN   The Presents   218

CHAPTER EIGHT   The Wedding   251

With Apologies and Best Wishes to the Bride   285

Index   289

Precision marching is less important for the bridal party than maintaining the proper facial expressions: The bridegroom must look awed; the bridesmaids, happy and excited; the father of the bride, proud; and the bride, demure. If the bridegroom feels doubtful, the bridesmaids, sulky, the father, worried, and the bride, blasé, nobody wants to know.

Preface

GENTLE READERS:

The rules in this volume have thrice been personally test-driven. Lofty and idealistic as they may sound, there is proof that they actually work.

The first such demonstration, because it took place fifty years ago, is bound to be dismissed as coming from a time when the entire populace was so inhibited and unadventurous as to be unfailingly polite for lack of any more imaginative ideas. It was my own small but formal wedding, in my parents' house.

Ten years ago, the same standards were observed at my son's wedding. As documented in the original version of this book, *Miss Manners on Weddings*, the greed and exhibitionism encouraged by an engorged bridal industry had already hugely influenced the format of the American wedding. It was then considered eccentric of us to ignore those practices, but the wedding guests still mention how unusually charming they found the result.

By now, however, certain forms of wedding rudeness have become so commonplace that real people actually believe that etiquette requires bragging (known as "personalizing" everything, including religious and civic ceremonies) and extortion (known as "saving guests the trouble" of deciding how to spend their own money).

Therefore, my daughter and co-author felt it necessary to supply a section called Troubleshooting to deal with fending off pressure, often from well-meaning relatives and friends, to do the wrong thing. (She also had a wicked time satirizing the timetables and injunctions she found in what she delicately calls "bridal porn.")

The third instance, her own wedding, took place just a month after the completion of this revision of the book. Once again, we found that behaving well has its rewards:

- If you invite only people who you have reason to know really care about one or more members of the two families (and you may be pleasantly surprised at how many there turn out to be), they will go so far as to find their own paper and stamps to tell you whether they are able to attend.
- If you choose your attendants because they are the relatives and friends to whom you are closest (perhaps finding that they do not strictly separate along gender lines), and treat them as such throughout, they will surround you with warmth—and the women will look and feel good if each is trusted to approve or select her own clothes.
- If you refrain from injecting jokes and courtship stories into the wedding ceremony (by now everybody you know has heard them anyway), you will find that your guests will be able to register the importance of the occasion—and several of the women will confess that they feared for their mascara.
- If you celebrate with a real wedding reception—perhaps a festive tea—instead of a festival featuring nightly dinners in a strange place, you will easily be able to accommodate a variety of food requirements, adjust to last-minute cancellations, and move around to spend time with all your guests—and you will have earned their gratitude for being able to attend your wedding and also have their vacation time and money to spend as they like.

- If you give no thought to what presents you might receive, the guests will do the thinking and you will have the fun of opening surprise packages that may turn out to be even more delightful than you might have hoped, and will be forever linked in your mind with their donors. Plus if you write your thanks immediately, in your first burst of enthusiasm, not only will you have no chore hanging over you, but you will put your generous guests into shock.
- Finally, if the bride wears a wedding dress, instead of a cartoon princess's ball gown or a taxi-dancer's slinky come-on dress cut down to here and slit up to there, and the bridegroom does not attempt to spice up his formal clothes, your children will still be amused by your wedding portrait, but they will not be quite so embarrassed.

Nor will you.

Judith Martin

CHAPTER ONE

The General Principles

WEDDINGS ARE NOW the biggest and only formal festive event (mercifully overlooking the high school prom) in most people's lives. Multiple experiences at being wedding guests and attendants, not to mention multiple experiences of being married, have made everyone an expert on wedding etiquette.

The result is that couples with the innocent intention of having a wedding get plenty of advice. Not so much the optional kind of advice, such as "You should have flags made with your entwined initials to fly over the reception hall," but the threatening kind, stated as "You have to have . . ." and "Everybody expects . . ." and "If you want to do it right . . ."

If only these pronouncements had to do with behaving decently—never mind properly; we will get to that—Miss Manners could retire to her porch swing and confine herself to wishing all bridal couples well (and yes, just a touch more champagne, please). But here are some of the most commonly held ideas that are passed around as "etiquette":

- That the bride is granted dictatorial powers that hardly exist outside of prisons: how everyone is to look, dress, and behave, as well as control over others' money;
- That all the arrangements, including the location, the timing, and the menu, be dictated by the bridal couple's preferences, regardless of the convenience, comfort, or budgets of family and guests;
- That no matter what the ages, financial circumstances, and previous marital histories of the bride and the bridegroom, their parents are responsible for financing the events of the wedding weekend, and that the attendants must finance the other events;
- That it is outrageous for the couple's mothers to seek any input, but that weddings are sufficiently complicated that a professional wedding planner must be hired to provide the guidance and experience mothers offer for free;
- That a wedding consists of a series of events—a showily staged proposal, an engagement party, multiple showers, separate risqué outings for bride and bridegroom two nights before the wedding, organized sports and a dinner party for everyone the day before, an all-night party after the ceremony for anyone still standing, and a brunch the following day;
- That only guests whom the couple know and approve will be invited, regardless of kinship or friendship with their parents;
- That it is essential that the couple choose their own wedding presents, which can include cash and sponsorship of parts of the wedding or honeymoon, and that this is a thoughtful way to save their guests the trouble of being thoughtful;
- That the recipients of this largesse need not acknowledge receipt, let alone register gratitude, for an entire year; and
- That the ceremony is a biographical extravaganza about the couple and their courtship, and need not coincide with the solemnization of the marriage, so it may be repeated in different venues and for different viewers—the most important viewer being the camera.

By no means does Miss Manners mean to suggest that these tenets are held only by bridal couples. Wedding guests not only also hold them (and sprinkle their tales of exploitation with the pathetic admission, "I know it's their day . . ."), but have additional ones of their own:

- That it is the hosts' obligation to supply the means of responding to the invitation, so an absence of self-addressed fill-in cards signifies that the hosts don't much care to know who will attend, and that in any case, the hosts should know that attendance will depend on the mood of each guest at the time of the event;
- That guests need to bring guests of their own, because watching friends get married is not sufficiently entertaining, and certainly no one wants to socialize with the couple's relations and other friends;
- That expectations of formal dress violate our basic freedoms;
- That guests must come to the wedding with their presents under their arms, and that the money they spend on presents must equal the cost of refreshments they consume, but that these guests deserve some return on their own expenses, in the form of welcome baskets, goody bags, party favors, and alcohol;
- That if the couple does not announce what they expect their guests to buy them, they are requiring cash donations; and
- That the principals are too busy to notice whether their guests have said hello or goodbye, or even whether they showed up.

They dare to call these exploitative instructions *etiquette*? A system that squelches etiquette's fundamental obligation of consideration of others with the mantra "Remember, this is all about you"? Behavior that suspends the most basic and timeless forms of politeness in order to violate the solemn nature of the ceremony and cancel the obligations of hosts and guests?

Well, yes—and the bridal industry is successful at passing it off as that. It is almost enough to make Miss Manners regret that she revived the word *etiquette* from comic limbo many decades ago, when the peculiar idea was prevalent that the world would be a pleasanter place if we all behaved naturally.

What sustains Miss Manners is the belief that there are still couples in the world who want to have lovely weddings, and

- who value dignity above self-glorification;
- who do not live beyond their means and do not expect to be reimbursed by their guests;
- who choose their guests through bonds of family and friendship and try to arrange matters so these people will enjoy themselves;
- who take the ceremony seriously as a ritual of the society, not an advertisement for themselves; and
- who therefore confine their merrymaking to the celebration that follows.

When subjected to all the widely disseminated wedding advice to the contrary, such people do not fail to notice how egotistical, greedy, and expensive it sounds. But relatives, friends, colleagues, strangers, and, most emphatically, wedding vendors and their publications assure them that these are the customs and traditions they must follow.

Calling vulgarity *proper* is doublespeak, of which there is an amazing amount in wedding literature. *Tradition* is invoked to whitewash a self-serving action that was considered appalling a decade or two ago, sometimes selectively plucked out of the context of an unrelated situation. One hears often about ersatz "traditions" of a bride's collecting money in various ways during the festivities, but never about the ancient tradition of her mother-in-law's checking the sheets the next morning to see if she had been a virgin. As for those other horrid "customs," they are indeed now unfortunately as customary as other common forms of rudeness.

In Weddingspeak, "gifts" are specific items on a shopping list compiled by the expectant recipients who distribute said list to people whom they expect to do the buying. The most expensive new items are justified by being called "heirlooms." "Candid pictures" are posed from a detailed list of directed actions (*Bride kisses her dog goodbye before entering limousine—oh, you don't have a dog?*) that together constitute the "memories" of the occasion, as opposed to whatever happens to stick in the mind. "Personalizing" the wedding means devising a ceremony that plays like the couple's respective press releases, and stylizing the party in a manner alien to the couple's actual way of life.

IS THAT EXPENSE REALLY NECESSARY?

DEAR MISS MANNERS:

I am 25, mostly financially sound, and trying hard to become more so. I have been seeing my future husband for a year and a half now. He is also mostly financially sound. We very much want to marry, but are unable to make any solid plans because of our lack of means. (At the moment, we are looking at a two- to four-year wait from this point—if we must depend on ourselves alone.)

Eloping is not an option, as our families (and our mutual friends) would never forgive us for the slight, and we would feel terrible to offer insult by leaving them out of our happy day.

My mother is the crux of the problem. It is the bride's family who traditionally pays for the wedding. How do I find out from my mother if she is able to pay, or even contribute? I know she would be willing, but I also know she is not rolling in cash.

I love my beau, and very much want to marry soon, but I also love my mother and do not wish to cause her discomfort by asking her to reveal if she is impoverished. Should we bear with the current lack of means and rely on ourselves to wed later? Or is there a tactful and loving means of determining what my mother wants to (and is able to) do?

GENTLE READER:

Has the price of a marriage license gone up so much that it will take you years to save the money for it? Will the cost of giving those relatives and friends a glass of champagne or punch, a slice of wedding cake, and perhaps a few tea sandwiches put you in the poorhouse?

Otherwise, Miss Manners cannot understand why two financially sound people who want to marry find themselves in the midst of a Victorian tale of poverty and deprivation.

A truly proper, festive, and enjoyable wedding is not the financial and social burden that you seem to suppose. It is not a one-chance excursion into a fantasy of royalty, film stardom, or childhood fantasies that wrecks not only your budget but your emotions. Few people can handle with equanimity being propelled into unfamiliar territory, taxed with designing a ceremony and a large formal party that showcase their personalities and taste, and directed to produce a complicated day that is perfect.

Instead, you could exhibit truly good taste. That would mean following the time-honored civic or religious ritual in which you believe and then having a gala celebration that favors conviviality over pretentiousness and incidentally stays within your means.

However, if what you two really want is to stage a wedding extravaganza that you cannot afford, Miss Manners will wipe away her tears at your tale of woe. Save up for it, and tell your mother that you are doing so. If she wants to help, she will volunteer.

IT CAN BE DONE

DEAR MISS MANNERS:

I received an invitation to a June wedding which stated the parents of Miss Bride-to-Be and Mr. Groom, of This City, would be honored by my presence at their wedding at this place on this date at this time. There was no list of where the happy couple is registered, no hinting about what they would like me to help pay for the wedding; there was not even one of those cards for me to return (in the pre-stamped envelope provided) for me to respond with my terms of acceptance of their invitation.

I was thrilled. I think this was the first time I've seen what an actual wedding invitation is supposed to look like, outside of examples in etiquette books. I sent off my reply immediately and am now shopping for silver candlesticks. I also thought you would like to know there are people who do remember how it's done.

Gentle Reader:

Miss Manners thanks you. She, too, has been fortunate enough to witness charming weddings, untainted by crass assumptions and bad theatrics.

However, please read on.

UNPRINCIPLED NOTIONS

Weddings still make people cry, Miss Manners has discovered. But not, it seems, for the traditional reasons.

The spectacle of an innocent young couple inspired by love to leave the homes and protection of their respective parents and create an irrevocable bond used to set off the sensitive souls among their guests. When people of experience emerge from their own home to create a negotiable bond subject to cancellation, it may still be touching, but perhaps not to a tear-jerking extent.

However, among the people associated with modern weddings, there are still plenty on the verge of tears:

- The bride, because after a year spent planning this wedding she has discovered that the flowers for the table are a deeper pink than she ordered and don't match the sashes on the bridesmaids' dresses.
- The bridegroom, because he's had a lonely year and is not sure the solution to it is that executive-level events planner who has been ordering him around.
- The mother of the bride, because she has been told that she didn't put enough money into the wedding to entitle her to have any opinions about how it should be conducted.
- The father of the bride, because he has been told that he cannot bring his second wife, who is home crying.
- The mother of the bridegroom, because she has been forced to wear a dress in a color she hates.
- The father of the bridegroom, because he paid for his daughter's

wedding in its entirety, having been assured that this was traditional, and has now been told that tradition demands that at his son's wedding he pay for a dinner party for the entire guest list the night before and for all the liquor being consumed during several days of festivities.

- The bridesmaids, because their time, money, and patience has been freely consumed for events, clothes, and demands to which they never consented.
- The groomsmen, because they've had too much beer all week. (The bridesmaids have had just as much, but they hold it better.)
- The guests, because they realize they have blown their vacation time, as well as great sums of money for transportation, hotels, and several rounds of presents, only to be left standing around endlessly, doing nothing, while the wedding pictures are being taken.
- The bride's colleagues, because they had to chip in to give her a shower and weren't even invited to the wedding.

So who, exactly, is enjoying this ordeal?

Miss Manners still believes in happy weddings and has been to more than a few. But she is beginning to understand why observers of the wedding scene—other than those who are there for love or money—assert that there is an inverse relationship between the elaborateness of the wedding festivities and the success of the marriage. A number of sociologists, divorce lawyers, and members of the clergy have said publicly that the more lavish, complicated, and prolonged the arrangements, the more likely the marriage is to end in divorce.

Here is what makes Miss Manners teary: The spectacle of a couple—perhaps not so young and not so innocent but nevertheless in love—who feel obliged to devote untold amounts of time and money to producing an elaborate festival that is beyond their experience and capacity and leaves everyone cranky.

◦─ *Parent Abuse* ─◦

DEAR MISS MANNERS:

Plain and simple . . . My fiancé's mother is remarried to a man who has two adult daughters. My fiancé and I barely know them. Sometimes we can't even remember which one is which!

My fiancé's mother *insists* that we invite both of them, along with their significant others that we *really* don't know, to our wedding. We were not planning on inviting them, but now that his mother has said something . . . do we invite them because it's the "right" thing to do . . . or do we stick to our guns about only inviting people that are special to us to our wedding?

GENTLE READER:

Stick to the guns that you are pointing at relatives to prevent them from trespassing on your private territory?

Miss Manners hopes not. Plain and simple, weddings are not "about" the bridal couples to the exclusion of the feelings of others. As proud as you may be of not being able to tell your fiancé's stepsisters apart, they are in his mother's family. And she is in his, and about to be in yours.

◦─ *Bridesmaid Abuse* ─◦

DEAR MISS MANNERS:

Is it impolite for one of the bride's attendants to wear an engagement ring during the festivities (given that the bridesmaid is newly, within days, engaged)?

GENTLE READER:

No, but Miss Manners is puzzled about the thinking that prompted this question. Is it the idea that bridesmaids are a chorus line back-up for the bride, suppressing their individuality for aesthetic unity, even down to their own symbols of attachment? Or that the excitement of this lady's new engagement would some-how detract from the wedding?

Either notion would be a sorry negation of what bridesmaids are really supposed to be: the bride's dearest friends, all of whom are individuals with lives of their own. The bride is supposed to care enough about them to wish them happiness and should be especially disposed to appreciate the happiness of love and marriage. Nothing detracts from a wedding as much as a self-centered bride.

⁓ Guest Abuse ⁓

DEAR MISS MANNERS:

After my relative was married in a lavish affair with copious amounts of food and drink, the bridal couple compared what all the relatives had given for wedding gifts.

All had given money and the amounts were disclosed, along with complaints about those who had not given enough. Some relatives gave hundreds of dollars while others gave thousands of dollars.

What do you think of this? I don't know what was spent on the wedding reception, but are the guests required to "reimburse" their hosts for the cost of their meal by the largess in terms of the wedding gift? It seemed to me the wedding reception was a bit overdone.

GENTLE READER:

Well, doesn't that sound like a good time was had by all.

Or, considering the countless and shameless money-shaking schemes that bridal couples have disclosed to Miss Manners (in the idiotic hope that she could whitewash them with bogus etiquette), maybe this couple was just franker about what seems to be the chief purpose of such weddings.

No, of course guests shouldn't calculate the cost of their dinners when selecting presents. The very notion that wedding guests, or any guests, owe their hosts for what they ate and drank is a disgusting perversion of the notion of hospitality. People who want to charge admission to their weddings, rather than simply to share the occasion with those about whom they care, should sell tickets.

P.S. What were your relatives' reactions to this attempt at public shaming? Did they rush to pour more money into those grasping hands?

MISS MANNERS TO THE RESCUE

You begin to see why Miss Manners has to put down her champagne glass and go rescue well-meaning couples who are bombarded with mean-spirited misinformation. She will begin by administering some instant relief.

⌐*Things a Bride Need Not Trouble Her Pretty Head About*⌐

1. Do not worry whether the gentleman with whom you have already planned marriage has sufficient dramatic flair to devise a proposal that will astonish everyone you know, and preferably also public onlookers. The ability to hire a blimp trailing a banner declaring love is not indicative of whether he will be a good husband.
2. Do not worry that you need devote a year of your life to planning a festival that will showcase your personality and squander everyone else's vacation time and resources.
3. Do not worry about who is going to give you showers and other parties. The shower is a lighthearted, nonessential element of an engagement (as opposed to, say, the fiancé, who is essential and whose heart should be fixed at this point). In any case, it is voluntary on the part of the bride's friends. They either throw one (or more) or they don't, but she can't suggest it.
4. Do not worry about whether you like your relatives. You have to invite them anyway.
5. Do not worry about how many guests you can invite and still afford

your dream menu. The proper formula is to count up the relatives and friends first, and then figure out what you can afford to serve to that number of people.

6. Do not worry about what you will receive as presents. You are inviting people to witness and celebrate your wedding, not to furnish your life, and it is not up to you to tell them how to spend their money. When guests ask what you want (and they will, as registries have gotten them out of the habit of thinking about what would please their friends) you may reluctantly admit to a preference for a certain style or category that includes modest items, or, if you must, to being registered at stores.

7. Do not worry about finding other ways to recoup the money spent on your wedding from your guests. You cannot do it. Beggars in formal clothing and lavish surroundings lack the pitiable aspect that inspires charity.

8. Do not worry about deluging your guests with constantly updated information through multiple mailings and a Web site, all artfully designed to share your history, emotions, thoughts, and color scheme. Guests need to know the date and place early enough to search for airfare bargains and make hotel arrangements and, when the time comes, might need to be reminded of where they are expected to be when. They do not need to know how much in love you are.

9. Do not worry in advance whether the people you invite to your wedding will attend. You can encourage attendance by minimizing the inconvenience and cost, or you can indicate, with an exotic location, that you want only guests who have time and money on their hands. Then it is up to them to decide, once you send them the invitation. Later on, you can worry when they don't respond.

10. Do not worry about developing a "theme" for your wedding; the theme of a wedding is marriage. And nobody notices or cares whether the postage stamps on your wedding invitations pulsate with love.

11. Do not worry about whether your bridesmaids will match one another, or whether there are the same number of them as there are groomsmen. This is not a parade or a public matchmaking. The idea is to have your friends around you, regardless of whether the effect is symmetri-

cal. The attempt to form auxiliary couples for a wedding recessional has driven the affianced crazy with demands of "Well, I have to have Chris, so you've just got to find somebody else." Nor is there anything wrong with having pairs of bridesmaids march together at the recessional. Anyway, no one is watching by then, because their eyes are still misty from sentiment at the ceremony itself, or because they are looking around for the bar now that the ceremony is over.

12. Do not worry about whether your mother will match the bridegroom's mother. They are not a set either, and can both be trusted to dress properly for the occasion. Or not, but then there is nothing you can do about it.

13. Do not worry that every minute of the wedding day be captured by every electronic means available. It can ruin the occasion, and your friends will not long allow you to make yourself tedious by whipping out your telephone to display wedding pictures and expecting them to sit still for wedding videos. Love you as they may, they do not crave their own copies of your wedding portraits—only the pictures in which they happen to appear.

14. Do not worry about "limousine" (there is no polite word for distinguishing pretentious automobiles from ordinary ones) privileges, pew seating, or dancing order. Aside from the general ideas that it is nice for people who are feeble or who are wearing long delicate dresses to get rides, that family watches the ceremony from up front, and that the bridal couple opens the dancing, there are no persnickety rules for doling out such honors.

15. Do not worry about whether you have outfitted your life with everything you have ever coveted, all brand new. The stores will still be open after the wedding. Anyway, in the first few months of marriage a proper bride is too busy writing thank-you letters, and nagging the bridegroom to do his, to put everything away.

16. Do not worry about whether the bridegroom is sufficiently interested in the wedding. He may or may not be, but this is not indicative of whether he loves you and whether he is ambivalent about getting married. The earliest you would ever need to consult him about such matters again is a whole generation from now, and Miss Man-

ners assures you that your daughter will not be all that interested in whether her father thinks the wedding cake should be vanilla, chocolate, or peanut brittle.

OVER THE BRIDAL BRINK

A virulent strain of Wedding Fatigue has become increasingly common and dangerous. Although it has not been shown to cause permanent damage, it nibbles away at otherwise healthy brains, rendering them useless for months.

As Miss Manners recalls, the old form merely affected that part of the brain that was designed to participate in debates about which shade of peach the bridesmaids' shoes should be dyed and whether Grandma's beau should be seated up front. The relatives and friends of brides and, not infrequently, the bridegroom were typically the first to succumb.

But now that couples insist on doing all the planning together, Wedding Fatigue has begun to attack them both. Rather than producing paralytic boredom, as it does in others, this strain deprives its victims of even a modicum of common sense. So here, in the spirit of healing, are answers to questions Miss Manners has received, questions people in their right minds would not have had to ask:

Q: "On the invitations do I have to list my last name? It is still my name from my first marriage; I did not change it back due to my child. I really would like it if there was some way not to have it on the invitation."

A: Yet your prospective guests would really like to know who is getting married. What makes you think you are the only Madison they know?

Q: "I would like to ask for my g/f's hand in marriage, but due to the nature of things now, her parents are divorced and her father lives in another state, and she currently resides with her mother and siblings. I would like to do the traditional thing of asking her father, but I do not know his phone number and I would like for it to be a surprise. What should I do?"

A: Consult an online telephone directory.

Q: "What is the rule of thumb for wearing the man's wedding ring prior to the wedding day? Can the man wear the ring on his left hand, third finger, or should it be put in a safe place till the wedding day?"

A: It is not his ring yet; it is the bride's. Read the wedding ceremony—she gives it to him then. And the thumb has nothing to do with it.

Q: "My wedding dress is ivory and the tux shop and dress shop recommend ivory shirts, ties, and vests for the men. They say that since the wedding dress is ivory, the men should be in ivory so as not to make the dress appear dirty. My fiancé is sure that we will lose that formal evening flare if he is wearing ivory with his tux."

A: The groomsmen can only make the bride look dirty if they get drunk and make off-color jokes about her. But if you want to be absolutely safe, you had better skip the wedding cake so its bright white icing doesn't make you look soiled.

Miss Manners apologizes for any signs that she might have been impatient with these questions. She wishes all these brides and bridegrooms great happiness and a speedy recovery.

OPTING OUT

An increasing number of couples are said to be eloping because they can't bear going through the ordeal of a conventional wedding. Far from disapproving, Miss Manners would be suspicious of anyone planning a big wedding who didn't sigh at least once about how much nicer it would be to elope. Someone so seduced by the envisioned glory of the occasion as to fail to remark, "Darling, don't you just wish the two of us could slip away without all this fuss?" (not necessarily putting down the three-ring notebook with the e-mail addresses of florists and bands) probably shouldn't be getting married.

Yet Miss Manners would also like to caution against impetuous elopement, and not only because wily wedding vendors have come to require a deposit. Elopement may indeed be the kind way to avoid all-out warfare between irreconcilable factions, and the lasting animosities that would obliterate the fact that marriage is the joining of two families. But that would be something more than the couple's wanting a rock band while the parents want old show tunes.

However, avoiding fuss is something she can understand. So let us talk fuss. In some cases, it is the competing desires of relatives and friends that are thought to create too much fuss. Families want the wedding held in one place, friends in another; the bride and bridegroom come from different cultural or religious backgrounds, perhaps from more than one each; the older generation's idea of festivity is different from the younger's; everyone seems to have enemies among those who ought to be invited. This merely strikes Miss Manners as an excellent opportunity for the couple to learn how to placate others and negotiate compromise, major requirements for family life.

The fuss that others want to avoid is the time and energy, not to mention the money, involved in putting on a lavish production. They are quite right. Running a three-day show for hordes of business acquaintances is neither necessary nor tasteful.

What does seem to be necessary to the human spirit is some sense of ritual connected with so momentous a step in life. It amuses Miss Manners that people who have talked for years about getting married, and very likely already share a household, are deeply interested in the rituals of the formal wedding. It touches her, too. Presumably there are people who never regret having skipped any semblance of ceremony when they married. But Miss Manners keeps hearing from those who made the decision to marry without any fanfare and are now complaining that they missed out on an entitlement and asking how to make up for it.

Miss Manners seems to have missed the section of the Constitution that guarantees every couple an elaborate wedding. A proper wedding is simply a dignified ceremony followed by a happy celebration for those who care about the couple, done in a somewhat more formal version of the way they usually entertain. It also seems to her that those who married without ritual are free to have post-wedding receptions and then anniversary parties that are as elaborate as they like, but should not feel that the world has cheated them. What is marriage, if not the ability to make a decision and then stick by it later?

～Eloping～

DEAR MISS MANNERS:

Believe it or not, I have no desire for a big, traditional wedding. My dream is to elope while on vacation, getting married on a tropical beach. No hassles, no outlandish costs, no pomp and circumstance. How do I handle family and friends who would expect the traditional wedding? Mom, my best friend, would be devastated (I think). I'm the only daughter. What sort of after-event could we have to share our joy with everyone? Is there elopement etiquette?

GENTLE READER:

The traditional reason for an elopement was to thwart the hopes, plans, and dreams of the bride's parents, which is why the entire rest of the world sympathized with elopers. Thwarting parents has always had a wide sentimental appeal, even by people who don't know the elopers, parents, or anyone else concerned.

It is also why the traditional elopement was sometimes followed by the traditional annulment. When the mean and unromantic parents pointed out that the bride was supposed to be in junior high school and the bridegroom was wanted in four states, happily ever after could be prematurely terminated. But even now, when parents are considerably less vigilant, couples elope.

There are many reasons for an elopement, some of them nicer than others. Perhaps the couple wishes to spare their parents (or themselves) the expense. Or they have been married before and wish to spare others repeating the fuss that may have been made over one or both of them at previous ceremonies. Perhaps they are eluding unromantic employers with an anti-nepotism policy. Perhaps they are thwarting parents in a modernized way—rejecting parental ideas of a proper wedding, rather than parental ideas of the proper spouse. Or perhaps they consider the choice of wedding scenery more important than the people who would otherwise be the wedding guests.

Miss Manners has no desire to talk people into big weddings, pomp and circumstance usually being more threatening than encouraging to proper wedding behavior. But pray, what do you call a hassle if it is not an action that causes devastation for your mother (and thus, as you gracefully say, for your best friend)? That you may be satisfied with a vacation wedding is not enough if it would cause her genuine distress.

That is not to say others cannot be talked around. If your mother would be satisfied with a big wedding reception upon your return from elopement, Miss Manners certainly has no objection.

⸺ Eloping Locally ⸺

DEAR MISS MANNERS:

I fear this sounds silly, and indeed I consider it so myself, but is there actually any rudeness in not holding a big wedding when one can afford it?

As soon as our engagement was announced, my fiancé and I started fielding questions from friends about when and where the wedding will take place, always with the assumption that they would be invited.

The truth is, we will probably go to city hall with our parents and a handful of very close friends as witnesses, then go get celebratory ice cream sundaes. When we try to explain we won't be having a big ceremony and reception, many seem to take offense and consider us cheapskates.

That's the thing, you see—theoretically, we could afford a giant wedding, but neither of us would enjoy such an event, nor would we consider that good use of our savings. I know it's possible to hold a reasonable, tasteful reception on a budget, but it requires enormous amounts of time and planning, and I must admit that organizing social events makes me terribly anxious and I dread the very thought.

The way I see it, we can either hire someone to plan everything, and spend more than we'd like, or organize it ourselves and thus make ourselves miserable, or . . . have our tiny dream wedding and send our friends a postcard from the honeymoon.

Is it actually rude not to hold a reception? You'd think friends would be grateful to be spared another night of bad catering, not to mention the cost of travel, attire, and gifts!

GENTLE READER:

Perhaps your friends are so overcome with love for you and pleasure in your marriage that they long to witness it. In that case, you might consider a wedding that is big in the guest list but otherwise simple—an afternoon ceremony followed by ice cream sundaes, for example.

Yet Miss Manners does not believe that is the reason you are being importuned any more than you do. Now that weddings so often comprise multiple extravagant events, people have come to regard them as put on for their entertainment. You do not owe them that. Her only addition to your plan is to suggest that you refrain from announcing it beforehand, and describe it in your postal cards as an elopement.

⁓Downsizing⁓

DEAR MISS MANNERS:

I am happily engaged to be married soon. I would like my wedding and reception to be a true celebration with friends and family who love us and wish us well, but I have a very limited budget.

To that end, I have resorted to a buffet-style luncheon to be eaten with paper and plastic products rather than china and silver. I will use traditionally worded, plain ivory invitations; however, they will be printed, not engraved, and will not include that superfluous bit of tissue or (you will be happy to hear) those monstrous response cards. I will have only one attendant, and family and friends are helping prepare the food, cakes, and decorations.

When you have recovered consciousness, perhaps you could reassure me that I am not a disgrace to well-mannered brides everywhere. My distress, which is quite acute, stems from my feeling suddenly that etiquette is the purview of the well-off, of which

I am not a member. As a well-mannered Southern girl, I desperately want my ceremony and festivities to be proper and feel that perhaps I am operating outside these bounds. Please help.

GENTLE READER:

The proper thing for you to do is to help Miss Manners up off the floor first. She fell into a faint all right, but not over the idea that not having a big vulgar wedding is a violation of etiquette.

What sent her crashing—her smelling salts, please; there's a dear—is your notion that etiquette is some sort of luxury cultivated by the rich. You must have met very few of them.

Etiquette has nothing to do with gaggles of chorus-line bridesmaids, groan-producing dinners, endless revelries, and the other over-done ingredients of the debt-ridden wedding. The simplest weddings are, in fact, the most likely to be proper. For example, engraved invitations are merely the traditional substitute for handwritten ones. Rather than printing imitations of engraving, the more charming, not to mention cheaper, alternative is to write them out by hand.

The greatest improprieties occur when bridal couples ignore the comfort and convenience of their guests in their efforts to aggrandize themselves. Miss Manners trusts that your friends and relatives volunteered to help with the cooking, rather than being assigned to do so. And when she suggests firm plates and flatware, she is not hoping for a commission from the sale of china and silver—any reasonably attractive ceramic and metal will do—but rather thinking of how nasty it is to eat from paper.

⌒ The Re-enacted Wedding ⌒

DEAR MISS MANNERS:

My boyfriend and I need to get legally married now for immigration purposes in order to stay in the same country after I graduate medical school. We cannot afford a wedding right now and the timing is bad because of an intense medical school schedule.

For the two of us, this civil marriage feels like our engagement. We would also like our family and friends to think our wedding is meaningful, when we do have the "real" ceremony in a year or so. However, we didn't want to keep such a serious decision from our parents, who are traditional and upset about this split setup.

What should we tell friends who kindly inquire about our future plans and engagement status? What should we ask our parents to say when faced with the same questions? I dislike lying, but I also feel that this is private information.

GENTLE READER:

We can only hope that your reluctance to face the facts and your conviction that you can manipulate reality and suppress inconvenient information will not carry over to your medical career.

Miss Manners is aware that many couples have now separated getting married from what they are pleased to call "having a wedding." They throw the party at another time, which would be fine in itself, but they include a fake ceremony, as if that made it as important an occasion as the real thing.

That Miss Manners is not the only person who considers this fraudulent is evident from your realization that your guests will not find the rerun as meaningful as actually witnessing your marriage. And you cannot make your legal marriage into an engagement by declaring it so. Rather than tangle yourself further in this deception, Miss Manners recommends admitting to your friends and family that you are married but that you will be inviting them to a delayed celebration later.

⁓ The Subsequent Wedding ⁓

DEAR MISS MANNERS:

When my daughter was married five years ago, the marriage lasted two years and ended in divorce. She has been living for two years with another young man, and they are planning to be married. She wants a large church wedding, complete with white flowing wedding gown and veil and several bridesmaids.

At her first wedding, she received many, many beautiful gifts from our generous family, friends, and business associates. She was well supplied with fine and casual china, silver and stainless flatware, and crystal in her chosen patterns. She intends to select and register new patterns of silver, china, and crystal. I question the propriety, and am embarrassed that our family, friends, and associates will feel pressured to give another nice gift.

GENTLE READER:

Your daughter quarreled not only with her husband, but with her silverware? My, that is anger. Or did he manage to clean her out during the divorce?

No matter. Miss Manners is addressing her answer to the part about wedding presents to the guests. Since your daughter will of course only admit to being registered when she is specifically asked, it is they who need to decide whether they need help in figuring out what to give her.

Wedding presents, particularly elaborate ones, are not as customary with subsequent weddings as with a first. There is nothing wrong with seeing someone married twice (or however often she plans) and sending only a token present after the first time, or even just a letter wishing her well.

The truly proper second wedding is small and relatively informal—the bride wears a perfectly smashing suit, in a delicate pastel color rather than white, and an even more smashing hat instead of a veil. She has one honor attendant, not a parade of them, partly because all her old friends now know that her previous promise to them—never mind her promise to her previous bridegroom—was false: They have not had other occasions to wear those bridesmaid dresses she made them buy.

Before Miss Manners is attacked by starry-eyed brides who made one little mistake and now want to go all out for what they insist is their first true marriage, notice that she is waving a tiny, white, lace-edged handkerchief. She is neither so vulgar as to associate the white dress with inexperience, nor so mean as to throw etiquette brickbats in place of rose petals. Like true well-wishers, she is inclined to be indulgent.

UPDATING TRADITION

Can weddings be run without sex playing a significant part?

Oh, dear. That does not at all sound like what Miss Manners intended. What she means to discuss is whether the division of tasks and honors by gender, which has always characterized weddings, should be overhauled in the light of gender enlightenment.

Oddly enough, this does not seem to be as much of a problem when wedding principals do not match the traditional definitions. State legislators enjoy working themselves into a lather over that issue, but Miss Manners has noticed that same-sex couples have been using the sensible and (she would think) obvious solution of presenting themselves as two brides or two bridegrooms.

But good sense does not often apply when many couples assemble their wedding party. Gender is considered to be such a defining characteristic of giving the bride away, or serving as maid of honor, best man, bridesmaid, or groomsman that most weddings maintain the division to the exclusion of other qualifications.

Some of the questions that keep arising are:

- Why are the bride's parents' names, but not the bridegroom's parents', on the invitation?
- Why do the bride's parents get to have the wedding in their hometown? (That question from bridegroom's parents.)
- Why do we get to pay for everything? (That question from bride's parents.)
- Why is it the bride's previous marital history, not the bridegroom's, that determines whether it is classified as a first wedding?

- Why are there domestic showers for brides and hilarious drinking parties for bridegrooms?
- Why is she given away, while he just donates himself?
- Why do the attendants of each have to be the same gender as they are?
- Why does everyone look at her and no one at him?

Rather than await Miss Manners' pronouncements on these questions, many bridal couples have taken matters into their own hands, or sometimes fists. It is not uncommon now to see lots of parental names on invitations, to hear that the bride's friends took her out to a male strip joint while the bridegroom's friends had a quiet dinner at a respectable restaurant, for the bridegroom to wear attention-getting clothes and for everyone concerned to claim that everyone else concerned (and some people who just happened to be briefly passing through the family) should contribute to paying the bill.

It is high time that Miss Manners made some order out of all this. She is not against change. Etiquette is continually evolving and always has been, as life changes. Full dignity for ladies is one of the best changes to come along in centuries.

But tradition also has a claim. Why else are all these hysterical people involved in putting on this spectacle? Customs that have outlived their original reasons may nevertheless still carry emotional weight. Orderly change consists of adapting tradition to the actual situation it is to adorn.

A small lesson in social history seems to be in order.

The Anglo-American wedding format that is more or less current did not really begin until Victorian times. Before then (and long after for those who had neither the funds nor the habit of lavish personal ceremonies), couples, perhaps accompanied by a few relatives and friends, merely donned their best clothes, and after the formalities of the marriage, returned home for a festive midday meal.

As more prosperous people expanded the occasion, they did so to fit the circumstances of the time. The bride's parents traditionally gave the wedding because she went from their home and support to her husband's. Their names alone were on the invitation because they were the hosts.

She was more likely to have a father than a mother (childbirth being a perilous business), and even in a two-parent family, a father who believed himself (the silly man) to have total control over his daughter gave her away because her fate was in his hands.

And in those days, neither bride nor bridegroom had any trouble explaining being "just good friends" with a person of the opposite gender, because they weren't. Her attendants were all female because her friends were, and similarly, the bridegroom's attendants were all male. One of the great social advances of our time is the realization that not every tie between a lady and a gentleman is brimming with erotic excitement.

Miss Manners is all for retaining charming old traditions, provided that the deeper meaning is not sacrificed to superficial considerations.

Certainly both sets of parents, or the bridegroom's alone, can give the wedding, or the bridal couple themselves or their friends. Parents' names may be retained as sentimental figureheads, even if the couple does all the planning and paying. However, considering that brides seldom grow up next door to their bridegrooms, the identity of the latter becomes necessary in a way it never used to be. Miss Manners does not object to an invitation saying whose son he is, although she prefers that the bridegroom's parents merely slip a formal card with their names into invitations for their side of the list.

What no one concerned can do is to assign bills to other people, or sell or withhold wedding honors. Any offers to contribute, especially if there is a need, are gracious, and qualify as strictly family business with which etiquette would not dream of interfering.

If a bride wants to retain the symbolism of being given away, it should be by someone to whom she feels she belongs. It could be her father or stepfather, or both parents, or a guardian. But if she was reared by a single mother, the mother should do it.

⁓The Best Person⁓

DEAR MISS MANNERS:

I am to be involved in a wedding in which two of my dearest friends will marry each other. In lieu of a best man, the groom has asked me, a female, to act as "best person." This is an honor and I am touched as well as proud of my friend's openmindedness.

It has come to my attention that some of the other women in the bridal party are apprehensive in regard to my role in the wedding, a formal church ceremony. I wish to be sensitive to the feelings of those who may be uncomfortable with this break with tradition, as well as being correct in my behavior.

GENTLE READER:

It troubles Miss Manners to think why these bridesmaids are apprehensive. Do they imagine that one of them will have to dance with you at the reception? Do they think of the recessional as a parade of pseudo-romantic couples?

All this would be silly. Traditionally, the bridegroom is attended by his best friend, friendship being the chief selection factor, not gender. Of course you will dress as a lady and dance with gentlemen. You will not offer any lady your arm, but merely march at the maid of honor's side as paired bridesmaids do in a processional. But if the bride's honor attendant is a gentleman, he may offer you his arm.

⁓ Pilfering Traditions ⁓

DEAR MISS MANNERS:

I recently received an e-mail invitation to the wedding of a family friend. While I considered this improper, I realize the times are different and often young people don't take the time to find out the proper etiquette for these things. Within the wording of the invitation, however, was a headshot of an engagement-type photo of the happy couple—dressed in traditional Muslim garb! The bride-to-be, a beautiful young woman, was totally unrecognizable, since, of course, only her eyes showed.

This is not a Muslim couple. He is Protestant and she is Catholic. Needless to say there had been much discussion among the receivers of this invitation. Is this some new trend? I understand the photo was taken on a recent trip, and I found it to be offensive, but perhaps I am old school.

GENTLE READER:

The new school would find it even more offensive to mock other people's religions by playing dress-up, Miss Manners assures you.

Through immigration, assimilation, and intermarriage, American rituals are legitimately a mixture of many cultures. Routines, such as the Unity Candle, that seemed to creep in from nowhere, she finds less charming, but all right, if you must. Masquerading is not.

⁓Discarding Traditions⁓

DEAR MISS MANNERS:

What do you think about receiving an invitation to a wedding but not the reception? A friend and I were discussing another friend who was invited by a neighbor to a wedding for the neighbors' daughter, but not included in the invitation was the invite to the reception.

The friend and I felt it is extremely rude to invite people only to the wedding, and feel that it appears as if a gift is desired, but that the host is not interested in paying for a meal. We both feel that if one is not close enough to be invited to the reception, she should not be invited to either. What is your opinion?

GENTLE READER:

That it is a fine and useful example of etiquette's not being enslaved by tradition. For indeed, it was once commonplace to discriminate among the guests at what were considered fashionable weddings. Some received reception cards in their invitations, others did not.

Why the latter group did not think, "Why would I want to witness their marriage when they don't want to see me afterward?" Miss Manners cannot imagine. It was rude then, and it is rude now.

TROUBLESHOOTING

DEAR MISS MANNERS:

The man I have been seeing and I have decided to get married. We are both graduate students. His family lives close to where we are attending school, and my family is large and very spread out. I have many siblings, and most of them have small children and infants, so it is not easy for them to travel. I am very shy and have never been fond of the idea of having a wedding, especially the kind that are so prevalent today, where people seem to put on a spectacle. I feel that a marriage is a very private affair, and while I am close to my family, I am not comfortable with the idea of having a wedding ceremony in front of them.

On the other hand, I don't want to be selfish. My mother and siblings have expressed dismay and told me that they would be hurt if I had a wedding ceremony that did not include them. They are not pressuring me to have a big event, but since it is so difficult for everyone to travel, I am afraid it would become an event.

Further, we don't have any kind of a budget for a "real" wedding. It is such an intimate occasion to me that I would feel embarrassed if anyone were there who doesn't have to be (my fiancé and me), even if it is just family. I don't know how my fiance's family feels about this issue, but I will certainly take that into account. I love both his family and mine and would not want to hurt them, but the idea of a wedding where I am half the focal point is almost excruciating.

Am I just being like everyone else who is getting married lately and making this into "my day," when I should be taking the families' wishes into account?

GENTLE READER:

If you are, you have certainly put a unique twist on it. A bride who doesn't want to be the focus?

You have left us speechless. Well, almost. We do wonder what you imagine goes into the ceremony that would cause such profound embarrassment in front of your own family.

You can simply go down to the local courthouse, which might meet your family's definition of a non-event they wouldn't mind missing. It is crucial that you find out about your fiancé's family's feelings, however. Not including them might set the precedent for lifelong tension and resentment. Please see the following.

DEAR MISS MANNERS:

Recently my husband and I eloped. Realizing that there were conflicts between who we should invite (some of my family are estranged), and who we wanted to invite, we opted to marry with only my son, the minimum two witnesses, minister, and photographer. Instead we have managed to upset everyone. Particularly my new parents-in-law. While we get along in every other instance, every visit occasions a mention of how they were not invited to our ceremony (we did not hold a reception due to lack of funds).

Is there a polite and graceful way to point out that this was not an intentional slight to them, but rather an extremely intimate ceremony for us? Or do we have to accept that they are hurt and we will hear about it from now on?

GENTLE READER:

Citing the occasion's intimacy only emphasizes to your family that they are not among your intimates. Since you had a photographer present (which begs the obvious: how exactly do you define "intimate"?), perhaps you can make amends by showing them how brief a moment they missed.

DEAR MISS MANNERS:

The idea of the "selfish bride" who is "overexposed to the commercial wedding literature" is one of many negative stereotypes about women. It contains the following false assumptions:

1. That women are passive victims of commercial literature rather than adults who think and speak for themselves,
2. That women are motivated by petty selfishness rather than by genuine concerns,
3. That parents are never motivated by status anxieties, and that mothers are never "wedding-crazy" and profligate themselves,
4. That comfort of parents is important but the comfort of the bride is irrelevant to the success of a wedding,
5. That parents are never domineering, and
6. That parents never couch selfish desires in language of appropriateness and consideration.

I've been involved in six weddings in the past two years (including my own), and in five cases the bride was very sensible and the mother was wedding-crazy. Here are some quotations from brides in those five cases (not including my own): "My Mom told me that the wedding had nothing to do with my fiancé and I," and "I'm licking my wounds."

An incredible amount of resentment can build when wedding-crazy mothers repeatedly assume domineering attitudes towards sensible brides. For this reason, I've come to view "bridal assertiveness" as healthy—it prevents resentment from building and strengthens family relationships in the long run.

The bride doesn't need to justify, she doesn't need to convince. She is allowed to just say no. She knows what is truly necessary for her happiness.

Weddings are three-family events—there is a new family being created—and on some level parents don't like this. They struggle to maintain dominant roles in their children's lives and they fight mightily to preserve the idea that "we know best." The ability of adult children to resist this and say no is important for the long-term health of their new marriage, in addition to actually promoting healthy family relationships over the long run.

GENTLE READER:

A little angry at Mom, are we?

But no, we don't wish to support a negative stereotype of women by depicting the pushy bride, just as we're sure you don't mean to advocate a negative stereotype of women by characterizing the overbearing mother.

Bad behavior knows no gender, age, or relationship. We do not wish to imply that any one party is the most prone to blame, which is why we like to give the brunt of it to the wedding industry. At least they are making money from it.

Family harmony is, indeed, the goal here and anyone pushing her agenda just to make a point is clearly working against this. There are ways to maintain one's ground reasonably without reciprocating bad behavior.

If a bride needs to use her wedding day as an excuse finally to assert herself against her overbearing mother, then she clearly wasted her teenage years. And her new husband can probably look forward to reliving them over the long run, as you suggest.

DEAR MISS MANNERS:

My fiancé and I feel strongly that our wedding plans should be accommodating to our parents' wishes. They've been dreaming about this day longer than we have, and weddings are really about families coming together. We want it to be joyous for everyone involved and are determined not to make people wear clothes they don't like or feel obligated to do anything they don't want to do. We have agreed to give in on the things that are not very important to us. However, we also want our wedding to be correct.

Although overall their ideas are lovely, occasionally a well-meaning soul enthusiastically suggests something that we do not want to do. Like ask guests to help pay for our honeymoon, or include "and guest" on the invitations, or order the bridesmaids to get matching haircuts. When it's someone not helping to plan the wedding, it's fairly easy to smile and say, "Hmm . . . Perhaps . . ."

and leave it at that, but it's hard to pretend to consider the wording on the invitation with someone who is directly involved with the wording on the invitation. So how should we respond, when it's one of our parents or closest family or friends?

GENTLE READER:

Sit your loved ones down and explain that you are so well brought up that you want to incorporate the family ideals into the wedding. No one is to be financially burdened, demeaned, put out, or otherwise embarrassed.

But (you add) you desperately need their help to pull off this highly unusual approach. Talk over each dreadful idea seriously, mentioning the dangers: Even if mandating identical haircuts didn't make the bridesmaids run from you clutching their heads, it would look cultish to your guests.

You live within your means, and fortunately don't have to swallow your pride and ask your friends for money. And you don't mind taking the trouble to find out the guests' romantic attachments' names so as to save them the insultingly anonymous "and guest" designation.

You might say that you have had your share of giggles over other people's attempts to be clever and original with their invitations. "But 'Hallelujah she's not knocked up!' or 'Jack and Martha want you to watch Sarah finally make it legal' will give Grandma a heart attack and we want ours to be serious. No nicknames, even— we will use our full names, as you gave them to us."

Your parents will have no choice but to be proud that they have reared children who can pay for their own vacations and relieved that their own wallets will not be exploited. (Talking point: The more gracious solution is usually the less expensive one.) A flattering and reasonable attitude should at least embarrass them into appearing gracious when they don't get what they want.

CHAPTER TWO

The Engagement

D IFFICULT AS IT IS to fathom the distinctions between friendship and dating, or, heaven help us, between, uh, "hooking up"—Miss Manners has trouble with that expression—and any form of acquaintanceship, it ought to be clear what constitutes an engagement. Well, no, apparently not. So Miss Manners must begin by clarifying the terms.

DEAR MISS MANNERS:

My boyfriend and I have been in definite agreement for a while that we would like to get married after I was done with graduate school. However, we felt that it would be in poor taste to announce an engagement for a wedding that is still years down the line, so few people know about our plans yet.

I have recently been hearing a lot of women say that you cannot be truly engaged unless a guy has bent down on his knee and given you a ring and said the magic words. My boyfriend never offered me such a proposal, but he has expressed his sincerity in many other ways. I do not see the point of having him get down on bended knee to propose to me now when we are ready to announce our engagement, considering that I already know he wants to marry me.

Plus, I do not want an engagement ring, as there are other things I would rather spend the money on. I was hoping to simply announce that we are planning our wedding on a certain date and leave it at that.

Everybody else I have known who had plans to get married down the line has either gotten officially engaged when they knew they wanted to get married, or else their boyfriends "surprised" them with a proposal as the wedding date drew near. I do not mind not receiving a proposal myself, but I am starting to feel that I must be doing things improperly. Who is right?

GENTLE READER:

Nobody.

A definite agreement to be married is indeed the definition of an engagement. Rings, bended knees, and announcements are all optional. But you are dangerously wrong in allowing the expectations of outsiders to make you doubt the decisions you and your fiancé make. Miss Manners hopes you will correct this before you find yourself in a marriage being run by gossips.

DEAR MISS MANNERS:

I have begun to notice that the definition of the word fiancé(e) is changing, and in my opinion, not for the better.

When I was growing up, the love of one's life whom one intended to soon marry was for a short period referred to as a fiancé. Young girls dream of one day being engaged and for a brief period becoming someone's fiancée. My boyfriend became my fiancé, and six months later he became my husband.

Now, however, it seems the term has become a catchall for a variety of uncommitted, open-ended relationships. Couples who have lived together for ten-plus years with no real intention of ever marrying refer to one another as "fiancé(e)." Young couples who find themselves to be in the family way but out of wedlock immediately raise the status of their relationship from boyfriend and girlfriend to fiancé and fiancée with no real wedding plans anywhere in the foreseeable future. I'm sure this is due to their desire for others to regard their relationship with more esteem, and I don't truly care what they want to call one another, but it's been an observation of mine and I thought perhaps you would have a comment.

GENTLE READER:

Well, yes. Miss Manners has noticed that in newspaper articles, the unmarried father of five children who is on amicable terms with the mother is identified as her fiancé. But if he beats her up, he is called her boyfriend.

Actually, long engagements were not uncommon in the past. But then the delay would be to accumulate enough money to support a household; now it is to accumulate enough money to support the wedding. The imminent arrival of a child would speed the wedding day; now it delays it, so that pregnancy does not interfere with the bride's figure or zest for partying.

Or, as you point out, there may be no connection between a declaration of being affianced and an intention to be married. Still, when children are involved, Miss Manners finds it more stabilizing to use a word suggesting at least that degree of commitment. There is always the possibility that some time after the arrival of that fifth child, the couple will decide that they are sufficiently compatible to risk marriage.

DEAR MISS MANNERS:

Would you please write about what constitutes a proper engagement? A young person recently told me that an engagement should be a year at least. She was referring to a couple we both know who are in their thirties!

In my youth, I seem to recall that an engagement of that length or longer might be proper if the couple was extremely young, still in school, completing military service, or not financially independent. This couple meets none of those conditions and is even living together already. What am I missing? Has the nature of engagement changed?

Gentle Reader:

Of course it has. As in the case you cite, affianced couples are apt to be sharing living quarters already. Engagements used to be shorter because the pair felt it was more urgent to be alone together than to plan an extravaganza for others. But if the engagements were really short, people would assume that the couple "had to get married," an expression Miss Manners doubts anyone even understands these days.

A proper engagement is one that lasts from the mutual decision to marry until the marriage occurs. How many hours or years that may be is something she is happy to leave up to the couples in question.

THE PROPOSAL

Which is the more up-to-the-minute and fashionable way for a modern couple to reach a definitive agreement that they will be married?

⏤Scenario One⏤

This takes place in the household that the couple already shares, at a time neither of them has scheduled. Either person can initiate the conversation, as long as this is done in an acrimonious tone. The subject is provoked by a piece of information from the outside—a wedding invitation from another couple, an inquiry from a parent, a photograph of a baby in a magazine, a newspaper feature declaring a trend in the way people live. If the possibility of marriage is not rejected out of hand, the next session is a businesslike negotiation. Terms are debated: Whose money would be whose? How would future work, such as child rearing, be divided? What contingencies would there be in case the marriage failed? If that negotiation is concluded successfully, discussions of wedding plans begin with the mention of an engagement ring. Will there be one? How will it be chosen? How will it be financed—by the gentleman alone, or should the lady contribute equally? Can she contribute more in order to upgrade what he might be able to afford, on the grounds that it is she who will be wearing it?

⌒Scenario Two⌒

The gentleman secretly plans a special occasion and lures the lady to conform with his plans without her guessing the purpose. If she does, she is obliged to preserve the illusion by pretending to be bewildered. The setting he has chosen has sentimental associations, or luxurious or romantic characteristics, or as many and much of these as his imagination and resources allow. He is on his most courtly and attentive behavior, but he draws things out for the maximum suspense. At the great moment, he brings out an engagement ring that he has chosen and bought by himself. Perhaps he hides it somewhere clever for her to find (food seems to be the hiding place of choice), or perhaps he just produces it dramatically as he pronounces the age-old formula, "Will you marry me?" She appears to be overcome with confusion and emotion. After a suitable period of blushing and protesting her amazement, she agrees to allow him to slip (or shove—one hopes he took the precaution of finding out her finger size) the ring on her finger. Then one or the other must bring up the next business at hand, which is when and how he will ask her parents' permission to marry her.

Which do you think is today's cutting edge form of marriage proposal?

Call her old-fashioned, but Miss Manners had thought it was Scenario One. Even her cloistered ears have heard that young people do not nowadays agree to marry after a mere kiss on the parental front porch and that they have perhaps not preserved their innocence about financial matters and other practical considerations.

Yet she seems to have been mistaken. Scenario Two is becoming more and more the prevailing tradition. True, those who practice it are not generally in their first youth or first stages of courtship. It has even been suggested to her that it is for that very reason that they want the trappings of romance and the ceremonies of the past.

Miss Manners is aware that the gentleman may have to remind himself not to conclude the meal by saying, "Don't think we're going to split this down the middle—you had dessert and I didn't." She knows that the following week, the lady who claimed to need her parents' permission to be married may be indignant that they think they have anything to say about wedding arrangements. But for the moment, Miss Manners would just like to bask in the charm of this anachronistic yearning for romance. She only hopes that they avoid ending up in the Emergency Room because the lady has swallowed the ring.

DEAR MISS MANNERS:

Why did the idea of a man proposing down on his knees originate?

GENTLE READER:

It is the traditional posture of begging and worship.

DEAR MISS MANNERS:

So my boyfriend (now fiancé I guess) of two years has just announced to his family and one random friend that we are indeed getting married.

The problem is that I have not ever been formally asked. We discussed the matter of marriage several times, and always agreed that we were meant for each other and would eventually get married when the time was right. This to me was not an agreement really, just more of a discussion about our relationship.

What I really want is to be asked and proposed to with a ring and experience the whole romantic tradition. How do I get this across to him? Can I still receive this, is it too late, or does my bringing it up ultimately ruin it?

GENTLE READER:

Are you planning to accept this gentleman?

Yes, yes, you plan to marry him; that is as clear to Miss Manners as it is to the gentleman himself. But can you accept him as someone who fails to see the point of the fad for stagy proposals between people who have already agreed to marry?

Only then could you good-humoredly confess your wish and ask him to comply. If you do it seriously, you are bound to be disappointed, knowing that he is only following instructions. If you make light of it, as his indulging your weakness rather than correcting his, you may—over the years—be able to train him to the point where he will think of romantic gestures himself.

But be warned about this first, perhaps frighteningly significant, request. You will have issued him a challenge, and if he blows the year's rent by hiring a skywriter to spell out his proposal, you will have only yourself to blame.

⁓ Her Proposal ⁓

DEAR MISS MANNERS:

During courtship, there is typically a period of "testing the waters" for marriage. In this day and age, I do not believe that a lady must necessarily wait for her suitor to propose, assuming that if he hasn't asked her, he is not ready to marry her. I think it would be romantic for a gentleman to receive an (albeit unconventional) proposal from the woman he loves.

What is the correct etiquette for proposing to a man? Does the lady still wear an engagement ring? If so, should it be bought in advance or after? By him, her, or both together? Should she offer her fiancé a ring or some other token of her commitment? Finally, does this alter in any way the traditional divisions of responsibility and costs of the wedding?

GENTLE READER:

Miss Manners wishes people would understand that there is a difference between one gender's claiming a privilege that was once associated with the other and completely switching genders. Proposing to the gentleman does not make her—if he accepts—the bridegroom. Nor would he wear the bridal veil at the wedding.

There is nothing wrong with a lady's proposing marriage to a gentleman; it is not even all that unconventional. That's what old-fashioned feminine probes to find out the seriousness of a suitor's intentions were all about.

As for the wording, a marriage proposal should concentrate on one person's passionate desire to be united to the other. Miss Manners might have considered that obvious but for all the people who believe that "It's about time," or "I'm not getting any younger," are just as effective. They aren't. Tell him that you can't wait to begin your lives together.

The part about the ring is best left out. Gentlemen do not wear engagement rings (Miss Manners is not listening to the cry of tradespeople who want to supply such items), and a lady's giving herself an engagement ring tends to suggest that the gentleman's role in the relationship will be negligible.

Having accepted a marriage proposal does not in any way prevent a gentleman from giving his fiancée an engagement ring if he feels so inclined. From the time he accepts, they become an engaged couple and proceed in their plans as they would otherwise have done.

~Parental Permission~

DEAR MISS MANNERS:

I was wondering the proper order of events, pertaining to an engagement. Does the groom ask her father for her hand in marriage, then ask her and give her the diamond? Does he ask her to marry him and then her father?

GENTLE READER:

He should not ask her father to marry him. Proposing to two members of the same family can only end in strife or bigamy.

If, however, you wish to ask the father's permission to ask the lady to marry you, you must do so first. Miss Manners warns you not to attempt this before being reasonably sure of a favorable reply from the lady. "Your father is okay with your marrying me," is not a persuasive argument these days.

DEAR MISS MANNERS:

My sister is hurt because her daughter's boyfriend did not include her when he asked the dad for their daughter's hand in marriage. Our son-in-law asked us to dinner when he asked to marry our daughter. Maybe ours was an unusual situation, but I thought it was nice to be included.

What is the norm? My sister talked to her daughter's boyfriend several times a week before this happened. She has not talked to him or returned his phone calls since. My sister and niece will be coming in a week and her fiancé lives in our town.

GENTLE READER:

Then perhaps you will have a chance to resolve this ridiculous misunderstanding before it wrecks two families and a wedding. The custom of asking for a lady's hand in marriage dates from long before ladies had the vote, politically or domestically, so the mother was not officially consulted. Among modern gentlemen who preserve the custom, some update it to address both parents, some do not.

It should be remembered that this procedure, although charming, is a mere formality now. The hand is only too likely to have been freely given long before, often along with the other parts. For that matter, it was something of a formality then, when even a draconian father was not likely to be able to stand up to a determined daughter.

So the prospective bridegroom is guilty only of having preserved an anachronistic custom. If you can explain to your sister that no insult was intended, and get her prospective son-in-law to do the same, you will have done the family a service.

DEAR MISS MANNERS:

My fiancée and I are both formerly divorced and each lives alone. We are both in our mid-fifties. My fiancée's parents feel slighted because I did not ask their permission to marry their daughter.

Since my intended is both divorced and a grandmother I did not consider it an obligation to ask her parents for her hand in marriage. Did I commit a *faux pas*?

GENTLE READER:

Did you ever. You brought to these people's attention the harsh fact that their little girl is no longer subject to their rules and protection. Miss Manners advises apologizing for your oversight and presenting yourself as a suitor for the lady's hand. You might also want to check with her grandchildren, since this is apparently a touchy family.

～The Engagement Ring～

DEAR MISS MANNERS:

What if the lady does not like the ring the man chose? Is there some etiquette or some rule that tells us if and how and when she can ask to exchange that ring for one that is more to her liking?

Some people think that rejecting the ring is tantamount to rejecting the proposal. Others vigorously defend the woman, saying that no true gentleman would foist a gaudy blob on the woman he loves, nor be so uncouth as to expect her to wear it day in and day out. Yet others automatically assume that the woman was expecting something more (bigger diamond, basically) and made disparaging remarks about a woman who would consider the price tag and status symbol more important than the ring's purpose as a symbol of the promise to marry.

So, suppose that two people are genuinely in love (and not driven by lust or other nonpermanent emotions) and ready for marriage (with each other) and the gentleman took it upon himself to buy/design an engagement ring, and did his best to get something she would like. Suppose he pops the question, on his knee, all romantic, with the velvet box.

Suppose she accepts with delight. *But* she does not like the style of the ring. Perhaps her idea of "classic" is different from his. Perhaps the giant diamond is just too unwieldy. Perhaps the styling does not work for hands of her size and looks disproportionate.

Should the lady simply keep her mouth shut and wear it and be grateful she has an engagement ring? Is it acceptable for a lady in such a situation to ask to get it exchanged? If yes, then how and when? Should a gentleman be offended by such a request?

If it is acceptable to exchange that unattractive engagement ring for another, how should the engaged couple do this? Shall they travel to the jewelers together? Shall the lady go alone (or with her friends)? Would the jeweler the gent bought the ring from take it back for a full refund? What if the jeweler's policy is no refunds, only exchange or store credit . . . and there is nothing in that store to the lady's liking?

GENTLE READER:

Okay, you've given Miss Manners enough to work with. You can stop now.

The surprise ring dates back to when the gentleman was likely to produce a family ring, and it fell into abeyance when gentlemen without family jewelry were nevertheless deemed eligible. Sensibly, then, the proposal came first; some time subsequently, the lady was taken to choose from a variety of rings in his price range that the gentleman had put aside.

Now that producing a ring is considered central to the drama of a proposal, it has become a package deal. To take one without the other would not only irk a gentleman who spent weeks learning about the Four Cs of judging diamonds, it would confuse him.

This does not mean that the lady is stuck with it forever,

although one hopes she sticks with him. In a happy moment, far from the proposal time, preferably after the wedding, she says musingly, "I always want to wear my engagement ring, but it's not comfortable for everyday. Do you mind if I have it re-set?"

By this time he has forgotten the Four Cs and his investment in them and probably prefers not to be troubled with the matter.

DEAR MISS MANNERS:

I am a divorced male whose fiancée is also divorced and marrying for the second time. What is the currently accepted protocol for engagement rings in second marriages? Also, must my fiancée's ring necessarily be larger than the one given by her ex-husband to his current fiancée?

GENTLE READER:

The correct formula is to multiply the size of the lady's first engagement ring by the size of the one you gave your first wife and add to it the size of the ring her former husband gave his fiancée. With any luck, you will soon reach a stalemate, with the gentlemen no longer able to afford to raise the stakes and the ladies no longer able to lift their hands, and Miss Manners will be able to turn her attention to sensible questions.

DEAR MISS MANNERS:

I have been engaged for nearly nine months, but my fiancé and I have recently bought my engagement ring together. My mother is upset with us, because she says that the ring is supposed to be given to me at the engagement party and that I am not supposed to see it until then. Is there any truth to this saying?

GENTLE READER:

No, Miss Manners is afraid not. She doesn't want to encourage you to engage in etiquette battles with your mother—the two of you have a wedding yet to get through—but she knows of no such custom. Presentation of an engagement ring is necessarily a private event. A party is to announce that the engagement already exists—not to allow people to witness its being made.

⌒ The Announcement ⌒

DEAR MISS MANNERS:

As of yesterday I became "officially" engaged to my long-term, live-in boyfriend. I use the term "officially" since I actually received the ring I had picked out approximately 18 months ago. I have been referring to him as my fiancé since that time.

Now that I've received the ring, I am joyful. I want to share my joy with others, including former colleagues who supported me during difficult times, but I am uncomfortable for two reasons:

1. Since I have been referring to him as my fiancé for so long, I assume that these folks might rightly wonder what the big deal is about the ring.
2. I fear that providing this information is the equivalent of soliciting congratulations. I am not comfortable being the object of attention, nor do I wish for others who are not very close friends to think that I am merely telling them as a means of bragging or of soliciting gifts.

We plan to have a small intimate wedding with only very close friends and family—these colleagues would not be invited. With all this in mind, is it appropriate to mention my engagement or to send an informal e-mail with a photograph of us together?

GENTLE READER:

Much as Miss Manners would like to help you prolong the excitement by declaring forty-seven stages of engagement, she is afraid that your forebodings are accurate. There are only so many times you can expect a burst of enthusiasm by announcing the same engagement.

Whatever terminology you and your fiancé enjoy using is fine between you, but you actually became engaged when you agreed to marry. You then went public with it and, Miss Manners trusts, received everyone's good wishes. You may now go around confiding to friends that you received an engagement ring, which is, indeed, tantamount to asking for admiration, but is generally indulged. But one is only allowed so many "Guess what!" moments.

Once you let go of the idea of "official" occasions, you will be able to revert to your normal polite consideration of who would like to know what, and to put it in a normally friendly form.

That you now have an engagement ring will be of interest only to those who are close to you, or those whose engagement rings you have admired. Relatives should be receptive to pictures of you and your fiancé, as should any good friends who have not met him. As long as you think of all this as part of the normal give-and-take of minor news that friends and family trade, rather than as An Announcement, you should be able to spread the word without undue self-aggrandizement.

DEAR MISS MANNERS:

I received a formal, engraved engagement announcement; the couple does not plan to be married any time soon. Is a gift required, or even appropriate?

GENTLE READER:

Traditionally, there is no such thing as a private, formal engagement announcement, as opposed to general announcements in newspapers. People are supposed to let their friends know the happy news by telephone, letter, or other informal means.

Miss Manners does not want to suggest that your friends had any ulterior motive for inventing a new form. Perhaps they fell under the influence of a stationer who had an ulterior motive of his own. Perhaps they have more friends than they can possibly keep in touch with using the normal methods, although that does seem to make nonsense out of the definition of friendship (and e-mail). In any case, the response is the same as if they had written that friendly note. Write back, congratulating them and wishing them happiness. No presents are necessary.

⌐⌐ *The Reaction* ⌐⌐

DEAR MISS MANNERS:

I am feeling incorrect. A colleague recently became engaged and was delightedly showing her ring to the women at work. Each one squealed "Congratulations!"

While I am as happy as the others are for her, it seems a bit like she won the grand prize on a game show, rather than committed to a lifetime of caring and responsibility.

What is the "correct" response? I settled for something along the order of "I'm *sooooo* happy for you!" which did not seem as celebratory, but was the best I could do on short notice.

There are many young, unmarried, women in my office, and I am sure to have to know the answer to this question in the near future.

GENTLE READER:

It is you whom Miss Manners must congratulate. You have accidentally stumbled on the correct approach. Strictly speaking, a lady should never be congratulated on her engagement or marriage, however charming the gentleman. It is he who is officially the lucky one, to whom congratulations are given. She is properly wished happiness.

DEAR MISS MANNERS:

I am a gay man planning to become engaged in the near future. While I'm looking forward to getting married, I am dreading the questions from friends and family about the legality of the wedding, such as "Are you going to go to Massachusetts?" or "Is that legal here yet?"

At best, the questions throw cold water on what should otherwise be a joyful and congratulatory moment. At worst, it puts our attention on the rather painful subject of marriage inequality. I do not wish to sound angry or confrontational in my reply by saying something like, "No, did you travel to a strange state to get married?" or "Well, I'm not waiting around for my state to get its act together!"

We intend to have a minister preside and to be as lawfully joined as possible, but I do not feel as if this is something I should have to justify to others, nor do I feel my wedding must be some sort of political statement. I've contemplated appropriate responses, such as, "Oh, of course not," but I worry that will only lead to further questions. What is a proper, polite, and effective response to a question about my pending marriage that I do not wish to answer?

GENTLE READER:

Precedent here is that most people love to talk about their wedding plans and take the slightest show of interest as license to go on and on until others are weak with boredom.

There is no reason that you cannot achieve this effect. Just follow Miss Manners' rule of answering the question you want to deal with rather than the one that was asked. It got her through school. "Right now we're talking about the cake," you might say. "He likes chocolate, but one of my aunts is allergic to chocolate, so I'm thinking that maybe we should have cake that she can eat, but chocolate pastries on the side for those who want them."

DEAR MISS MANNERS:

A friend of mine that I knew in high school recently became engaged. She is 20 years old, marrying a man in his late 20s who has a child from a previous relationship. They are planning a wedding after he gets back from military training and she is not only planning her wedding but preparing to move 15 hours away with him and his young child.

I personally do not approve of her marrying at such a young age and am concerned for her jumping into an "instant family" so quickly, since they haven't been dating for very long. It seems like nobody else finds this early and mismatched union strange except for me!

How do I respond to her excitement when she talks about her wedding? It wouldn't sit well with me to lie and tell her that I am "so happy" for her, nor would it be appropriate to express my disapproval. Help!

GENTLE READER:

Can you squeak out "I wish you great happiness"?

Surely this is true. Please don't tell Miss Manners that your lack of enthusiasm for the bridegroom and lack of belief in the success of the marriage translates into the hope that your gloomy predictions are right.

DEAR MISS MANNERS:

I am in my late twenties and a lot more of my friends are becoming engaged, and something has really been bothering me.

I am an activist and really have issues with diamonds due to their origins. It is actually one of the main reasons my husband and I did away with the idea of rings altogether until we could find a jewelry company who thinks along our lines (I have found several recently).

I am happy for all my friends' engagements, but when they go and show me the diamond and ask my opinion on the ring (i.e., "Isn't it beautiful?"), I really want to explain my position on these stones.

I know that at parties in mixed company, it is definitely not appropriate (nobody wants an activist to spoil a wedding or engagement party) and I usually end up stammering and saying "Very nice." This usually makes me feel very uncomfortable and hypocritical like I am accepting these stones as being okay.

How do I get away from the constant feeling that I should let them know how I really feel about the ring, but that it has nothing to do with the actual engagement?

GENTLE READER:

"Isn't it beautiful?" is not a question; it is a prompt to give the conventional compliment. If you used the opportunity to state your position, what do you think would happen?

Struck by the righteousness of your stand, the new fiancée would pull off her ring in horror and fling it away?

No? Then what would you hope to accomplish?

Miss Manners assures you that people do not absorb moral lessons from those who trample on their feelings. Rather, they forever associate the unpleasantness of the spokesperson with the cause itself. So if the certainty that you would hurt your friends' feelings is not enough to satisfy you into mere murmured politeness, how about the certainty that you would hurt your cause?

⌒ The Pre-Wedding Parties: Number and Composition ⌒

DEAR MISS MANNERS:

My fiancé and I are on a tight budget and are planning a small, family-only wedding. My mother would like to throw us an engagement party, a work buddy wants to give me a shower, and I'd love to have a bachelorette party with my girlfriends.

Many people that would attend these events would not be invited to the wedding. I've heard from several sources that to not invite these people to the wedding is the height of rudeness. Is that true? Do I really have to give up these special events because my fiancé and I can't afford a big wedding? Please help!

GENTLE READER:

Help with what? The notion that every bride is entitled to a series of parties? That people are happy to attend such events even if their presence is not sought for the wedding itself?

These people are, presumably, your friends, so you are in a better position than Miss Manners to guess their reactions. What you have to keep making clear is that you are not favoring some friends over others, in which case it would be extraordinarily rude to expect the unchosen to do the minor celebrations only to be excluded from the main one.

What you are doing, you must explain, is being married privately, with only family present. It would be in bad taste to plead budget considerations. Hard as it may be to believe, there are people who simply prefer not to surround their marriage ceremonies with hoopla.

Then talk to your mother about who, in her circle and yours, are close enough to be delighted if she says something like, "Emmeline will be married with just the family there, but I'm throwing a little party where she and Emmet can see the people we care about."

You should permit the work shower only if it is customary in your office to mark colleagues' weddings in this way without further expectations. And as for showers and other gatherings of your friends—they are not for you to propose. Should friends come forth and offer to give them, confining their guest lists to those who understand the situation, Miss Manners will not object.

~The Engagement Party~

DEAR MISS MANNERS:

I am puzzled over the purpose of the Engagement Party. Is it an occasion for celebration with gifts expected, or merely a celebration? I am of the generation that believes that only a wedding gift is required. Is this another event that is taken to extreme like holding graduation for preschoolers, flying children to Disney World for their birthday, etc.?

GENTLE READER:

The engagement party as such is a relatively new form and Miss Manners has the same suspicions that you do. It developed at about the time that adults started giving annual birthday parties for themselves.

That is not to say that relatives and friends did not give respectable parties for engaged couples. Please bear with Miss Manners while she attempts to explain the subtle difference.

One type of party was to announce an engagement that was not otherwise known. Guests were invited as to a no-particular-occasion party, and the host would surprise everyone by proposing a toast to his daughter and future son-in-law.

Another type could be given by either set of parents, or by friends, to introduce their circle to the person who was marrying into it. Before and after the wedding, friends might entertain in honor of the new couple, but—and here is the shocker—no presents were given, just lots of hugs and kisses and happy wishes.

However—please see the following.

DEAR MISS MANNERS:

My husband and I are planning an engagement party for our daughter and her fiancé this summer. Is it rude to enclose a registry list with the invitation?

We were married 25 years ago. We planned our wedding in three months and never registered for our wedding. Now we have four wonderful daughters and would like to give them a little more than what we could do for ourselves at the time. Can you help us?

GENTLE READER:

By chipping in?

If you have the kind wish of giving your daughters more than you had when you were married, there is nothing to prevent you from doing so. Miss Manners would hope that a modicum of sense and taste would prevent you from giving what you can beg from others.

DEAR MISS MANNERS:

I was invited to a brunch in honor of engaged friends, hosted by the parents of the groom-to-be. In addition to a gift for the engaged couple, does etiquette also require a gift for the host and hostess?

GENTLE READER:

No, but the question that is probably torturing you is: Where is all this going to end? There will be the wedding showers, the celebratory parties, the housewarming, the anniversaries, the re-enactment . . .

Are you going to have to furnish your friends' entire lives?

Miss Manners assures you not. Neither engagement presents nor host presents for parties are obligatory. You may want to bring one anyway, but two would be overdoing it.

DEAR MISS MANNERS:

My husband and I were embarrassed by the gift we brought to an engagement party—a funny relationship comedy DVD and a box of popcorn to pop while watching it. We thought it might be fun to enjoy during the stress of planning a wedding. The cost was probably $10.

However, when the engagees opened their presents in front of the group, we saw that they were receiving big-ticket items more typical of wedding presents, such as TVs and microwaves.

What is the appropriate gift for an engagement party? Especially if, as in my situation, you are close with the bride and will also be buying a bridal shower gift and then the wedding gift. Or perhaps you are even a member of the bridal party and will have further expenses. Buying so many gifts for the same couple can get a little tiring—and expensive!

GENTLE READER:

Thus making embarrassment sound like the best choice. But Miss Manners sees no reason for you to be embarrassed. You gave a thoughtful little present, appropriate to the occasion, and if others choose to give two or more sets of what are, in effect, wedding presents, do not let it bother you.

⌒The Shower⌒

In proper American etiquette, a bridal shower is a lighthearted event among intimate friends, not something required to call attention to a wedding in the way that a rain shower calls attention to the need to fetch an umbrella.

Bridal showers are incidental and optional gatherings that may be initiated and given by bridesmaids or other friends—or not. The bride should be pleased and surprised if one is spontaneously suggested to her. No one should be invited to more than one such event for the occasion. Presents should be mere tokens.

However, we live in an age of entitlement and all these rules are being violated right and left. In her darker moments, Miss Manners muses that the shower has become just one more opportunity to turn a milestone to material advantage.

This should not discourage guests from abiding by the rules of etiquette always available to them: They may decline the invitation, sending nothing more than their good wishes. Some couples used to think that in itself was quite valuable.

DEAR MISS MANNERS:

What happened to the "rule" that said family members do not host bridal or baby showers?

GENTLE READER:

Nothing happened to the rule; it's still there. It is the sense that it is cheeky to ask for presents for your relatives that something happened to.

⌒The Virtual Shower⌒

DEAR MISS MANNERS:

I have been asked to be maid of honor for a good friend who lives quite a distance away. Her fiancé lives in another part of the country, and nearly all the invited guests reside all over the country and in Europe.

How am I to throw a shower for the bride? Is it proper to have a "shower by mail," where people send gifts on a certain day?

GENTLE READER:

A shower is a party, Miss Manners feels it necessary to remind you. What you are describing is a mail solicitation, which is not regulated by etiquette but by the post office.

It is not an absolute requirement that the maid of honor give a shower. If you want to throw a party, it would seem more sensible to have a bridesmaids' luncheon when everyone is gathered for the wedding.

⌁The Double Shower⌁

DEAR MISS MANNERS:

Please help fast! Time is running out. A friend is having a baby soon, and she and the baby's father have agreed to wait until a month after the baby is born to get married. Can we combine a baby and bridal shower, or is it unethical to ask people to bring two gifts? We really don't have the time for two separate showers.

GENTLE READER:

How fast? Miss Manners is out of breath. It's not just from rushing (if her usual stately pace can be speeded up at all). Has the purpose of marriage so changed that it is more important how the bride looks at the wedding than that the baby be born within the marriage? Hand Miss Manners her smelling salts, and don't bother reminding her that this aspect is none of her business.

Yes, holding two showers for the same person would strain the patience even of friends. But so would expecting them to bring separate presents to one shower. As your friend has combined being a bride and being a mother, there is no reason that your shower honoring her should not do so as well, allowing people to choose items appropriate to either aspect of her new life.

⌒ The Endless Shower ⌒

DEAR MISS MANNERS:

I am a single, late-twenty-something just trying to make ends meet. Many of my friends are getting married and having multiple wedding showers—tool and gadget, lawn and garden, lingerie, etc.

I want to help all of these friends celebrate their milestones, but frankly, I'm broke. I also think it is kind of tacky and unfair that couples (who each own their own home and make more money than I do) are garnering gifts from single, struggling friends on a regular basis.

Is there any good way to show my appreciation and care for the couples without buying so many gifts? Is there any "rule of thumb" on number or frequency of showers?

GENTLE READER:

Of course there is. Miss Manners hopes that you do not suppose that etiquette says, "Whatever you need or want, just keep rounding up your friends and making them hand it over."

But your friends seem to think that etiquette does say exactly that, so the only way to protect yourself is to make your own rule: accept only one shower per couple. Your supposition that it is necessary to show your appreciation and care for a couple by doing all their shopping is excessive. You need only express regret when you decline an invitation—or six of them.

⌒ The Unfriendly Shower ⌒

DEAR MISS MANNERS:

I just came from a bridal shower with very nice food, very nice conversation, no one in the room without at least one academic degree. But, not once during the party were we greeted by the bride-to-be, or, the maid of honor who was listed as the giver of the shower. Neither did I see them thank anyone for coming, or, acknowledge that a gift was given.

Early on, I twice asked the mother of the bride where the bride-to-be was, and was ignored. The bride-to-be and the maid of honor hung with the bridal party.

The parents of both the bride and groom-to-be have good manners. Somehow these skills were not inherited. I truly believe that the two do not know that they were supposed to greet the guests, say thank you for coming, and acknowledge that a gift was brought. We in the United States put so much emphasis on academic accomplishments and so little emphasis on social skills and etiquette.

GENTLE READER:

Indeed. But your having been twice ignored by the mother of the bride suggests to Miss Manners that inheritance in this case would not have helped.

⌐The Prenuptial Contract⌐

"Daddy's being horrid," the bride-to-be would say in simpler times. "He wants to know about the money—as if I cared about money! All I care about is you. His stupid solicitors are even asking about dowager rights. That's disgusting. Why, if anything happened to you—or if I thought you didn't love me anymore—I wouldn't need any money, because I'd just kill myself."

Her fiancé would take her hand in his, glancing around to make sure no one was looking. "My parents are just as bad," he would confide. "Money, property—my mother wanted to know what would happen to the family pearls if I predeceased you and you married again. You wouldn't marry again, would you? I'm beginning to think they can't ever have been in love themselves. No one who understood how I feel about you could even think of material things."

Thus the happy couple could snuggle up against each other in perfect understanding and love while her family and his hammered out an agreement that represented each of their interests should the unthinkable occur.

Miss Manners does not recount this tale to suggest that all does not always turn out as the affianced imagine, nor even to warn that they should prepare themselves in case it doesn't. She believes in true love. She is merely pointing out that concern about the eventual disposition of money and property when a marriage begins is not a new phenomenon. The Victorians knew how to handle it a lot better than modern couples.

The modern approach is that the bridegroom (or whichever of the couple is richer) shoves a document into the bride's face the day, or perhaps only hours, before the wedding and says, "Here, you have to sign this." At any reluctance, he threatens to call off the marriage. By this time she would be only too glad to be rid of him, but she feels a sense of responsibility to the caterer. So she signs.

It is true that in the antique version it was entirely possible that the gentleman would eventually run off with the governess and that the lady not only did not kill herself, but, as he was able to show, had long since been consoling herself with the curate.

However, in the modern version disillusion and bitterness have set in before the wedding has taken place, whereas in the olden days, the financial arrangement was kept entirely separate from the courtship. The agreement by which she had to give back the pearls and he was unable to touch her family property had been cheerfully made between two parties, either parents or their representatives, whose business sense was unclouded by emotion.

Miss Manners suggests that anyone interested in a prenuptial agreement about finances return to the ancestral wisdom. Perhaps there are no parents around willing to involve themselves in the transaction, but one may still blame others for being unromantic, even if one has hired them for the purpose.

Miss Manners recommends a version of the following dialogue:

"Oh, darling, I wish we were married already. There's so much to do, and I just want to be alone with you."

"Mmmmm. Me, too."

"Did you call about the cake?"

"I thought you were going to do that."

"That's right—I will. I'm sorry. Oh, and then there's another thing. My lawyer has done up some property agreement—what happens if I die, or whatever."

"Don't even think such a thing. I couldn't live without you. What's in it? Where is it?"

"Darling, I don't even know. I find the whole thing degrading. I'm just going to have my lawyer send it over to your lawyer. Now come here."

TROUBLESHOOTING

DEAR MISS MANNERS:

Now that legislation permits, my fiancé and I plan to have a very small wedding, followed by a blessing of our marriage at the church we regularly attend at home and a small reception. We hope to do this in the same dignified and respectable manner with which we live, and we want those closest to us to witness our pledge to each other.

We are not entering into this lightly, and most of our beloved friends and family have been very supportive. However, some acquaintances, and sadly enough, some of my family, cannot resist pointing out that since this second ceremony isn't a "real" wedding, they are not obligated by love or duty to behave accordingly. Some have declined, others have indicated that we should not invite them to our reception, as they will not attend. Some have gone so far as to scoff and say, "Even if it is legal, I still think it's wrong. Can't you have it in a park or a hotel?" One cousin said she felt that it was an "abomination" to bless our marriage in a church. (Fortunately, the clergy at our church disagree.)

Miss Manners, my fiancé is a police officer, and spends every working day helping others. He is as kind and decent a person as ever lived, and I cannot understand why some people—including my own parents—can overlook this obvious fact. Further, I can't understand why my happiness—which my fiancé goes to great lengths to enhance—means so little to them. I have thus far managed to avoid political or religious discussions with those who have already made up their minds on the issue. However, I am having a difficult time containing my anger when I see the hurt look on my beloved's face after he receives yet another declined invitation or crass comment.

My responses have been limited to the breezy: "Well, we're going ahead with it anyway, and I'm sending an invitation to you anyway, because we would love to have you there. It's important to us. Please promise me you'll take some time to consider it before responding." Or I resort to the direct: "We will miss you, and I hope that at some point your feelings for us will help you overcome your [meaningful pause] preconceived ideas about our wedding."

Should I just accept the fact that the very act of us marrying is viewed as a personal insult by these otherwise nice people? Or must I embark on an exhausting campaign of explaining why we feel it is important that they be there in some capacity? Or should I just borrow my partner's billy club and bop them on the noggin? (I already know the answer to that last, but I'm striving for a sense of humor.)

Gentle Reader:

We are striving to keep up with your extreme generosity in still wanting to have these rude and intolerant people at your wedding. And if you can set an example for us, perhaps you will also be able to influence those who have so much more to learn.

⌒ Discouraging Presents ⌒

Dear Miss Manners:

As the mother of a bride-elect, I endeavor to guide her to a tasteful wedding which does not ignore proper conventions. We will be throwing a small engagement party for the families and bridal party. We did not include any mention whatsoever of gifts on the invitation, however, a relative has already inquired about what a proper gift would be. My response was that no gift was required, the pleasure of their company would be wonderful.

We are slightly uncomfortable even giving this party as we do not wish to seem to be fishing for gifts, in fact, we will be uncomfortable if any gifts are forthcoming, but also wanted to avoid the awkward "no gifts please" phrase on the invitation, which to my mind is another way of asking for gifts. I have been to social occasions before where this phrase was employed and then been the only person to actually honor the request.

GENTLE READER:

You are correct about "no gifts please." It is often ignored because it plants an idea where none might have been. If you merely give a party in honor of the bridal couple, not an "engagement" party, your guests will inquire whether they are expected to bring presents, and then you can say no, of course not.

⁓The Shower On Demand⁓

DEAR MISS MANNERS:

A friend I've known for nine years is now engaged to be married. She always came over for holiday dinners, etc., but now I hardly ever hear from her or get together. She is expecting me to hold the wedding shower at my house. Should I confront her about how I feel about our friendship or lack of, or should I just go ahead with her shower and be done with it?

GENTLE READER:

You won't be done with it. Not with a bride so brazen as to demand to be honored—and by someone she doesn't otherwise see.

Tell her that you feel sure that she would rather have a host with whom she is in closer contact and who will be better acquainted with her current social crowd. Thus your feelings about the friendship can be neatly and diplomatically inserted as you politely disengage yourself from hosting duties.

∼The Demand for Cash∼

DEAR MISS MANNERS:

I have encountered a couple of shower practices involving cash. One is the money tree, where people hang money on some structure for the honoree; the other is the practice of pinning money directly upon the person, well, okay, the raiment, of the honoree.

The first time I heard of this, I was astounded, but apparently the practice has spread to the point that I hear of it quite often and no one seems to give it a second thought.

I have yet to be invited to such an event, but if I were, unless I knew the person quite well, I think I would feel a bit silly pinning money to his or her clothing. How does one respond to such an invitation, beyond the raised eyebrow?

GENTLE READER:

What an antiquated notion that you would have to know the people quite well in order to pin money on their raiment. This practice is actually quite an acceptable and time-honored tradition . . . at strip clubs. If you are given advanced warning of such an event and it makes you uncomfortable, you may simply decline and send a small (read: token, not extravagant or registered for) gift, if you wish. If you find that the invitation to participate occurs only after you are already there, perhaps you can hold on to your gift, if they let you, and awkwardly shove it at them when they present themselves for money. Or you could make an elaborate show of getting out your wallet and going through your bills. Either response emphasizes the crassness of the whole thing—or, at the very least, occupies your hands while you are raising your eyebrows.

⌒The Demand for Laundered Cash⌒

DEAR MISS MANNERS:

Two close friends are giving my fiancé and me a creative and unusual shower. They have chosen our honeymoon as the theme and have suggested we register at an online honeymoon registry. While the gesture is thoughtful and generous, I am concerned about the propriety of the registry when the guests will essentially be contributing money, not giving a traditional gift.

When I relayed the hosts' suggestion to my mother, she balked, saying that it's inappropriate to "solicit cash." Since these sites allow guests to buy specific gifts (i.e., dinner at a bistro in Paris), it doesn't seem exactly like soliciting cash to me, though the waters are a bit murky for someone who is trying to follow the etiquette rules pretty strictly.

GENTLE READER:

Doesn't seem too murky to us. Paying for your Paris dinner is still soliciting cash; you've just provided a time and a place for it. Encourage your hosts to abandon this atrocious idea (or ask your mother to use her authority to run interference) and use their creativity for decorations instead. If the guests wish to participate in the theme, they can get you honeymoon-related trinkets instead.

⌒The Ceremonial Opening⌒

DEAR MISS MANNERS:

For my friends and me, this is the age of showers: bridal and baby (usually, but not always, in that order). These parties should be a great opportunity to celebrate and catch up with friends. Unfortunately, many of them become tedious due to the opening of gifts.

At larger showers, gift opening takes over the whole event, at least for the honoree. Expressing joy on receiving these everyday items, though they be welcome and necessary, must get exhausting. Moreover, since most of the presents were chosen from a gift registry, not even the color is a surprise.

I will be hosting a shower for a dear friend and would love to avoid having the party hijacked by the presents. I've suggested that it might be more fun and comfortable for her to open her gifts at home, so that she could enjoy her guests during the shower. Her mother was appalled. She insisted that everyone loves the gift opening and it would be mean-spirited of me to deprive friends and relatives of a chance to see the loot. Since I don't want to cross the mother of the bride, I suppose I have no recourse but to go with the public unwrapping tradition. Unless you have other suggestions?

GENTLE READER:

You are correct: As a general rule you don't want to cross the mother, and opening presents purchased from a list is not exactly a hootenanny.

You could reconcile this by suggesting that the present opening be saved until the end of the party. As hostess, you could begin this by thanking your guests for coming, alerting them to the fact that the bride and family will be staying on to open their presents, and that the guests are most welcome to witness the fun if they wish, thus providing a gracious opening for guests to miss the fun and take their leave.

Self-Thanks

DEAR MISS MANNERS:

What is the etiquette for preventing someone else from engaging in rudeness on my behalf? I am engaged to be married, and a dear family friend is hosting a bridal shower for me. At a friend's bridal shower several years ago, also hosted by this woman, she purchased thank-you-note stationery and set out the envelopes next to the guest book, with the instruction that each guest was to address an envelope to herself, to save the bride-to-be time. Apparently, this is now the "custom" in my area.

I believe this to be terribly rude and would prefer to address (and write, of course) the thank-you notes myself. But inquiring whether this practice will be followed and insisting that I would really prefer to address the notes myself seems inconsistent with the demureness the bride-to-be is supposed to exhibit. And waiting until the shower would seem like rejecting a gift, as the stationery would already be purchased.

I know this woman means well. What is a girl trying hard to be proper to do?

GENTLE READER:

Beat her to the I'm-saving-you-the-trouble punch by making a show of the stationary you purchased just for the occasion. Then ask her for the addresses in advance, or, since it's likely you supplied many of them yourself, show her that you've already addressed the envelopes. Your immediate expressions of gratitude to your hostess and the guests should be sufficiently demure.

CHAPTER THREE

Three Terrible Ideas

THE WEDDING AS "MY DAY"

That people should get married when they are old enough to know what they are doing seems to Miss Manners to be a remarkably good idea. She would think it reasonable to assume that, by that time, they also know enough about themselves, their families, their friends, and human nature, and also about how to entertain, to be able to plan an event that brings all these people together in harmony and delight.

Not necessarily, it seems. Wisdom often deserts even the most level-headed people when it comes to their own weddings. Having presumably learned life's most important lesson—that other people have feelings that must be taken into consideration—they have been known to regress for this one event.

Never mind that maturity had a lot to do with making them desirable as marriage partners. With the modern form of extended courtship (often extended beyond parental patience), there is ample opportunity to discover before marriage whether someone else is unselfish enough to take an interest in one's own happiness. It should therefore set off a warning when either one says (or hears), "Ever since I was small, I wanted . . ." or "This'll be a good chance to . . ." or "After all, we're the people who are getting married, so . . ."

Only a warning. Miss Manners, who always assumes the best, is ready to hear these openings properly completed:

> *"Ever since I was small, I wanted to marry someone wonderfully kind."*
>
> *"This'll be a good chance to gather all the people we care about and show them how much they mean to us."*
>
> *"After all, we're the people who are getting married, so we should take the responsibility and see to it that this doesn't unduly burden our parents."*

Here, for any brides or bridegrooms who are old enough to know better but may have forgotten, is a reminder list of wedding wisdom.

1. Secret fantasies should remain fantasies, if not secret. No good will come of their being acted out in public. Miss Manners has heard from multi-divorced grandmothers who confide that in their latest engagements they see an opportunity to hold the wedding of their childish dreams, designed for nubile brides shyly emerging from their parents' protection; she has heard from successful businesswomen who never would have dreamed of going into show business who now want to express themselves in wedding dramas of their own making. She sympathizes with both, provided they get a grip on themselves. Miss Manners believes all weddings should be festive, but one should not depend too heavily on the indulgence even close friends have for the showily inappropriate.

2. Parenthood is not exclusively a financial relationship and thus its privileges cannot be suspended when the payments cease. Grown children cannot reappear demanding that they are owed sponsorship of their weddings, nor can they announce that they plan to ignore their parents' feelings and opinions on this family occasion, since they themselves are paying the bills.

3. While most people are pleased to hear that their friends or relatives are getting married, few are so moved as to want to mortgage their

own futures in order to make all the couple's dreams come true. Anyway, it is the guests, not the bridal couple, who are supposed to come up with the idea of wedding presents.

4. Guests are guests, and must be treated hospitably, even when the hosts happen to be using the day to get married. "We're only having foods we like" is the wrong attitude; the right one is, "We're having special treats that we think everyone will enjoy," even if this is applied to the same menu.

5. A wedding is not an opportunity to boss other people around, whether this means assigning bridesmaids to buy dresses they hate, or divorced parents to behave as if they were still married. Neither, for that matter, is marriage such an opportunity.

⌒ Dissenting Views ⌒

DEAR MISS MANNERS:

The marrying age is increasing, brides and grooms are more independent, but the bride's parents are still responsible for the wedding. Parents have two or three decades to notice that they have a daughter, and to realize that someday she will probably marry. Saving for a wedding should be a priority, and a wedding should not take the bride's parents by surprise.

It seems that parents often dismiss this responsibility, as some dismiss their responsibility to plan for their children's college education. This is consistent with our self-centered society.

If parents have to go into debt to pay for their daughter's wedding, then shame on them for not planning ahead. Yes, the costs should be reasonable, and the bride and groom can contribute their own funds if they want something extravagant, but $10,000 to $20,000 is not extravagant for a middle- to upper-middle class family in this culture. Think of it as a wedding gift from the parents, instead of the dowry that was required from the parents in past centuries.

GENTLE READER:

You're joking, right? Surely the complaint about "our self-centered society" was the tip-off. Please tell Miss Manners—and more importantly, your parents—that you are joking.

DEAR MISS MANNERS:

What about inviting people verbally, say five months before, and then changing your mind? I realize that it's not right, but sometimes in the expansive mood of the engagement, these mistakes are made. In addition, I've known some sourpusses for many years. They could easily pout their way through the wedding and not share the happiness. Yet I've known them for fifteen years or so, and feel an obligation (somewhat). How much of my day really is this wedding day, anyway?

GENTLE READER:

You pushed the wrong button here. Miss Manners hates that bridal canard about My Day (even aside from the question, Why isn't it Our Day?)—as if getting married, of all things, gave one the right to suspend normal consideration of others. Here you are contemplating using My Day as an excuse to dis-invite guests (which would be a high insult) or to rate your friends and relations on whether they will be able to produce suitable facial expressions (which would be a new low in choosing bridal accessories).

⟶ Personalizing Your Wedding ⟶

Isn't your wedding already personal because you are the ones who are getting married?

The professionals strongly urge you to believe otherwise. "Show your guests who you really are through pictures, videos, blogs, programs, table names, and any other means possible," they declare. "Stick to a theme, a color palette, and foods that represent your unique wedding journey." "Mix and match ceremonies and customs to suit your personality." And, above all, "Don't try to be a people pleaser."

"It's your day," they insist. Cram it all in. Your tastes, color prefer-ences, and entertainment style should be fiercely cultivated and relent-lessly shared throughout your wedding and reception. Hour upon hour of highlights of your supposed lifestyle, reinforced by tint, taste, sight, and sound. Questions such as "What is your signature drink?" and "What do you mean, your bridegroom says he doesn't have a favorite font—he must!" are not allowed to go unanswered. Unless, of course, you just want to be like everybody else.

Unfortunately, personalizing your wedding turns out to mean de-personalizing everyone else. The bridesmaids have not only been dressed identically, but told to wear the same chin-length bobs and shade of blush because these look good on you. The guests all have to eat uncooked food because you've adopted a raw-food lifestyle. The older generation will be excluded from dancing because acid funk is the only accurate musical reflection of your union. After a lifetime of choosing friends and learning how to get along with your family, you are going to make everyone eat, see, listen to, and look like only what is in your taste.

That is not a wedding. It is a cult. Doesn't making your closest friends appear identical—or worse, colorized mini versions of you—defeat the purpose and pleasure of having multiple friends? And didn't you just give everyone you know a major demonstration of your taste by whom you selected to marry?

The good news is that a wedding is not your only chance to express your taste to a captive audience. You will have more parties. You will wear other clothes. You will have more stories to tell and food to share. A better way to share your personal values and good taste is by showing a sincere regard for other people's individuality and feelings.

Think of all the time, trouble, and money you would save. There would be no debating whether your names should be in silver or gold on matchbooks and paper napkins, which you don't need anyway, as your guests should be issued real napkins and are not likely to smoke.

You would not be saddled with the assignment of composing vows and other declarations in competition with great writers of the ages, and of reciting them in front of people who have a sentimental attachment to the time-honored words you rejected.

You would not have to think of a theme for the wedding, either the popular ones, such as (pseudo) Victorian or a medieval tournament, or something reflecting your hobbies or affection for your pets. The theme, as it were, would be A Wedding, the basic pattern for which has already been worked out for you over the generations.

You would not have to hire a master of ceremonies who patronizes your parents and milks the crowd to applaud you and the entire wedding party, and you would not have to worry about his getting your name wrong.

You would not have to design the invitations, as the form of the third-person, engraved invitation on white or ivory paper has been the same for as long as anyone can remember.

Nor would you discover the work involved in making an autobiographical video, or the disappointment of seeing its audience wandering off for drinks, leaving only a few relatives already familiar with the pictures and story, plus some engaged couples hoping to learn from your mistakes.

And while you will naturally exercise your taste in making the arrangements, you could save yourself a lot of flak if the food and music were to include not only your own favorites but take into consideration the pleasure of a variety of guests. It would be, nowadays, a highly unusual and individualistic way to approach a wedding.

The Indirect Defense

DEAR MISS MANNERS:

One of my brothers is about to be married to a woman I liked very much when we met. Since then, however, I have become appalled.

I observed her and her friends doing the "white glove test" at a dinner party. She has asked my parents to pay half the wedding costs (her parents have encouraged her to reduce her expectations). She called my mother to ask exactly what her future in-laws will give as a wedding present and, when told, said, "Oh, I guess that will be okay." I have been making a quilt and, when the quilt top was done, she strongly desired that I make the two-hour round-trip for her to inspect it. Everything is done with a cheerful voice and pleasant smile, but it makes her behavior no more appealing. I wish to be polite, but my stress level increases with each encounter. The wedding is three months away!

GENTLE READER:

Three months seems sufficient time for you, and perhaps your parents as well, to have a cozy little chat with your brother. It should go something like this:

"Tiffany is such a lovely girl, dear; we're all so happy for you. We're so much looking forward to having her in the family. I'm sure that she'll soon get used to our ways. But perhaps—since we don't want to get off on the wrong foot with her—you'd better tell her about us.

"As you know, we'd like you both to have lovely things, but we can't really see paying for a lavish wedding. And we felt funny about being asked about our presents. Tell her to have a little more faith in our desire to welcome her, even if she doesn't find us able to be as generous as you may have led her to expect. The quilt is a labor of love, but it's not reasonable to make a special trip to have it inspected. Tell her I want her to be happy with it, but I don't have that kind of leisure. Darling, I hope you didn't make her think we were rich, or had unlimited free time. But what we do have is lots of love to give your wife; see if you can make her understand that."

TROUBLESHOOTING

DEAR MISS MANNERS:

Through pure coincidence, it turns out that one of my cousins is getting married on the same day I am. We aren't very close, as she was very competitive with me while growing up.

She is getting married in the morning, and I am having an afternoon wedding with an evening reception. I assumed she wouldn't be able to make it to my reception as she would be exhausted and want to spend time with her new husband. However, I just received an e-mail from her saying she really wants to go.

I think it's great that she is considering it and would be happy to have her there. The catch is, she said she is not going to have enough time to change so she wants to wear her wedding attire (dress included) to my reception. I think this is terribly rude! I mean, how long does it take to change? Am I just being petty? How does one appropriately respond to something like that?

GENTLE READER:

With the gentleness you would use with a little girl who wants to wear her Halloween costume to school in September. While brides are not encouraged to dictate guests' clothing, they do get to be the only one in bridal attire at the wedding. Please tell her that you are sure that she will be more comfortable changing out of her wedding clothes, and that she is welcome to use your changing room to do so. Better send some family members in with her, though, so she doesn't return in your going-away outfit.

DEAR MISS MANNERS:

I am attending a wedding with my family next month and have received an e-mail giving the "attire for the ceremony and reception" as All White for women and girls, and khaki pants and white shirts for the men and boys. The e-mail states that this will make the wedding fit in with the couple's outdoor theme.

My questions: a. Is it appropriate for the couple to dictate what guests should wear to the wedding? b. Do guests need to go along with this? and c. Isn't it a *faux pas* for anyone but the bride to wear white at a wedding?

GENTLE READER:

a. no, b. no, and c. yes.

The idea of an "outdoor theme" just begs to be met with guests in hunting outfits and hiking gear. Or doing as the previous bride's cousin is attempting and wear your own white wedding dress. But you didn't hear it here.

THE WEDDING AS FUND-RAISER

When people used to speak of "marrying for money," it meant that one half of a bridal couple was plundering the other. Nobody, with the possible exception of the impoverished side of the aisle, considered that quite nice. But at least it kept whatever monetary exploitation was being practiced within the family—allowing for the fact that the family was actually being formed for that purpose.

Miss Manners has been told that brides and bridegrooms are not as inexperienced and innocent on their wedding days as they used to be. They have lawyers. But however much the possibility of greed between lovers may have been curbed by caution, the association of that nasty appetite in connection with matrimony does not seem to have been suppressed. Only now it is the guests to whom bridal couples turn when they think of making a profit out of matrimony. *Marrying for money* has come to mean making a profit from the wedding guests through direct cash contributions and wedding presents, after deducting the expenses of allowing them to attend.

Ever the romantic, Miss Manners has never actually believed that expectation of candlesticks is what motivates people to get married. She is quite severe with those who assume that other people only get themselves born, graduated, married, and pregnant for the purpose of extracting presents from them. But her Ghastly Wedding File is unfortunately bulging with anecdotes suggesting that guests are no longer considered people with whom brides and bridegrooms wish to share their happiness without regard to the possibility that they may be moved to give some token of their pleasure at the event. To wit:

- "I would like your opinion of the growing number of 'Jack and Jill' parties, often organized by the engaged couple themselves, who sell tickets for a dinner dance and keep the profits after expenses. Are these proper?"
- "The groom sent out an invitation by office computer, with a choice of entrées ($22 for steak, $19 for filet of sole or chicken Marsala), and the notations, 'No host cocktails,' 'Please R.s.v.p. with payment to ___' and 'There will be a money or gift basket available.'"

- "I was invited to a wedding dinner in a restaurant, where the check was handed to the groom, and without announcing the amount, he instructed everyone to pass down $75 a person. I did not drink any of the expensive wine, or coffee, and I split a dessert. The following day, I learned that my portion of the bill was less than $30 including tip."
- "A member of the bride's family passed a hat decorated with flowers and ribbons indicating it was for donations for the honeymoon. This is the second time this has happened to me."
- "I have been informed that an invited guest gives a money gift based on the cost of the wedding reception. In other words, if it is a nice, sit-down dinner with an orchestra, the guest is expected to give at least $100. Is a wedding reception now a charity event or an evening out which guests pay for, like the parties I attended at college, where you gave five bucks at the door to help the frat boys cut the cost of beer and snacks?"
- "The father of the bride, my relative, has informed me that my wedding gift (a museum-quality, handmade Native American work of art) was not appropriate. While refusing to assign a value to the item, he said it was not right, meaning not adequate, in view of the fact that four members of my family will be in attendance."
- "Just when I thought I'd seen it all, my daughter received a wedding invitation—not even from a close friend—with a card asking, 'If you would like to assist us in saving for the purchase of our first home together' and giving the name of their mortgage company. Thinking and hoping it was a joke, I called the 800-number. Sad to say, it was not."
- "Under the R.s.v.p., there was listed a money amount per person, with the notation, 'Includes dinner, dancing, and gift.' Is it considered appropriate for the invited guests to pay for the festivities and to chip in for a gift to be determined by someone else?"

In what one must presume to be an advance of delicacy, one couple offered a chart with a heart to be placed by the guest donor, indicating whether that person's contribution should be spent on such choices as "a night on the town," "a moonlight cruise," or "shopping for souvenirs." Another bride, eschewing the crudity of collecting cash, listed her demands and the catalog numbers with which they could be ordered.

It was Miss Manners' last illusion that people who engaged in such practices were aware that they had sacrificed any vestige of politeness and were just too greedy to care. Then she got the following letter, not even from the person who stood to profit:

> *Recently, I had a bridal shower for one of my girlfriends. I decided to have people send in $15 each for a group gift. This request was actually printed on the invitation. Now I know what is right, but I found that many people do not. Those who regretted did not send in their $15. I come from middle- to upper-class society, and I was just shocked at this. I know what is socially correct, so this is not a question, rather a reminder to those in my circles who need a refresher course on their manners.*

Miss Manners is relieved at the notation that this was not a question. It saves her from picking herself up from the floor, where she fell into a dead heap at the death of decency and hospitality—never mind romance.

FINANCIAL FRANKNESS

DEAR MISS MANNERS:

A couple in their mid-thirties, who will be married next month, have registered at a large department store for various household goods and china. However, they have made it quite clear that they do not intend to keep the china, but return it for cash to be used to purchase a stereo system. I am appalled. I am in my mid-thirties, too—am I *that* old?

Another bride, who has lived on her own for a few years, said that she wanted to have lots of showers so that she can get a lot of gifts. I just do not understand the greed. Money is not a problem for either couple, which is demonstrated by both brides purchasing expensive dresses and planning large receptions. Can you please explain what is going on?

GENTLE READER:

Greed? You want Miss Manners to explain greed? And then what? Lust and sloth? Instead, she will modestly limit herself to explaining why greed, always part of the human condition, is now so frankly expressed, rather than decently concealed.

The appalling idea that openness is a virtue, regardless of the sin being flaunted, has been around for a generation or so. That is why one hears ugly confessions accompanied by the self-righteous declaration, "But I'm not going to be a hypocrite," and why those who are timid about condemning dreadful behavior affect to be upset only by the transgressor's having subsequently lied about it.

In that spirit of total revelation, bridal couples are cheerfully admitting to their wedding guests that they are deeply focused on the presents they will receive and that, far from leaving the choice to the generosity and taste of their friends, they see the wedding as an opportunity to make others do their shopping.

Within this context, the couple willing to launder the money through some hapless store's china department may think themselves marvels of subtlety. Since they went and blabbed their scheme, Miss Manners can hardly agree with them.

All this frankness is highly unflattering to the guests, of course. They might have harbored the notion that the couple, being primarily interested in their friendship, was pleasantly surprised that friends, using their own taste and their sense of what the couple might appreciate, are also sending presents. This may never have been strictly true, but it was a pleasant illusion for the guests to have. Miss Manners cannot fathom why those who are disabused of this are still motivated to demonstrate affection.

~Sponsorship~

DEAR MISS MANNERS:

Will you please tell us where the custom originated of sponsors for weddings and debuts? Our neighbor is going around asking for money for an expensive wedding. We think it is awful for people to impose on other people for money for their sons' or daughters' weddings. If you can't afford an expensive wedding, settle for what you can afford. We paid for our daughter's wedding, down to the last flower or mixed drink. We all try to do the best for our kids, but why should we pay for others?

GENTLE READER:

The origin of this practice—Miss Manners refuses to dignify it by calling it a custom—is the strange idea that marriage is a justification for committing extortion. Miss Manners trusts that you will refuse to submit to this, without yourself being rude. You need merely decline the offer to be a "sponsor," and add that you send the couple your best wishes.

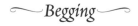

Begging

DEAR MISS MANNERS:

What is the proper way to request cash in lieu of gifts?

GENTLE READER:

Sit on the floor with a hat turned upside down on the floor beside you.

DEAR MISS MANNERS:

I was surprised that in this techno-savy age you didn't know there is a way to ask for cash, without begging. With all the wedding Web sites on the Internet these days some have actually become very helpful. One such Web site that my wife and I used very recently was TheKnot.com. On this Web site you can "Create a Gift."

The gist of it is, you put down something that you really want, but is not possible for someone to purchase; ex: new living room carpet. The Web site then allows you to set minimum amounts that people can contribute. A person could set the amount at $25, then when a guest goes on the Web site with no idea what to get as a gift they can give $25, or increasing increments of, towards your "living room floors." At the end, the newly married couple goes on to the Web site and is able to have all money deposited into their bank. I feel this is the new way to ask for money on a bridal registry, without begging.

GENTLE READER:
Do not go into the etiquette business.

⌒ The Bag Lady ⌒

DEAR MISS MANNERS:
HELP! My daughter is getting married soon—a formal wedding—and she has just decided to carry a "money bag" during the reception!! She hopes to make enough money for a down payment on a house!!!

I'm appalled! Is this telling her friends, our friends, his friends that their gift is not enough, or is this something common?? In my opinion, greed has overcome the young people and they don't celebrate the solemn occasion—they want to see how much money they can "make"!! If it is proper, maybe her father and I should carry one—a big one!!

GENTLE READER:
Do you think you have put in enough exclamation points to express proper horror? Miss Manners finds an excess of them still perilously lodged in her own throat. She had better dispose of them discreetly, because you have actually given her two questions to answer:

1. Is it common for couples to go crazed with greed? Yes, although Miss Manners congratulates this couple on taking the impulse to new depths.
2. Is it proper? Don't make Miss Manners laugh while she has something in her throat.

You might inquire of your daughter whether she is under the impression that your friends and hers will be so emotionally overcome by the event of her marriage that they will be moved to help her buy a house. And, furthermore, whether they will be too shy to accomplish such a wish unless she does them the favor of offering them an opportunity.

Otherwise, her scheme consists of simple social blackmail. She is counting on the guests to fork over under the threat of embarrassment. This is not exactly what we call hospitality.

Miss Manners is unfortunately not confident that if the real nature of what your daughter and her fiancé are doing is drawn to their attention, they will back down. Why should people hesitate to induce a profitable false embarrassment in their friends when they have shown themselves willing to give their own parents cause for the intense, genuine embarrassment of blackmailing *their* friends? Miss Manners urges you to refuse to be a party to this. People who treat wedding guests this way do not deserve to have any.

A Reply

DEAR MISS MANNERS:

Miss Manners (I am loath to call you that) needs to do more research into other cultures and customs before condemning the young lady who wanted to carry a money satchel at her wedding. Both you and her mother were horrified, but just because you have your nose in the air, the young lady hardly invented it.

In some communities (this includes many Polish, Russian, Italian, French, and, I just learned, Vietnamese peoples) gifts are reserved for the wedding showers. When you attend a formal wedding with a sit-down dinner, at a banquet hall, the proper "gift" is an envelope with cash or check, which is left with the bride, who places it in the money bag.

If Miss Manners thinks her uppity manners prevail everywhere, she has another think coming. Those of us who are happy to celebrate our own customs await your apology, and a hope that the overbearing mother of this with-it new bride sees this before she ruins her daughter's wedding day.

Today, a banquet hall reception can run $75 to $100 or more per person. Many couples, whose parents aren't able to underwrite this tremendous bill, pay for the hall out of these monetary proceeds. My wife and I did this ourselves.

GENTLE READER:

Miss Manners is not immune to the lure of tradition and would not interfere when customs are practiced among those who developed them. Please forgive her, but in this case she does not quite understand the argument about being emotionally attached to a heritage of which the young lady's parents have never heard.

She also cautions those whom you characterize as "with it" against pleading tradition too strongly. Miss Manners has heard of a great many wedding traditions from these and other cultures, few of which allow the bride to have any say about anything, including the choice of marriage partner. As life progresses, people weed out inherited practices they find offensive and dig up ones they find useful, such as you and this bride have done. By requiring guests to contribute toward putting on a wedding that the principals cannot afford, you are jettisoning the universal tradition of hospitality in favor of one called Living Above Your Means.

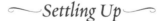

Settling Up

DEAR MISS MANNERS:

I know there's no remedy for my problem. My husband and I had a beautiful, simple wedding a year ago, which we planned and paid for ourselves. We're in our early thirties, were already living together, and have full-time jobs. Needless to say, the wedding was a lot of work and expense, but at the time we were happy we did it. The only thing marring a wonderful memory is that at least twelve of our closest friends who attended never gave us a wedding gift.

I realize it is verging on pettiness, but I wonder how many other couples experience this. Is this common, or do we just have an unusually large number of inconsiderate friends? I know I should never mention it to them, but my husband and I both find that we feel resentful toward these people. I am sure they probably figured they had a year after the wedding to get a gift and then just forgot, but I can't help it. I now look at these people and think they're selfish. I find I don't call them much.

One of these friends is getting married soon and I find myself evilly thinking, "This is our chance to not give them anything." Is this completely out of line? How do my husband and I get rid of this resentment that is now marring our friendships? I now wish we'd eloped.

GENTLE READER:

Miss Manners doesn't know how many couples experience bitter regret at having had a simple and beautiful wedding because it did not achieve the goal of collecting tribute from every single person present. Nowadays, probably lots.

What is the point in getting married without a 100 percent return in donations? As you may imagine, Miss Manners does not much care for this line of reasoning, which she agrees you have accurately characterized as evil. The remedy is to enjoy what ought to be your own happiness.

However, after your year of brooding, the situation has changed. You now find yourself in the position of being invited to be wedding guests, and therefore the question of whether to give presents or not is one that you may legitimately consider.

The custom of giving presents to help establish a new household has indeed been eroded, both because many bridal couples, such as yourselves, already have fully stocked households and because the potential recipients have become so frank about their expectations as to take the pleasure out of giving. Miss Manners would like to see the custom survive as a symbolic expression of goodwill on such an important occasion as marriage—but only if it can be maintained as a voluntary gesture, prompted by affection.

Should you no longer feel affection for your own wedding guests, you have no business attending their weddings. Should you still care for them, it seems to Miss Manners that you would want to participate in their happiness, not seize on an opportunity to slight them in revenge.

～The Charity Solicitation～

DEAR MISS MANNERS:

Since my fiancé and I are in our late thirties and have maintained households for many years, we do not need many of the things that people often give as wedding gifts. We are both active in volunteer activities and we thought we would ask our friends and relatives to make a donation in our name to our favorite charity in lieu of a wedding gift. As we made this known, we found that several friends said they intend to give us a gift anyway.

Do you have any suggestion as to how we can tactfully discourage these people? How should we handle the people who bring gifts to the reception? We do not wish to embarrass them, but we also don't want people who followed our wishes to see a number of gifts and wonder if they, too, should have given a gift rather than a donation.

GENTLE READER:

Miss Manners has a wonderful suggestion for you: Take all that time and effort you are putting into improperly denying others their privilege to decide what, if anything, they want to give you and donate it to your favorite charity. As for people who do give you presents, your job is to thank them. The items are then yours to use as you wish, which could include donating them to charity.

DEAR MISS MANNERS:

I am getting married in October. My fiancé and I are wanting to adopt a child from Guatemala; however, the cost is preventing us from doing so.

We currently have a house and are living together. We really have no need or want for wedding presents like a toaster and china.

Many of the adoption agencies that we have contacted have given us information about setting up our own foundation in order to have friends and family donate money toward the cost of the adoption. How do I let people know that I do not want wedding presents and instead would like money donated toward the adoption?

GENTLE READER:

If only it were a question of how touching and worthy the cause, you would have a sympathetic case. Miss Manners would certainly put you ahead of all those couples who want their guests to give them money for the wedding itself, for the honeymoon, for paying off their debts, or for taking out a mortgage.

But how is she going to make everyone understand that their guests are not their creditors? And that decent people do not instruct their friends to pay their bills?

Yes, yes, she has heard the argument that you are only saving them all from buying toasters. (And by the way, why is it always toasters that people cite? If there is one item that is easily returnable after the thank-you letter is written, and whose absence will not be noticed by the donor, it is a toaster.)

Wedding presents are voluntary tokens of affection from people who should care enough about you to put some thought into the selection. They are not intended to be a source of income for the bridal couple to count into their budget and allot as they wish.

Children are worth sacrificing for. As you have a fully equipped house, Miss Manners gathers you are not destitute, so perhaps you could find a way to pay for the adoption by sacrificing—for example, by having a modest wedding and honeymoon. But she urges you not to sacrifice your dignity.

TROUBLESHOOTING

⁓Generosity⁓

DEAR MISS MANNERS:

I have recently become engaged, and I have decided to ask three of my closest friends to be bridesmaids.

I have been blessed in life, with a wonderful family, and now wonderful in-laws. I also have a great job, and my fiancé and I both make significantly more money than one of my bridesmaids, who is not very well-off. The other two bridesmaids are fairly well-to-do.

The wedding will be a small one, and I would like to pay for all the bridesmaids' dresses, as I know that would be an imposition on my friend—it is important to me that she stand up for me, and I do not want money to be the reason she is unable to. I also do not want to single her out, and since I can afford to, I would like to pay for all three dresses.

Both my mother and my mother-in-law feel that this is inappropriate, as it is traditional for the bridesmaid to buy her own dress—they feel it might be seen as a sign of a bride gone over the edge, requiring control over all the details. Is this correct? If so, what can I do?

GENTLE READER:

It is a lovely gesture to offer to pay for the dresses, and since you are able to do so for all three, there hardly seems to be a conflict. We only ask—although we feel sure you know this—that you phrase it as, "I would like to make the dress a gift to you," rather than, "Don't worry, I'll foot the bill."

How sad that your almost unprecedented kindness and regard for other people's life situations is considered going over the edge, but demanding that others pay for and wear a dress they cannot afford is thought less controlling.

⟞ Generosity Abused ⟝

DEAR MISS MANNERS:

My fiancée and I planned to attend a friend's wedding with mutual friends, who would be staying with us. Two weeks before, I was surprised to receive an e-mail from the bride saying, "By the way, it turns out the price of wedding cake is exorbitant, so we're asking friends to bring cakes to the wedding. I know friends are staying with you, so I thought maybe you could whip one up together on Friday night. Love, the bride."

I admit that I felt rather shocked by this last-minute request that I "whip up"—and bear the cost of—something the bride and groom have deemed "too exorbitant" to pay for. I would be happy to celebrate with them regardless of what food they provide.

I would not have planned to bake a cake either on Friday between coming home from work and picking up my guests at the airport or on Saturday morning before going to this wedding.

But, after asking my guests (who received similar e-mails), we agreed that the bride is a sweet girl who has, perhaps, behaved thoughtlessly but who we like nonetheless and are willing to forgive, and we will plan to get up early enough to make her her cake on Saturday morning.

My fiancée and I had planned to buy the couple a gift from their registry. Is it appropriate for us to provide the asked-for cake in lieu of the gift we had planned to purchase? I can't decide if this is reasonable, or if it's an indication that I'm still irritated and need to work a little harder on the forgiveness part. I don't want to respond with another transgression.

GENTLE READER:

We won't tell anyone if you don't get the couple a gift. Demanding that you provide accommodations, food, and items off her shopping list is beyond unreasonable and your forgiveness and generosity commendable. If your conscience won't rest (or worse, you fear that she will call you out on it), get her a token gift. We suggest a cake pan and baking mix.

THE WEDDING AS SHOW BUSINESS

Miss Manners may be the only person who remembers when people got married by putting on the best clothes they already had and going with a few similarly attired friends and relatives to their regular place of worship, where they followed a solemn and traditional ritual set by their religion.

Queen Victoria herself started the practice of costuming the bride in white (although we do not hold the dear lady responsible for the vulgar notion that this advertised that the body inside was untouched). From then on, it was all downhill, from solemnity and tradition to the flash and gimmicks of show business. There have always been similarities, theater having originated by copying the pageantry of religion, but now the direction has been reversed and the process accelerated.

Since the Academy Awards ceremony has been televised, it has been the quintessential modern ritual, setting the pattern for all others. The ingredients are: outrageous clothing mixing all degrees of formality and informality, a pathway cleared for grand entrances, on-the-spot opinions solicited from bystanders, a patter of jokes and teasing from one or more masters of ceremonies, introductions of participants summarizing their biographies, intermissions and other inconveniences to accommodate the requirements of filming, choreographed chorus lines, rehearsed outpourings of gratitude and sentiment, standing ovations, sly references to the love lives of those present, presentations of trophies, acknowledgment of sponsors, and at least one impassioned plea on behalf of someone's favorite cause.

This has produced significant innovations in the wedding ritual.

- Everyone is costumed, but none of it matches. The wedding party may be in formal clothes, but not even of the same degree of formality—for example, the bridegroom in white tie (or more likely, an "original" variation thereof) while the groomsmen are in black tie, and the guests dressed at an even less-formal level, from business suits to jeans, on the grounds that they are audience, not performers.
- Direction, jokes, and background anecdotes are offered at the reception by a professional master of ceremonies, while during the ceremony, the officiant tries valiantly to be equally entertaining and self-revealing.
- The stars, seeing this as their moment in the spotlight, subordinate the form to showcase themselves and are given the leeway of high temperament and indulged in whatever whims and selfishness they may care to exercise.
- Family members and friends are cast into set roles, regardless of whom this includes or excludes: a man to give the bride away, even

That is the unfortunate result when a bride cares more about having matching bridesmaids and costuming them to match her personal taste, such as it is, than that her bridesmaids be her dear friends, however dumpy, and suitably dressed.

if there is no father—the mother not being considered for the part—and attendants chosen for the right look and number, rather than solely for being close friends.

- The bride's mother's entrance has become a staged event, a prelude to the bride's entrance, which pulls people to their feet. Applause and ovations are common, especially for the first marital kiss (which also draws laughter, as if it were a love scene viewed by an audience of early adolescents) and the pronouncement of the marriage (or maybe that round of clapping is because the show is ending).
- Presents are regarded as admission tickets, and there is a lot of anger at those who try to get in without them. These are brought to the event and handed over, regardless of the logistical difficulties this creates, because paying admission has become so important a part of the occasion.
- Capturing the event on film for another audience is treated as superseding any need to accommodate those actually present. Guests may be shoved aside or made to endure long blank waits, or cast without warning as extras if the film script calls for candid reaction interviews.

Miss Manners is only too aware of the unpopularity of the position she is taking. Nobody loves a critic. Why shouldn't a wedding be entertainment and draw on the experience of professionals in the business?

Her first reason is that this is often bad theater, and she is not the only critic. Not every amateur, no matter how in love, can produce a good original script. It is one thing to have friends murmuring "I thought the church needed more flowers," and quite another to hand them your courtship and philosophy to critique.

The second is that a wedding should be a joyous but serious occasion, not lighthearted entertainment. It's marriage itself, not the ceremony, that is supposed to be a scream.

The Program

DEAR MISS MANNERS:

It has come to my attention that I must have a program at my wedding, because "everyone" has a program at their weddings. Quite frankly, I cannot recall one at the weddings I have attended, but most likely I would not have kept it. The examples I have been given not only have the wedding ceremony, but a "list of characters," from the bride and groom down to the hostesses (not necessarily the parents, but rather a wedding consultant or caterer) and "acknowledgments," listing the florist, travel agent, facility, etc. I've been told that they help guests identify who's in the wedding and they can refer back to them should they forget a name, but the idea of having a program is not sitting quite well with me.

GENTLE READER:

Where else would you put the plot summary? And the synopsis of what happened in the prequel? And the preview of the sequel? How else could you credit the sponsors? Or introduce the supporting actors ("Sherrie is a newlywed herself and a new mother," or "Mike especially enjoys watersports")?

The only excuse for a program is to give the order of the service, which is not necessary at a wedding. Miss Manners congratulates you on resisting.

The Script

How you met: It's a fascinating, romantic tale, full of twists and turns, a Jane Austen novel mixed with *The Matrix*. The combination of fate, destiny, coincidence, near misses, hilarious mishaps, and sentimental anecdotes is something that everyone wants to hear (stories!), see (pictures! videos!), read (wedding columns and blogs!) and experience (your entire themed wedding and reception!) before, during, and after your big day.

Except it isn't and they don't.

Because we're guessing that you actually met online or at a bar. All right, maybe you met at college or at work or through friends. There's nothing wrong with predictability. There is, however, something wrong with yanking a bio-epic from the slim plot of your courtship and forcing it on your friends. Over and over again.

Considering how many years that family, friends, and mere acquaintances have asked "Have you met anyone?" and "When are you getting married?" it is not unreasonable to suppose there is huge demand for the details of your now-successful love life. Finally, you have gathered some, perhaps all, of the material for the three-picture deal called Courtship, Marriage, and Family. Your script is distinguished by the eerie intervention of fate ("The numbers in his profile username were my half-birthday!"), coincidences of commonality ("He likes beer. I like beer!"), and the all-important suspense ("We broke up for a while, but there was no one else who really got that sometimes I need me time.").

The truth is that in the course of your courtship and wedding preparations, maybe a few people will ask you how you met. Your close friends or family members heard it at the time and are already tired of it or, worse, will know when you're embellishing. So why deprive yourself of party chatter to others (complete with adorable arguments between you about who made the first move) by making it the relentless subject of your wedding or fodder for the Internet or local paper?

The Cast

DEAR MISS MANNERS:

My son by a previous marriage is to marry soon. His mother died while he was a minor, and two older sisters became surrogate mothers in her stead. He wishes to acknowledge this at the reception by announcing them together with myself as a part of that ceremony. My present wife feels slighted by this, and feels emphatically that a provision should be made to present her as my wife as well. She refuses to attend otherwise.

GENTLE READER:

Announcing? Presenting? Does Miss Manners understand you to ask who gets the public credit for being the bridegroom's surrogate mother?

See the trouble people get into by treating their weddings as show business award ceremonies? A wedding is a family gathering, not a contest. There is no need to announce, "And in the role of mother . . ." Why shouldn't the four of you occupy the front pew, sit at a family table at the reception, and receive his toasts of thanks?

The Extras

DEAR MISS MANNERS:

My fiancé and I are trying to find a mature and nice way of requesting on our invitation that there be no crying children at the wedding, due to the professional videotaping. What is the best way of telling guests without offending them?

GENTLE READER:

What makes you think that your younger guests are more likely than the older ones to be overcome with sentiment on the occasion of your marriage, and to weep throughout the service? Anyway, wouldn't this add a tender note to your professional videotape, bound to touch the hearts of audiences everywhere when the tape is released in neighborhood theaters?

Or is it, Miss Manners finally understands, that you assume that all children cry, simply as recreation, especially when asked to sit still for an hour? In that case, don't invite any children to your wedding. Should their parents inquire whether this was an inadvertent omission, you must say, with a tone of regret so as not to seem a monster, "Oh, I'm so sorry, but we're not having any children there. I know yours would behave perfectly, but others might find it tedious." This is more acceptable than "I'm not using children in my show."

⌒ The Set and Costumes ⌒

DEAR MISS MANNERS:

Within hours of their engagement, my nephew's betrothed joined the congregation of a very picturesque church to provide a suitable venue for her special event. The wedding is almost upon us, and the bride has announced that hats are *not* to be worn.

Other than the fact that my two young daughters and I have already purchased lovely bonnets to complement the chosen setting, how can we enter a house of worship for an afternoon wedding, bareheaded? Is it no longer customary to cover one's head in a church? Would a lace handkerchief or designer tissue do?

GENTLE READER:

If your prospective niece has changed her church merely to acquire the background scenery she wants, nothing is going to persuade her that she cannot costume the extras.

As you have noticed, the bride's idea about hats is wrong, in addition to being impertinent. It is proper, although no longer mandatory, for ladies to wear hats both for any church service and for any afternoon wedding. So perhaps you are entitled to wear two hats. It would be even worse to appear with patterned nosewipes on your head, if Miss Manners understands you correctly, or with lace handkerchiefs (although many a lady made do with such back when the Catholic Church barred bareheaded ladies from the door).

Nor do you want to start a family feud with a new relative who is unpleasant enough without provocation. Miss Manners would therefore suggest either sending back the message about your already purchased hats through your nephew (who supposedly knows how to deal with this person) or simply wearing flowers or ribbons in your hair.

⌒Facing the Audience⌒

DEAR MISS MANNERS:

My daughter faced the audience during her wedding vows, as did the rest of the wedding party. It was a treat to see the ceremony, the facial expressions, and the beautiful bridesmaids and the men. I realize that some ceremonies must be conducted with certain rites that must have the wedding party's backs to the viewers. However, some ministers or pastors would not object to having their backs to the audience. Perhaps you could suggest this?

GENTLE READER:

The "audience"? Is that how you categorize the people who gather in a house of worship to witness a sacred ritual?

Miss Manners has been increasingly aware that, weddings now being regarded as a popular amateur branch of show business, not only spirituality but also ties and duties to family and friends have become secondary to the production values. Your suggestion, however, is original enough to manage to shock her. Since you are dabbling in theater, she suggests that you analyze the symbolism you plan to convey: In facing their audience, to Whom would these star-for-a-day performers be turning their backs?

⌒Audience Reaction⌒

DEAR MISS MANNERS:

What is your opinion about the practice of clapping loudly for the newly wedded pair? I have seen a number of weddings on television, and each time I am surprised to see the ceremony end in applause. For what? For whom? For the adorable couple, I assume, and yet I feel upset that the solemn moment is treated as an entertainment. Does this surprising ovation occur in a church, too, or in a synagogue, or a mosque? I feel that applause is more appropriate in a theater.

GENTLE READER:

It is fortunate that, for this particular form of entertainment, the house, so to speak, is papered with friends. Audiences sometimes boo when they are insufficiently entertained.

⌒Playing to an Empty House⌒

DEAR MISS MANNERS:

This is a worst-case scenario: A wedding is planned and the bridesmaids, having bought their expensive dresses, are thrilled at being asked to participate in such a socially prestigious event. But then the invitations arrive and the wedding is to be held in the bride's home town, 200 miles away. The groom's relatives live in the opposite direction. Arrangements have been made to accommodate out-of-town guests (and the wedding party) in a nearby city; the rates are reasonable as weekend rates go, but the guests pay their own way. Times being hard and distance and expense outweighing fond sentiment, the regrets are 100 percent.

Then what happens? Can the bridesmaids and ushers bow out? The mother of the groom certainly would, if given half a chance, and she is not at all certain her dress will arrive in time. Do the bride's parents send out cancellation notices and let the couple marry in their own city and among their close friends?

At least the hosts will be spared the problem of what to do about the wedding presents people bring along to the reception, and the problem of the uninvited guests people bring along because there won't be anyone they know to talk to—supposing one could talk in the ear-shattering din of loud dance music.

Wouldn't it be a welcome end to all the show-biz extravaganza? And might not a return to the small, intimate, and meaningful ceremony result in lower divorce statistics?

GENTLE READER:

Miss Manners is no fonder of the show business mentality toward weddings than you are, but she finds herself unable to gloat at the picture of people who discover that no one cares enough about them to attend their wedding. The idea that even their intimates would then be tempted to bail out is pathetic.

However pretentious the bridal couple may be, surely it is such guests who have the more distasteful attitude. As you point out, convenience and price have outweighed sentiment. Had they cared, they might have hopped a bus and inquired about staying with the couple's local friends and relatives.

One does not absolutely require an "audience," as it were, for a wedding of any style. If they were planning this wedding to dazzle others, yes, it should be canceled if those others won't be there. If they were doing it for their own satisfaction, Miss Manners does not see why they should not go ahead with it.

—Also Playing—

DEAR MISS MANNERS:

My boyfriend and I announced our engagement four months ago. We have not set a date yet, as we are still trying to figure out the wedding details, but we told everyone that it would probably happen in October of next year, although we weren't certain.

My fiancé's closest sister, who is older than he and is not married, was happy for us when she heard the news, but also a bit jealous. You see, she has been living with the same man for 10 years and she very much wants a family and he has yet to commit.

Much to everyone's surprise, she suddenly announced that she too was getting married and the wedding would be next January! I am very upset because I feel that she is being inconsiderate by not waiting for my fiancé and I to set our date and now their family has to attend two weddings in one year! What is the proper etiquette, if any, that she should have followed in setting her wedding date?

GENTLE READER:

Are you suggesting that since she has waited ten years for a husband and children already, she might as well wait another year so that you can have the spotlight all to yourself? Or rather, that she should do so out of courtesy to the poor relatives who might face the hardship of attending two weddings in a single year?

Miss Manners finds it imprudent of you to have brought up the question of jealousy. Let us assume that your prospective sister-in-law is getting married because she wants to, as you acknowledge, and because the gentleman is willing, which you oddly fail to acknowledge but is surely a prerequisite.

Let us also assume that she sees her marriage as living her life, rather than trying to top yours, and that she wishes you and her brother well, which she has indicated. Miss Manners is hoping to hear that you can manage to behave as if you had the same attitude.

TROUBLESHOOTING

DEAR MISS MANNERS:

My daughter does not want video cameras at her wedding or reception—she finds them to be intrusive, they make her feel uncomfortable. There will be no professional video photographer for the same reason. We agree with her decision, but the question is, is there an acceptable way to say "no video cameras, please"?

GENTLE READER:

In an age when everyone wants to be televised doing absolutely anything, on or off reality shows, it is almost incomprehensible that someone would not want to have her every breath caught on film. That a bride would not want it is even more rare.

Good for her. Now she must convince the rest of the world. As small as video cameras have become, they should still be fairly easy to spot. Ask a trusted and otherwise unoccupied relative or friend to run interference ("I'm so sorry, but we are asking that there be no filming.") as the guests arrive, and to keep an eye throughout on wily guests brandishing cell phones. Better yet, give this assignment to those who crave attention, offering them a sense of importance and perhaps distracting them from providing running commentary.

DEAR MISS MANNERS:

My fiancé would like to sing and play the guitar during the wedding ceremony, but my mother says to perform at one's own wedding is impolite. My instinct agrees, and my fiancé graciously agreed not to perform. I'd like to be able to tell him why it is impolite, but I don't know the reason.

GENTLE READER:

While etiquette does not specifically dictate a rule against the performing bridegroom (it didn't think it had to), its close cousins, good taste and propriety, do. A wedding ceremony is a solemn occasion, and its rituals oddly do not include covers of "Can't Get Enough of Your Love, Babe." If your fiancé must sing, ask him to do so at the reception. If he isn't very good, encourage a karaoke setup so he won't embarrass himself. Or your mother. Or you.

CHAPTER FOUR

The Plans

B Y THE TIME you become engaged, it is too late to plan a wedding. Or so you will be told by those who believe that a lifetime is too short to prepare for such a momentous occasion. And by the way, while you were dithering around about making a lifetime commitment, everything got booked up.

They try to help by providing a timeline:

TWENTY YEARS BEFORE

Decide what your dream wedding would be and lock it in for future use so that it cannot be altered by changing times, altered circumstances, maturing tastes, or input from the bridegroom.

TWO YEARS BEFORE

Make sure the targeted bridegroom understands exactly what you expect in the way of a marriage proposal and that he must make it a surprise.

ONE YEAR AND FIFTY-ONE WEEKS BEFORE

Display ring to all and start vetting your friends—making new ones, if necessary—in order to create a devoted and attractive wedding party. Flaunt your new status to those who are single.

ONE YEAR AND FIFTY WEEKS BEFORE

Buy all available wedding literature and discover long lists of things that you should already have done if you expect to secure a location, officiant, photographer, florist, videographer, and caterer. Spread panic.

EIGHTEEN MONTHS BEFORE

Enlist support-service personnel, making sure that parents and brides-maids understand the chain of command. Explain dream wedding to all. If anyone raises money problems, cry.

SIXTEEN MONTHS BEFORE

Develop a personal taste, style, theme, and two favorite colors (become familiar with the term Wedding Palette). Decide what foods and Signature Cocktails best represent you as a couple.

ONE YEAR BEFORE

Conduct exhaustive hunt for wedding dress, being told at each place that you must decide and buy immediately, because there is barely enough time to get the dress made before the wedding.

ELEVEN MONTHS BEFORE

Do the same for the cake and the flowers.

TEN MONTHS BEFORE

This is your last chance to make sure that your friends and especially bridesmaids aren't getting pregnant. Babies could ruin your big day. On the other hand, check up on the cuteness factor of existing children you know for potential flower girls and ring bearers.

NINE MONTHS BEFORE

Develop family traditions and ethnic customs now that facilitate asking for money later.

EIGHT MONTHS BEFORE

Inform bridal party of what clothing they will be wearing, what duties they will be performing, and what parties they will be giving (and in what states or countries). Avoid the mistake of asking for their ideas and budgets.

SEVEN MONTHS BEFORE

Go to every possible store, grab a pricing gun, and point it at every material thing you've ever wanted in your entire life—and the less-expensive things you didn't (you must have a price range for your guests). Accept the store's offer to place this information on all forms of communication.

SIX MONTHS BEFORE

Take a romantic moment with your fiancé to plan your fantasy honeymoon. Figure out a way for others to pay for it.

FIVE MONTHS BEFORE

Fight with a parent or friend with whom you haven't yet fought.

FOUR MONTHS BEFORE

Nag a parent or friend about a party you haven't yet had.

THREE MONTHS BEFORE

Devise ways to make simple things really expensive. There is a fortune to be spent on maps, party favors, escort cards, table markers, personal trainers, and dance lessons. Ask around; there are things you didn't know existed.

TWO MONTHS BEFORE

Forget to register for your marriage license, so that you won't really be getting married on your wedding day. The important thing is that you have your friends and family celebrating your love. And giving you presents.

ONE MONTH BEFORE

Worry that your registry isn't yet bought. Remind your friends and family that there are only thirty more shopping days to go.

TWO WEEKS BEFORE

Panic. Realize that you are no longer the size of your dress and develop a sensible plan to lose twenty pounds in fourteen days.

ONE WEEK BEFORE

Nag all your vendors and friends one last time and think of new and complicated things for them to do for you. Consider firing someone.

THE DAY BEFORE

Get really, really drunk so that tomorrow you'll have a pounding head-ache, puffy eyes (all the better to justify the expense of your flown-in makeup artist), and a nagging feeling that you might have broken up with your fiancé after making out with his brother.

THE DAY OF

Relax. It's your wedding day.

Here is an alternate timeline:

SOMETIME AFTER PUBERTY AND BEFORE SENILITY

Fall in love.

SOMETIME AFTER THAT

Get engaged.

BEFORE EVERYTHING GETS ALL PLAN-Y

Figure out how many friends and family members you have and which of them would likely take pleasure in seeing you get married.

AFTER THAT

Pick a venue and entertainment style that will accommodate them all without putting you or your family in debt, resulting in unpleasant arguing.

ANYTIME AFTER THE ENGAGEMENT AND BEFORE THE
WEDDING (FOUR TO SIX MONTHS SHOULD BE SUFFICIENT)

Choose vendors who will help you select a tasteful dress, flowers, music, food, and invitations and who won't up-sell you (see "Useless Wedding Paraphernalia," page 119). Get your family involved, letting them help choose the things that are important to them, quietly encouraging them to be as mindful of taste and practicality as you are.

THE DAY OF

Enjoy what we can only hope is not the best day of your life (because that would mean that your married life would all be downhill), but a very, very good one, and genuinely relax, knowing that your familial and other relationships are secure.

THE PROPER PROCEDURE

All right, you've had your moments of privacy. Oh, you remember: It was when you chose to plight your troth over the loudspeaker system of a packed football stadium during halftime. Now other people are getting involved. Lots of them.

The pleasant thing about those girlish wedding fantasies is that you had no one to please except yourself. Well, things have changed, including, let us hope, your taste in clothes. Now you naturally want to please your betrothed as well. And his parents. And his other relatives on both sides. And your parents. And all relatives on both sides. And the stepparents. And your friends. And all their friends.

Miss Manners understands why even the most tenderhearted bride may throw up her hands at the hopelessness of pleasing everyone; indeed, many will advise her to do so. After all, it's her . . .

See where that leads? And we are not going to go there.

Miss Manners does not advise following all such suggestions. Not everyone gets to vote on the choice of flowers, a lesson some should have learned when they found they did not get to vote on the choice of bride-

The Bridegroom's Clothes

A polite bridegroom takes care not to be more eye-catching than the bride. He may wear white tie (above, center) or black tie (right) if the wedding takes place after six, morning clothes (left) for a formal daytime wedding, or a business suit (bottom) for an informal wedding at any time. He does not dress differently from the other gentlemen in the bridal party, and the wedding guests are supposed to dress formally if he does, as surprised and indignant as they may be to hear this.

groom. She merely stipulates taking some basic human requirements into consideration so as not to leave a trail of unhappiness.

The so-called destination wedding often does that. Since grown children started setting off on their own to places where they met strangers, attending weddings has involved travel for many. But choosing a remote place to be married simply because the couple would like to go there should be left to those whose entire circle of family and friends finds time and money hanging heavily on their hands. After the wedding, the couple is free to go alone to its dream destination—it's called a honeymoon—while everyone else gets to go home from the wedding with money and vacation time left over.

Then there is emotional hardship. The most difficult conflicts are when religion is involved. Miss Manners would not presume to say when accommodations can be reached between the couple's beliefs and those of their respective families, as that is a moral dilemma. The manners aspect is to head off last-minute shocks by patiently explaining to relatives who may be prone to shock, what will happen at the ceremony and why.

The reception can also draw on surprisingly deep-rooted differences. One family may feel that it is not really a wedding unless everyone leaves nauseated from five hours of eating and drinking, and the other may feel that anything more than tea sandwiches, wedding cake, and champagne is vulgar. Besides, nowadays there are not only food likes and dislikes, there are deeply held food philosophies.

And so it goes. Indeed, you cannot please everyone. But you can do your planning with others in mind, rather than consulting only your own taste and if they don't like it—tough. You can use compromise and variety to mollify objections. And for heaven's sake, you can seat the older generation far enough from the loudspeakers so they can hear themselves think.

DEAR MISS MANNERS:

I am getting married soon and some issues of tradition have become apparent, in particular, the retrieving of the garter by the groom. My fiancé is Hispanic, which means his family has Catholic roots; however, they never attend Mass. Anyway, he fears that his family would be offended by this tradition. He has also asked me to make sure my dress is particularly white, again because of his family's roots.

The dress thing was no big deal but the retrieving of the garter is a fun tradition. I am not saying he has to get it with his teeth like

some grooms, but I would like to include the activity in the festivities. You know, I throw the bouquet and he throws the garter.
How can I get him to compromise and explain to his parents that
the tradition is in no way meant to be vulgar or sexual, but lighthearted and fun?

GENTLE READER:

How can you persuade your fiancé that it would be fun to
offend his family? The question that occurs to Miss Manners is,
Why would you want to?

There are countless traditions associated with weddings, many
of which you would not care to follow. The custom you mention is,
at best, trivial. Offending your new family would not be.

UPSIDE-DOWN PLANNING

With all the lists, notebooks and Web sites that people use to plan weddings, they still keep getting the proper order upside down. And Miss
Manners isn't even counting the widespread notion that consummation
should occur before a commitment even to courtship. She is referring to
the common practice of deciding on the wedding arrangements before
compiling the guest list.

When the invitations go out, those who could reasonably expect
to be invited ("reasonably" meaning relatives, friends, and those who
issued invitations to their own weddings, not office colleagues and
other volunteers) but who were cut because of space limitations, are,
with reason, hurt.

Others, who are invited and would dearly love to attend, discover that
they must buy an entire holiday package, planned by others, in order to
attend, and that doing so would commit them to enormous additional
expenses in the way of preselected presents at successive events and
expectations to contribute to the wedding costs.

To avoid this sort of trouble, the couple need only turn their planning
notebooks upside down. First compile the guest list. Then go over the

possible arrangements you might make in terms of what most people—
especially key people—would find manageable.

DEAR MISS MANNERS:

I love my baby brother dearly, but he announced last month
that he is getting married at a resort on Key West. All of which is
lovely, except that he and his fiancée live in Dallas, my spouse and
I live in Seattle, and it's going to cost us a couple of grand just to
get there and enjoy the nuptials with him.

There is no way I would miss this landmark event in his life, but
I'm worried about showing up with (or without) a gift. Not only
would he have to lug it back to Dallas—possibly not a worry since
his fiancée's family is wealthy and presumably paying for everything because I know he and our dad are not—but my spouse and
I are on a limited income. We have been planning and saving for
a year to visit spouse's family for several weeks in Southern Italy
the week after Baby Brother's wedding. Does proper etiquette still
require that we bring an expensive gift?

GENTLE READER:

Surely you want him to have something of yours to mark the
occasion. Other than your change-of-address card to the poorhouse. Miss Manners suggests a family photograph in one of those
nice frames from the drugstore.

THE FAMILY

⟶ Chief Duties of the Bride's Parents ⟵

1. Welcome the bridegroom to the family, and relieve his anxiety by
   telling him how they now expect him to address them.
2. Gently explain the facts of life to the bride: That the wedding must
   be within the financial capabilities and general style of the way the
   family lives; that the ordinary considerations of respect for parents,

obligations of relationship and friendship for family and attendants, and concern for the comfort and pleasure of guests are not to be suspended; that marriage is supposed to be forever; and that yes, in this day and age, people still expect prompt, handwritten thank-you letters.

3. Act as hosts to the extent agreed upon in family council with the bride (who must bear in mind that presiding is not indissolubly linked with paying or even with doing the actual work of making arrangements). Duties include planning the rehearsal, wedding reception, and any auxiliary entertaining; issuing the invitations and announcements; arranging for the site, flowers, music, food and drink, transportation, and clothing of the bride and her attendants; and suggesting accommodations for the wedding party.

4. Restrain their own temptation to use the occasion to settle old scores, for example, against each other's present spouses.

5. Veto black dresses or period costumes, head off any attempts by the bride to request showers or dictate wedding presents, remind the bride never to drink to herself when she is being toasted, and brief her on what to expect on her wedding night if she does not have her own children to do this.

⟜ Unmarried Parents ⟜

DEAR MISS MANNERS:

I never married my daughter's father—he never divorced and I never married. I've seen etiquette rules for divorced parents at their child's wedding, but not for those who were never married.

He still lives with his wife and their grown daughter. He has visited us over the years on a rather regular basis, and he has never missed a special occasion. He and my daughter keep in touch, and he and I speak occasionally on the phone over family matters. We hold no animosities.

At the wedding, my guest will be my "beau" of two years. My daughter's father will be walking her down the aisle, but he will be attending alone. He has never been accepted by most of my family, although he is respected and acknowledged as a true human by my aunt and uncle and by the groom's parents.

What is the proper seating for the church ceremony and the reception? Both men are congenial types, always willing to talk with anyone (and hopefully to each other). We don't want to offend anyone, but most importantly, we do not want to make her father feel unwanted—he is wanted. We also don't want to make my guest feel in the way.

GENTLE READER:

Among the things that etiquette is much too polite to pay attention to at a wedding is whether or not the bride's parents were ever married. The marriage that is of interest is the one taking place at the moment, and the relevant characteristic of the parents is that they are her parents.

Normally, the bride's family is grouped together, both at the ceremony and if there is seating at the party afterward. The only reason that ways have recently been found to keep them apart is the fear that they will kill one another. Those parents not currently married are neither required to pretend to be a pair for the occasion nor to keep their distance, unless they and their current partners are not to be trusted together.

In your case, you have an amiable set of people, all presumably focused on the bride's happiness rather than on any previous dissatisfactions of their own. By all means, sit together. Your disgruntled relatives will simply have to accept the harmony among you. Perhaps it will set them an example.

⟶ The Birth Mother ⟶

DEAR MISS MANNERS:

Our daughter gave up a son at birth for adoption. Now, twenty years later, this lad has looked us up and we are delighted. He was looking for more family. He found his birth mother, two aunts, two cousins, and us, a set of grandparents.

Where do we fit in at his coming wedding? His adopted mother is dead. He has his adopted father, grandmother on one side, and an aunt. I don't think it fair to the adoptive father for the birth mother to be in the receiving line. In fact, I wonder if we should be at the wedding at all?

Gentle Reader:

As you have sensitively considered, a newly discovered mother should not play hostess to receive the intimate circle of a family with whom she has never been acquainted. Can you imagine the explanations that would be necessary?

"I'm Jonathan's mother. No, I had nothing to do with his father here. His birth father is—oh, never mind. It was someone else; let's just leave it at that. Of course I know Mrs. Tunis was his mother, although I never actually knew her. But she's dead, you know, and then he went and found me . . ."

The receiving line wouldn't budge after the first person started to receive this interesting news. The entire focus of the occasion would be on this relationship, rather than that of the new couple.

This is by no means to say that Miss Manners is opposed to your family's attending the wedding if the bridegroom's adoptive relatives agree. They may even approve a minor fuss being made over you—say, his toasting the newfound relatives at the reception, by way of announcement. But this, as your instinctive courtesy tells you, is not for you to suggest.

Your proposal might be that the lad ask his father how he would feel about any or all of you going to the ceremony only, or attending the reception but merely identifying yourselves as relatives of the bridegroom without going into detail. Even if he welcomes you, it would be well to be careful to show that the father is the one with the parental authority (or what can be said to be left of it by the time any child gets married), not your daughter, who turned it over to him.

⌒A Disapproving Mother⌒

DEAR MISS MANNERS:

My son is getting married in another part of the country. The bride-to-be and her mother are bubbling with excitement over the fancy wedding reception they are staging. They were so determined to hold it at a particular site that the wedding date was delayed by two months.

I don't care for ostentatious wedding-day arrangements. Certainly I will not stand in a receiving line. Nor will I allow my picture to be taken. (I do not like the way I photograph lately; recently, I had my silhouette done, rather than submit to the embarrassment of another picture.) Obviously, I am going to make someone angry if I hold to my principles at the reception. Thus I am thinking of just going to the wedding and not to the party afterward.

Which do you think would be least offensive to the bride and her mother—attending the reception in a way I can tolerate, or just skipping it altogether? If I do attend, I will not make any negative remarks, but neither will I pretend enthusiasm for anything I don't like. My husband, on the other hand, will jovially go through the motions at the reception and then come home and have a great laugh over his phoniness.

GENTLE READER:

Those are interesting principles you have. As Miss Manners understands it, they require sabotaging your son's wedding reception and publicly, if passively, insulting his bride and her family—out of respect for your sense of style and an odd whim or two.

Miss Manners refuses to recommend either of your solutions. If you are surly at the wedding reception, the inevitable assumption will be that you hate the bride. If you boycott the reception, the assumption will be that it is the bridegroom, your own son, who has done something so appalling that you cannot forgive him.

In neither case could you expect to have much of a relationship with the couple after the wedding. The wound you so righteously talk of inflicting will be a serious one. Miss Manners suggests you adopt your husband's solution. The parents of bridegrooms often laugh as they congratulate themselves on how superior their taste is to the other family's. But the principled ones do this strictly in private.

∼Chief Duties of the Bridegroom's Parents∼

1. Call on the bride's family (in person, if possible, otherwise by letter, e-mail being not formal enough for the occasion), propose a meeting, and declare how lucky they believe their son to be.
2. Keep up that tone, true or not, pronouncing everyone and everything perfectly lovely, while channeling any complaints about the arrangements through their son to the bride.
3. Supply an accurate copy of their guest list, without abbreviations or question marks, and keeping to the limit set, knowing that they can always give a party during the engagement or after the marriage to introduce the bride to their hordes of other friends.
4. Joke about how unfair it is that the bride's family has so much more to do than they and offer to help out, usually by entertaining the bridal party, officiant, all their spouses, and, if possible, the out-of-town guests the night before the wedding.
5. Spare the bride the necessity of reminding the bridegroom to buy her engagement and wedding rings, to get the license, to order the bridal bouquet and boutonnieres, to pay the officiant, to choose the best man and groomsmen, to talk them out of protesting about what they are expected to wear, to give them presents, and to sanitize the plans for the bachelor party.

DEAR MISS MANNERS:

Please explain the duties of the groom's parents after the announcement of their son's engagement to a girl whose parents are divorced and unfriendly. I know it is our duty to have the girl's parents to our home. Should we have each parent over separately? Since we have briefly met each one, is it necessary to have them over at all?

GENTLE READER:

Miss Manners hopes that you mean that the bride's parents are unfriendly to each other, not to you. She has an unpleasant picture of people whose response to "We're thrilled to hear that our son is to marry your lovely daughter" is a snarl.

In any case, you do want to do what you can to establish a friendly relationship with each of them. This is necessary on one level because etiquette requires that the bridegroom's parents create an occasion to tell the bride's parents how happy they are over the match. On another level, you need to establish a basis of sociability with people whose lives will be so much connected with yours over such matters as holidays, celebrations, and grandchildren, should there be any. Two occasions to do this does not seem excessive to Miss Manners. Obviously, if they can't stand each other, it will not be a good idea to attempt to see them together.

⟶Chief Duties of Stepparents⟵

1. Step into parental roles when invited to do so but refrain from sulking if not.
2. Maintain a graceful balance between parental pride and deference to birth parents, no matter how unworthy of honor the one you are not married to may be.

DEAR MISS MANNERS:

My husband's daughter is getting married and I want to do what is best for all. I have told my stepdaughter that I will give her a bridal shower for her father's side of the family.

Am I supposed to invite her mother and grandmother? How am I to dress for the wedding day? Do I dress as though I'm the mother of the bride? Should the color of my dress match the bridesmaids' dresses? Do I wear a corsage? Where do I sit in church?

Is my husband also expected to have pictures taken with his ex-wife? Are my parents to be considered as grandparents? (My stepdaughter does not call them Grandma and Grandpa, but Mr. and Mrs.) My husband and his ex-wife divorced on unfriendly terms, and he and I have been married for three years. What about when the bridal party is called to the dance floor and then the parents—is my husband expected to dance with his ex-wife? Or do I?

Gentle Reader:

You certainly are not expected to dance with your husband's ex-wife. Miss Manners is happy to be able to provide you with instant relief from that worry.

She can also get you off the shower hook, so to speak, if it is not too late. You are her stepmother, and may give a luncheon or reception in her honor, but not a shower, because the last is characterized by the giving of presents, and one is not supposed to be greedy on behalf of a relative (see "The Shower," page 54).

As for the other activities—costuming the relatives, deciding the dance order, and posing for pictures—etiquette cares less than you think. There is nothing wrong with consulting about clothing so that no one seriously clashes in style with anyone else, with wearing flowers, with signing up the bride for early dances with her closest male relatives, with having pictures taken. But these are not mandated wedding rituals. There is no rule of etiquette requiring mothers of the bride and bridegroom to match anyone, even each other; there is no rule that certain female relatives must be distinguished with corsages; there is no rule that certain people must dance together, or must appear together in photographs.

There is a rule that everyone must be polite to everyone else, no matter what the previous family activities. This may very well mean pretending that they don't dislike one another, but it does not extend to pretending that the original couple is still married. The lady accompanying the father of the bride is his wife, not his former wife. Brides who wish to display such a charade at their wedding must be gently discouraged.

⌒ The Big Give-Away ⌒

When Miss Manners hears about stepfathers, it is usually as their stepdaughters are about to trade them in. "Who should give me away?" they ask when they are planning to be married.

Well, dear, who has you? Never mind that it is usually the bridegroom. Miss Manners does not believe in spelling everything out on ceremonial occasions, even symbolically. Wedding guests are neither as innocent nor as easily titillated as young couples excitedly imagine.

The odd persistence of the archaic gesture of giving away a bride has often come to mean that, on the threshold of starting her own married life, a young lady who has been reared and sheltered by a gentleman unrelated to her by blood will inquire how to explain to him that she is dividing the tasks of fatherhood—and that his lot is to pay bills, not to give her away.

Mind you, Miss Manners is not going to argue otherwise. If the bride's mother and her husband are giving the wedding, Miss Manners cannot relieve them of the responsibility of paying for whatever they (they!) decide they can afford.

Nor is Miss Manners opposed to having the bride's original father, or whatever we call such people nowadays (being referred to as biological parents sounds as if the act were performed for a science-fair demonstration) assume the charmingly anachronistic function of "giving her away." Finances aside, the bride's father is the bride's father. There may be circumstances that have made her feel that he has destroyed that tie, but otherwise it is the lot of a kind stepparent to yield gracefully to prior claims, rather than to force the bride to make a wrenching choice.

That said, Miss Manners hopes those stepdaughters will take into account what a beautiful thing it is for someone to parent another person's child. Or to consider that family participation in a wedding is not a matter of casting preset roles, but of arranging things to fit the particular families involved.

For this reason, Miss Manners was delighted, rather than shocked, at the Gentle Reader who "couldn't pass up an opportunity to tell you about my granddaughter's wedding. She was 'given away' by four fathers!"

One was her stepfather, one was her natural father (who had been divorced when she was an infant and whom she had located a year or so before the wedding), one was my husband, who is her grandfather, and who had always been there for her while she was growing up, and one was the grandfather she had just found, her natural father's father. The murmurs and looks on the faces of the guests in the church would have made a hilarious movie. What exactly is important, anyway? To me, this was her way of expressing her love and her appreciation of the "fathers" in her life.

The correct answer is, of course, that love is important. But Miss Manners, who also finds tradition important, is as charmed and amused as the guests. It is not exactly traditional to have four fathers give a bride away, but if the tradition is adapted to the family, rather than the other way around, this bride ends up with a nontraditional quartet of fathers. Miss Manners is not making this a general recommendation—you must have a family and friends who have as much good nature and humor as this bride's grandmother.

When the choice is made and explained tactfully, it behooves the one not chosen to be gracious. A bride who tells her stepfather that she loves him dearly but feels she should have her father with her, or one who explains to her father that she loves him dearly but her stepfather was the one with whom she grew up, should be met with an example of magnanimous acceptance.

DEAR MISS MANNERS:

What is the proper role of the father of the bride when the bride chooses her stepfather to walk her down the aisle? There is no estrangement between father and daughter, and he has provided financial and emotional support from infancy through college. The bride simply feels closer to her stepfather, having lived with him and her mother almost all her life. Surely the father's role does not just become that of a guest. But I have heard no alternative offered that would give an honored role to the father at the wedding and/or reception.

GENTLE READER:

The proper role of the father in these circumstances is to beam. He must project this beam so that no one has any excuse for believing that his daughter or her stepfather has slighted him, or that he is miffed at either of them.

He may certainly be in the receiving line, if the stepfather and the father of the bridegroom are; if they choose to circulate as hosts instead, he may do the same. This consists of welcoming guests, seeing to it that no one is stranded, and confessing to them that he can hardly imagine his little girl is old enough to be married. He may also assume—not necessarily exclusively—such fatherly privileges as offering a toast to the couple, enjoying an early dance with the bride, and enjoining the bridegroom to take good care of her.

DEAR MISS MANNERS:

What do you do when an only daughter has her mother (a redneck) escort her down the aisle instead of her living father? The mother is the force behind this.

Her mother's side is more controlling. As aunt and uncles, we all sent gifts, but all went unrecognized. We have excused this with lack of manners from parents.

As a young couple, the two divorced early. My brother went his way and she did also. Over the years, he supported the child monetarily and not as much physically.

Should we lower ourselves as rednecks and take care of them in restroom? Or pretend their actions are not a slap in the face to our family, especially my brother, who did the best that he could as a young dad and adult? It leaves me to believe that they are vindictive and money grubbers.

Please help me understand their ignorance. Your comments and suggestions are important and much needed.

GENTLE READER:

It strikes Miss Manners that what is much needed is a security guard in the restrooms. Her suggestion is that you all calm down and not hurl charges of ignorance (along with other insults) that could better be used against you.

Galling as you will find this, having the parent who actually reared the daughter give her away at her wedding is traditionally correct.

DEAR MISS MANNERS:

My daughter, who is thirty-five, is having a large second wedding and has informed me she wants her two sons, ages eighteen and eleven, to give her away so that they will be part of the ceremony and not feel left out.

Where does this leave her father? We are a loving family, and she loves her father very much, but she said he gave her away at the first wedding. Shouldn't the boys be ushers, or the eleven-year-old a ring bearer (or is he too old for that)?

GENTLE READER:

Although Miss Manners admires the motivation for featuring children in a wedding that will make them part of a new family, she has to say that the symbolism of having a bride given away by her own children is not good. Far from leaving them for her new husband, as she does her father, she is taking them with her.

As for her father, she has already left his household, and the symbolism of his giving her away a second time is not great either. It looks as though he plans to keep doing this until he finds a permanent taker.

A wedding can be just as legal and charming when that particular ceremony is omitted. She can be escorted to the altar by her sons or her father anyway and, especially in a case such as yours, where feelings might be hurt, simply have him or them stand at the altar with her as she takes her vows.

This might be better for the sons. While they should not be left out, they may not be as eager to acquire this new relative as their mother is and should be allowed to participate without solemnly and publicly taking part in making it come about.

THE BILLS

⌒Money and Happiness⌒

It is a firmly held notion that when a young woman falls in love, her parents will fall in debt. According to this not-so-funny folklore, parents who care for their daughters should not hesitate to capitulate to such possibly ruinous demands as $2,000 wedding cakes and $250-a-head dinners.

It is not Miss Manners' function to save people money they want to spend. So she would happily ignore this attitude were it not for the accompanying insinuation that the driving force behind such spending is poor old etiquette. Etiquette thus becomes the villain—the handmaiden of commercialism, whose insidious ceremonial and emotional arguments always favor the spending of extravagant sums of money. It is called rude to ask prices for commercial services and incorrect to limit wedding expenditures, even when they include planting tulips in the snow and making live swans waddle across the lawn.

Miss Manners is outraged. Etiquette does not practice extortion. Etiquette loves simplicity. And most of what is demanded in its name is exactly the sort of excess that etiquette condemns as vulgar.

Useless Wedding Paraphernalia

Expensive and Unnecessary	Reasonably Priced and Proper	Cheap and Charming
Save-the-date balloon-grams	Save-the-date cards	Telephone call or word of mouth
Welcome baskets with elaborate itineraries, hand-calligraphied maps, gourmet truffles, and personalized water	A map and a cookie	Good directions
Monogrammed lighting design at the reception	Monogrammed place card holders	Monogrammed paper for letters of thanks

Expensive and Unnecessary	Reasonably Priced and Proper	Cheap and Charming
Passed hors d'oeuvres, full open all-night bar, five-course dinner, and any food item followed by the word "station"	Lunch or tea with finger sandwiches, sweets, and champagne	Cake and punch
Floral centerpieces with Hawaiian orchids, South African lilies, and French roses highlighted with crystal accents	In-season, locally grown bouquets	Flowers from your garden
Commemorative platter signed by guests	Receiving line	Receiving line
Loud, jokey and controlling DJ	Local/student string quartet or jazz band	Family musicians or iPod (with volume control and songs appropriate for older generations)
Master of Ceremonies announcing when everyone should dance, toast, and talk	Parents and relatives gently coaxing guests to do the same	Guests figuring it out themselves
Twelve-foot designer wedding cake with themed icing sculpture	Simple wedding cake with fresh flowers	Grandma's cake recipe
Three-camera videography capturing every moment from every angle	Discreet photographer	Memories

⸺Her Parents' Obligations⸺

DEAR MISS MANNERS:

Is it still customary for parents to pay for their daughter's wedding? She already has two kids from different fathers and is now pregnant with the guy she plans on marrying. This would be her first marriage.

GENTLE READER:

The law requires you to feed and clothe your minor children, but not to sponsor their marital adventures. Etiquette would never step in to make that demand.

Even when young ladies married while still in their parents' custody and it was the custom for the family to give the wedding, doing so was up to them—as a young lady quickly found out if she chose the wrong bridegroom. Even with approval, the parents would celebrate in a style they chose and could afford.

A lot has changed since then, as Miss Manners needn't remind you. But parents have never been required to lose control over their finances. If you would like to pay for your daughter's somewhat overdue wedding, you should begin by telling her how much you intend to spend. Apparently you cannot count on her to know when to stop.

⸺His Parents' Obligations⸺

DEAR MISS MANNERS:

When my fiancé and I got engaged, his parents got ecstatic. It was nice that they were so happy, but his mother mentioned going on a honeymoon together. Any other vacation we've gone on, we've gone with them (they basically pay for us).

My parents are paying for the entire wedding and are not going to ask them to pony up, but in any case, does the groom's side pay for the honeymoon?

I'm assuming that it's either have them tag along and they'll pay for it, or say no and they won't pay a dime. So how can I politely decline their offer to go on a "family honeymoon" without sounding ungrateful and without losing a paid honeymoon?

GENTLE READER:

Where did you get the idea that it was ever the bridegroom's "side" who pays for the honeymoon? Traditionally, it is the bridegroom. The idea is that he is a solvent adult (or he would not be getting married), and that when he takes his new wife on a trip, he naturally pays the expenses. He also pays for the officiant and the bride's wedding ring and bouquet.

For parents, the cost of marrying off a son was free until a sense of fairness made it common to offer to contribute to the wedding costs. But that is voluntary, and the fact that your parents are being generous does not mean that his parents are in your debt.

The honeymoon has also changed, in that it is unlikely to be the couple's first chance to room together. No doubt that is what is behind your prospective in-laws' bizarre offer to accompany you. Of course you should start out married life independently. Independently—do you understand? So thank them prettily and say you'd love to vacation with them another time.

⌒Everybody Else's Obligations⌒

DEAR MISS MANNERS:

My best friend is getting married, and we want to know is there an etiquette way to ask for donations to the newlyweds in lieu of presents. They have everything they need, but the cost of the wedding is going to put her in debt for a long time.

First we thought to open an account for family and friends to make a deposit, but we wouldn't know who gave what. Now we thought of having a nice decorative box for the envelopes to go in. We feel this is tacky asking for money, but it's really what they need. Can you help us?

GENTLE READER:

Yes, because Miss Manners knows what your best friend really does need. She needs to know that there is no polite way to say "We plan to spend beyond our means, and we want to stick you with the bill."

THE ATTENDANTS

⁓ Chief Duties of the Maid or Matron of Honor ⁓

1. Continues to act as the bride's best friend to the extent of listening to confidences and helping with tasks even when driven to distraction by the repetition of petty worries and details.
2. Attends all wedding-related functions and may become spontaneously moved to gather bridesmaids and other intimates of the bride for a shower.
3. Fusses over the bride on the day of the wedding, helping her dress, telling her that her doubts about the bridegroom are only traditional bridal jitters (or helping her escape if they are not), keeping an eye out in case the bridal finery needs straightening or the bride's new mother-in-law has left lipstick on her cheek, holding the bride's bouquet during the ceremony, gracefully straightening her train, and producing the bridegroom's ring at the appropriate moment.

DEAR MISS MANNERS:

I am trying to plan a minimalist wedding. My problem comes with choosing a maid of honor and bridesmaids. My dearest friend lives four hours away and would not be able to help much in "maid of honor" duties. My other dear friend, who lives closer, is a scatterbrain and I couldn't rely on her to help plan or carry out any plans made. My third choice is a wonderful girl whom I've known my whole life, but she and I aren't as close as the other two. I'm afraid if I ask her to be my maid of honor, the other two friends will feel snubbed and insulted. What should I do?

GENTLE READER:

The chief thing you should do is to rethink the position of maid of honor. Miss Manners would like to disabuse you of the idea that it is unpaid employment. You need not consider the candidate's ability to perform various duties. The person to ask is your dearest friend. If she feels she cannot do justice to the position as she defines it, she may demur, and you could ask her to be a bridesmaid and the next dearest to be maid of honor.

Miss Manners realizes this will shock you, but you don't have to have a maid of honor. You could simply have them all be bridesmaids.

DEAR MISS MANNERS:

I am a 53-year-old mother whose oldest daughter is getting remarried next year in a large church wedding, with her sisters and her best friend as the bridesmaids.

My lovely daughter has asked *me* to be her matron of honor! I was absolutely flabbergasted and cried when she said, "Mom, there's no one I'd rather have." A friend mentioned to me that, of course, the traditional place for the bride's mom is the honored place of "mother of the bride" which I will be . . . but is it proper etiquette for the mother of the bride to also stand in as matron of honor?

My heart says, "Who cares what anyone thinks!" but part of me still wonders . . .

GENTLE READER:

What makes you think that etiquette, the sacred purpose of which is to make people happy—well, at least to prevent them from shoving one another—might object to such a charming arrangement?

It is not uncommon for a bridegroom to have his father as his best man. It is less common, but no more peculiar, Miss Manners assures you, for a bride to have her mother as matron of honor.

And there is no reason it should interfere with your duties as hostess of the reception following the ceremony.

DEAR MISS MANNERS:

I am considering getting married again. The time before, my sister was my matron of honor. I would dearly love her to fill that role again, but in discussing it, we thought that this might be frowned on or socially unacceptable.

GENTLE READER:

What, pray, is your reasoning? That when changing husbands, it looks backward to retain the same sister?

DEAR MISS MANNERS:

I am a widow, and my friend has asked me to be her honor attendant in her wedding. Would I be called the matron or maid of honor?

GENTLE READER:

Miss Manners does not want to be the one to break the news to you that maidenhood is not renewable. So she will confine herself to saying that a widow would have to be a matron of honor.

⌁ Chief Duties of the Best Man ⌁

1. Delivers the bridegroom to the ceremony at the proper time, correctly dressed, and in a suitable frame of mind—which is induced by a.) sending him home early the night before, and b.) reminding him that he adores the bride and is not making a mistake.
2. Supervises the ushers, checking out their clothing, encouraging them to invite the bridesmaids, and especially the junior bridesmaids, to dance, and vetoing any ideas for jokes that would disgust the guests or disable the going-away vehicle.
3. Offers a flattering toast to the bride, omitting any details about the

courtship or the bridegroom's character that the bride's grandparents might not want to know.

4. Produces the bride's ring during the ceremony (either from his pocket or by nudging the ringbearer) and the tickets for the wedding trip at the conclusion of the reception.

⌐Chief Duties of the Bridesmaids⌐

1. Being good sports about the bride's taste in their dresses, jollying her into a compromise that they can both stomach and afford, and then putting up with the results.

2. Hanging around the altar during the ceremony, paying attention and looking pleased or moved (both, if they can manage it without getting so carried away that they stand on the bride's train).

3. Smiling charmingly, not only while marching up the aisle together, but also while marching back down it on the arms of groomsmen they may not fancy, while standing in the receiving line, and while going around the reception being asked when they are getting married.

⌐The Fertile Bridesmaid⌐

DEAR MISS MANNERS:

Among my granddaughter's bridesmaids will be a lady who will be nine months pregnant, walking along with the other bridesmaids. My opinion is that she will be out of place among them. Is her presence in the bridal party in good taste? I am eighty-three years old, and my children believe I'm old-fashioned.

GENTLE READER:

Indeed, pregnancy was once considered to be in poor taste and signs of it best concealed. This was a tremendous inconvenience to ladies who got pregnant anyway and is a fashion that Miss Manners is delighted to see gone.

Presuming there is no question of physical difficulty for the lady in question, she should properly take her place as a bridesmaid by virtue of being one of the bride's friends. Her own family situation is irrelevant to the occasion.

⌒ The Decorated Bridesmaid ⌒

DEAR MISS MANNERS:

I am to be a bridesmaid and the bride let us pick out our own dresses, as long as they were velvet and not strapless. Wheee! I found this elegant off-the-shoulder dress.

I have a tattoo on my right shoulder that shows. I don't know if I should cover it with special makeup (the bride's sister thinks I should) or leave it alone. The tattoo is now a part of me and they should accept me the way I am. I am a middle-class woman, well groomed, clean, not the biker type.

The bride really doesn't care if I cover it or not, but I feel as if she's not telling me her real feelings about the matter from not wanting to hurt my feelings. She's a really good friend. I feel if everyone at this wedding is so offended by my tattoo and not more interested in the wedding day, then they have a problem.

GENTLE READER:

Okay, what's the tattoo look like?

Never mind. Unless it is positively nauseating or obscene, Miss Manners is going to surprise you by defending it. Wheee! (as you would say).

The notion that the bride can make bridesmaids restyle their hair or change their weight or throw covers over them in the hopes of standardizing them into a matching set is as insulting as it is silly.

This bride has done nothing of the kind. She has been faultlessly polite—and yet you are goading her to tell you her true feelings. Miss Manners feels that if you are not more interested in your friend's wedding than in her opinion of your tattoo, it is you who have a problem.

⁓Grounds for Quitting⁓

DEAR MISS MANNERS:

I am at my wits' end. Over a year ago I happily accepted when my best friend of nearly 12 years asked me to be a bridesmaid on her special day. When I agreed, I had visions of hosting a lovely party, buying a sentimental gift, and tearfully helping her into her dress . . . not the nightmare of financial stresses that have ensued.

My friend is 25, and four out of her six bridesmaids are still in school (myself included) and don't have lots of money. Surprisingly, she has managed to ignore this fact in her bridal planning. The dresses she asked us to buy cost over $300 dollars (not including alterations, which averaged $100 more per person), and because her wedding is not local, each bridesmaid will be spending over $300 on accommodations.

Where I had planned on hosting her one "young person" bachelorette/bridal shower, there are now three parties that I am expected to attend, chip in for, and buy a gift for in addition. Never mind the normal things bridesmaids are expected to pony up for: shoes, hair, makeup, and the all-important wedding gifts. The latest e-mail I got, from a bridesmaid who is not in school, tells me to shovel out another $300-$500 on her bachelorette party.

I have had the awkward job of attempting to discuss financial stuff with the bride. At best, she brushes me off; at worst, I am chewed out for bringing it up and giving her "a guilt trip."

Her wedding is during the holidays, and I don't want to be too broke to buy gifts for my family . . . or pay for my next semester of classes. As happy as I am for her—and as much as I am wanting to share in the joy of her wedding, I am in over my head financially, and need suggestions on how to proceed. I know she's the bride and we should keep mum to make her happy, but I am not in the situation where I can happily shut up and put up over $2000 for one night. Please help!

GENTLE READER:

Have you and the other student bridesmaids considered a class action suit?

Since bridesmaids are, by definition, the bride's closest friends, Miss Manners is amazed at the callousness with which they are commonly treated. Unfortunately, they usually buy into the expensive—and morally outrageous—idea that they are under the total command of the bride. Even you voiced the idea that you are supposed to "keep mum" and sacrifice your welfare for her whims. Is that really your definition of friendship?

Individually—or better yet, collectively—bridesmaids should speak up about the costs they may be incurring. Don't you think that the bride and her family are carefully weighing their own budgets with every decision they make? For example, you should have said that the dress was lovely, but out of your reach. The bride could then have chosen a less expensive dress or a richer bridesmaid. Or paid for the clothes herself.

Gathering the other bridesmaids who are in the same predicament would make it easier to confront the bride with your inability to finance her fantasy. But if you must do it alone, you must still do it, offering to withdraw from the wedding party and expressing satisfaction at being merely a wedding guest. If the bride is truly indifferent to your problems, you should be resigning anyway, because she is not really your friend.

DEAR MISS MANNERS:

My two best friends are engaged to be married. Most of the group we hang out with all agree that these two should not be getting married.

I already agreed to be a bridesmaid, but now I am regretting the commitment. They fight every week and break up, and then, three days later, they get back together. One time I got a phone call because they were fighting over if there was a difference between fireworks and firecrackers. They almost broke up over this fight.

I do not want to support a marriage that I know will not go well. How do I tell my friends that I don't want to be part of the ceremonies because I don't support their union? Should I just mind my own business and be there for my friends, or stand up for what's right and refuse to participate?

GENTLE READER:

Do you and the group have a record for predicting the success of marriages? These two strike Miss Manners as made for each other. People who care that much about the precise meaning of words are not easily found.

In any case, bridesmaids do not have veto power over the choice of the bridegroom. Nor are they responsible for the success of the marriage. If you decide not to stand up for your friend, at least do not fool yourself that you are standing up for "what's right."

⌁Grounds for Firing⌁

DEAR MISS MANNERS:

What's the politest way to kick someone out of your wedding party who has repeatedly not held up her end of the "deal"?

GENTLE READER:

What was the deal?

If it was that your friend must accept the honor of waiting on you hand and foot while surrendering control over her own time and money and wardrobe, it was an illegitimate deal. Those terms exist only in the minds of brides who have worked themselves into a state of self-inflation that has rendered them thoughtless toward their own closest friends. Miss Manners is not going to help you fire a friend for refusing to turn into an indentured servant.

However, if your bridesmaid has been telling you that you can do better than marrying the gentleman in question and that she hopes to make it to the wedding but can't promise, it is she who has broken the deal. In that case, you could say, "I don't think you realized what you were getting into when you kindly took this on, and I can see it's becoming a burden to you. You know how dear you are to me, and I'd be just as happy to have you at the wedding without your having to go through all the business of being a bridesmaid."

DEAR MISS MANNERS:

I am getting married next spring and have a dilemma. Soon after getting engaged, I impulsively asked a friend from college to be one of my bridesmaids. Now that a few months have passed (the wedding is still 8 months away) I have realized I asked her in haste. We have grown apart since college, and I no longer feel it would be appropriate to have her as a bridesmaid. I am only having two.

What do I do? I would hate to have her in the wedding simply because I am too chicken to tell her I changed my mind. What is the appropriate way to tell her I have changed my mind?

GENTLE READER:

Congratulations on being too chicken to tell a friend that you have changed your mind about having her in your wedding. Miss Manners dearly hopes that the underlying reason for this is that you are too kind and too polite to fire her. So congratulations, also, on having three bridesmaids to attend you.

Miss Manners would also like to wish you well on your marriage. But you now have her worrying about your ability to make an emotional choice and stick with it.

THE EXPLANATION

DEAR MISS MANNERS:

I hope you can help with this sad case of being kicked out of a wedding party. In January, I was invited by the bride to be in the wedding and be a bridesmaid. Since we were friends and we saw each other often at social gatherings, I thought everything was fine.

In April, the bride finally decided on the dresses, got us measured, and did the first fitting of sample dresses in our sizes. Then back in May or June, my e-mails got no responses from the groom or the bride.

I went down in July to see the dresses at my friend's house. I was so excited to be in my first "beach" wedding. I of course felt so honored to be part of this wedding, knowing I was the Matchmaker and I was the one who introduced them to each other.

Only this past weekend, I was told by the groom, who is my second cousin as well, that I was no longer to be in the wedding party but only a guest. Their reasoning was that I brought too much stress in their lives and the planning process.

So I was technically kicked out of the wedding party. My happy and exciting feelings were sent out to sea. What should I do next? Everyone who has been invited to the wedding knows that I was supposed to be in the wedding party as a bridesmaid.

My aunt told me the groom and bride have no tact or decent diplomacy in this decision. Everyone around me told me not to attend any of the wedding festivities, including the wedding shower and the wedding itself. What is your opinion?

Gentle Reader:

It depends on how bighearted you care to be.

Your choice is between not going and having to participate in apparently cheerful conversations that go something like this:

"I thought you were supposed to be a bridesmaid."

"Oh, I was."

"What happened?"

"I was fired."

"Fired? Why?"

"They said I was causing them stress. [pause] I introduced them to each other."

Miss Manners admits that she would be tempted to have these conversations. But perhaps you are a nicer person.

⌒ Chief Duties of the Ushers ⌒

1. Keep their right arms bent before the ceremony to seat the lady wedding guests while the gentlemen follow behind, and again at the ceremony's conclusion, to escort the bridesmaids down the aisle.
2. Be good sports about restraining their sense of fun on the grounds that the occasion may seem a complete joke to them, but apparently has a serious element for their friend the bridegroom.

⌒ The Ring Bearer and Flower Girl ⌒

DEAR MISS MANNERS:

My fiancé and I are trying to finalize the members of the wedding party. Should the ring bearer and the flower girl be a certain age, or is it up to each couple to decide?

GENTLE READER:

The ring bearer and the flower girl are supposed to be of an age to make everyone smile and nudge one another and say "Awwwww, looooooook" during the processional. A mere "Don't they look cute?" with no extra letters in the pronunciation means that the young people are old enough to be either a junior bridesmaid or usher. What age produces the desired effect is something that the bridal couple may decide.

Whatever their ages, Miss Manners urges you to fuss a bit over the younger members of your bridal party. Children in weddings usually treat their roles with great seriousness and share the bridal couple's sense of the importance of the occasion. They also frequently retain vivid memories of such events, which they trot out a decade or two later when they want "a wedding just like Cousin Adelaide's."

TROUBLESHOOTING

DEAR MISS MANNERS:

Since the happy announcement of our engagement, my fiancé and I have been bombarded with demands from his parents. We are recent college graduates, so money is tight, but we feel that we should pay for our own wedding because we are adults.

My parents are giving us money to ensure we have a nice honeymoon and to help defray some of the wedding costs. While we both wanted the traditional dinner reception, we simply do not have the money. So we changed our idea and will serve cake and champagne/sparkling cider immediately following the church ceremony.

According to my future mother-in-law, I will be horribly offending everyone by this simple reception afterwards and the small amount of money that has been given to me by my parents should be used for the reception. Now mind you, with the simpler reception, we have the ability to accommodate an additional fifty people (she was throwing a fit that we closed the guest list at family and very close friends, even though that was over a hundred people).

So is it rude to ask people to be satisfied with a simple reception if the wedding is held in the early afternoon and the invitation states "Please join the bride and groom for cake and champagne following the ceremony"?

GENTLE READER:

Not in the slightest. In fact, the "traditional" dinner wedding is only of the last decade or two. Really traditional (and fashionable) weddings are held during the day with the sort of reception you describe. Please (gently) tell your future mother-in-law for us that you are offering a rare chance in life to have her cake and eat it too.

DEAR MISS MANNERS:

"Will you be one of my bridesmaids?" I dread that question! I've done it enough to know that I never want to do it again. I view marriage as a holy sacrament and think a line of bridesmaids in matching dresses is unnecessary. Besides, it's expensive, you can never wear the dress again no matter what they say, the brides turn into "bridezillas," the time commitment is a hassle when you're a busy mother of young children as I am; and for some reason my friendship with the bride always seems to wane afterward, which then becomes a source of guilt when you think, "I was in her wedding? I should be a better friend."

What is the best way to decline the offer but not hurt the friendship? I'm still recovering from the last wedding party I was in. The couple planned a semiprivate ceremony without the wedding party but had us spend $200 on a dress and stand in for pictures during a reception a few weeks later. My husband thought the whole deal was a farce. And once again, my friendship with the newlywed is showing signs of strain.

GENTLE READER:

Hurting the friendship may prove to be a moot point, since it seems accepting the offer does more harm than not. Until brides start behaving better (and we're doing our part here), the gracious out is to say that you are thrilled to celebrate with her but don't have the time or resources to do justice to being a bridesmaid. If you find yourself weakening, this allows the bride to counter with promises of a more reasonable experience.

DEAR MISS MANNERS:

My fiancé and I, being impoverished college students, are having a fairly small, yet tasteful wedding. Our families have been incredibly generous, assisting both fiscally and offering to help out with everything from the cake to the bridesmaids' dresses and decorating. They could not be more amiable in considering everyone involved.

How, apart from the obvious copious thanks and invitations to share their marital wisdom over ramen noodles, can we show our appreciation to them? (Other than by perhaps splurging and buying real pasta for their dinner.)

GENTLE READER:

Your happiness will be thanks enough? Perhaps not, but being gracious, equally amiable, and responding in kind with reciprocal offers of whatever kind of pasta you can afford will show both families your appreciation. Adding a desire to hear their marital wisdom is a lovely touch. Knowing that they have reared a rare breed—the appreciative daughter and (even more rare) the gracious bride—may truly be all the thanks they need.

CHAPTER FIVE

The Guest List

F OR YEARS MISS MANNERS let pass without comment (or much interest) the key rule of planning a wedding that she knew bridal couples are commonly told: Figure out the size of your wedding. This is determined by your taste, but limited by your budget. When you know what you want the style of the wedding to be and what you can afford to spend to make it so, you will realize how many guests you can invite. That number should then be divided evenly between the bride's family and the bridegroom's.

Not exactly fighting words, Miss Manners had supposed. Wedding size is not a decision based on etiquette, she told herself to assuage her conscience about her wandering attention. A proper wedding can consist of only the principals, or can include an entire nation lining the streets, simultaneously cheering and memorizing the design of the wedding dress for cheaper reproduction.

Certainly no one should be financially strained for the sake of a wedding. Contrary to unpleasant belief, etiquette has never tried to dictate who should spend what on a wedding. The only stake that etiquette has in the wedding size is that people who legitimately expect to be invited (there are a lot of illegitimate expectations floating around society these days, and their possessors are not shy of mentioning it) are not hurt.

Careful readers will have noticed the omission that so long escaped Miss Manners. Suppose the size you decide upon, either because you prefer it or because that is all you can afford, or both, is smaller than the number of people who will be hurt if not invited?

Miss Manners said you couldn't hurt them, not that you had to invite them. To avoid doing both, you must limit the list by categories unrelated to individual likes or dislikes. "There are so many close friends we would love to have, but we're having just a private ceremony with members of the immediate family," is a polite explanation that ought to satisfy any reasonable friend. So is "We're not inviting children," or "We've had to define 'family' only as far as first cousins, not second cousins."

What of the common variation of this—"We'd love to invite everybody, but we can only afford to have X people?" It has belatedly occurred to Miss Manners that there is something inherently rude in allowing style and cost to prevail over emotional bonds. When something has to be cut, it should be the menu and frills, not the guests. Let us say, for example, that you have a large family or a huge circle of friends who truly care about you and with whom you would like to share your wedding, but feeding them all dinner is prohibitive. The solution is to feed them all wedding cake and punch, rather than to feed everything to only a few. All that is required is not to set the wedding near a mealtime.

While the idea of dividing the list between the two families—or four sets of parents, as can easily happen nowadays—is a fair one, polite people will be flexible enough to count guests by relationship, rather than number. If he has six uncles and she has none, it would be thoughtful to fit the list to his family without the bride's demanding to throw in six extra acquaintances to make things even.

Miss Manners would like to hear of the two families planning together, first asking, "Whom would you like to have?" and only afterward, "Well, let's see. What can we afford to feed them?" It would be an excellent introduction, Miss Manners believes, to the special definition of fairness and generosity essential to a successful marriage.

PROBLEMATIC CANDIDATES

⌒Her Mother's Relatives⌒

DEAR MISS MANNERS:

My fiancé and I are taking a six-month moratorium before starting our wedding planning (which I am dreading a little, having seen friends do it and pay for it). Meanwhile, my mother is pressuring me for an invite list that does not yet exist.

Am I obligated to invite my aunts/uncles (her brothers and their wives) and cousins who I see once every five years, at most? She seems devastated at the thought that they might not be involved.

GENTLE READER:

Does the idea that your mother is devastated carry any weight with you? Shouldn't that affect you more than anything Miss Manners might have to say?

Your marriage will be all about the two of you, although Miss Manners hopes that you will have a warm group of relatives and friends. Your wedding, in contrast, is a civic, optionally religious, ceremonial, social, and family occasion. As a member of your immediate family and nominative hostess of the wedding, your mother should be allowed to invite not only her—also your—relatives, but her own close friends as well. Realizing this will help you avoid the stress of personal clashes that are at the bottom of most of that stress your friends have been experiencing. So have a nice little furlough and start jotting down names.

⌒Her Mother's Friends⌒

DEAR MISS MANNERS:

Because my mother and father are graciously paying for our wedding, I don't mind that the majority of the list are friends of hers. But I have objected to her wanting to invite some church friends that both my fiancé and I have never even met and don't have much desire to meet, but she insists that it would be rude to leave them out.

All I can think about is how awkward the receiving line will be when my fiancé and I will both be saying, "Nice to meet you." I want a wedding that will be on a smaller, more intimate level so I don't think that I'm wrong in this. Would you please help us?

GENTLE READER:

Not if it involves telling your mother that you have no desire to meet people she feels ought to be there.

Miss Manners can relieve you of the worry about meeting new people in the receiving line. Unless you have already been introduced to every one of your bridegroom's cousins and his parents' friends, you will be meeting many people for the first time. Since they will all be telling you how beautiful you look, it should be a pleasant experience.

⁓ His Mother's Friends ⁓

DEAR MISS MANNERS:

Due to finances and my choice of location, I have limited my upcoming wedding to 100 guests. This means that some of my future mother-in-law's friends will be excluded. She is therefore insistent on including them in the rehearsal dinner at her home the night before, to which she has invited my bridesmaids only verbally through me, and ignored the clergy entirely. She also will not permit me to send wedding announcements to any of her friends.

These are only four examples of her endless lack of cooperation with my plans. I feel that rules of etiquette exist to protect all parties, prevent present anger and future discord. Am I justified in seeing these as breaches that put my parents and me in a very awkward situation?

GENTLE READER:

There is an unpleasant thought that is preventing Miss Manners from entering sympathetically into the denunciation of your mother-in-law, which you kindly pair with a declaration of belief in etiquette.

It is that your case for courtesy seems to be built on the idea that you may blithely omit this lady's friends from wedding plans that you identify as yours, rather than both families'. Miss Manners is not saying that an exaggerated list cannot be argued down, but that those who are truly close to the family should not be easily dismissed.

You could limit the wedding to the families and throw related parties for friends. Had there been more sympathy shown all around, it could have been suggested that your mother-in-law give a party to celebrate your marriage after the wedding trip, for example.

Miss Manners gathers that instead, this lady was merely assigned to entertain the night before the wedding and is awkwardly trying to make the most of it. For the sake of your future family relations she urges you to work out a compromise that will recognize the legitimacy of her wanting to include her friends without harping too much on the unfortunate way she has been trying to accomplish this.

Newly Recognized Relatives

DEAR MISS MANNERS:

Is it proper to send a wedding invitation to first cousins whom I've never met? I would like to get to know them and want them to come to my wedding if at all possible. Should a personal note be included with the invitation, explaining how we are related?

GENTLE READER:

You are going to have to explain more than that, Miss Manners is afraid. You are going to have to explain why you never thought of getting to know them before, and how you plan to do so now, all while presumably tending to other matters on your wedding day.

⌒Former Relatives⌒

DEAR MISS MANNERS:

My son died several years ago. His widow is being married soon. Is it customary for the family of the deceased spouse to be invited to the wedding? They are having a large wedding. If we are not invited, should we send a gift?

GENTLE READER:

It is not customary, for fear that the family of the deceased spouse may find such a ceremony painfully reminiscent of the previous wedding. Your question suggests that you are on warm terms with your daughter-in-law, and it would be kind of you to let her know that you wish her happiness. This can be done with a letter and, if you wish, a present.

⌒Former Loves⌒

DEAR MISS MANNERS:

My fiancé has a female best friend who he coincidently used to date years ago. I told him I think that we should invite her to the wedding, but he begs to differ. He says that no man in his right mind would ever invite an ex-girlfriend to his wedding. I think that if they are such great friends it would only make sense to be a part of one of the biggest days in his life. Miss Manners, should this lady be invited to the wedding?

GENTLE READER:

Why? Her best friend doesn't want her there, and he presumably knows better than you how she would feel about it.

Or perhaps you do know. Miss Manners hopes you merely want to extend hospitality to your fiancé's friend and have not the least notion of relishing her witnessing the end to any romantic feelings that may linger. There will be plenty of opportunities for you to invite her to be a part of your joint social life later.

PROBLEMATIC INVITATIONS

⌒Far-Flung Invitations⌒

DEAR MISS MANNERS:

My husband's and my relatives and friends live so far away that it will be an expense for them to come out to our daughter's wedding, much as we would like to have them. Is it correct to include a note acknowledging that we will understand if they cannot attend? Are we to provide hotel rooms?

GENTLE READER:

Please stop thinking this way. Miss Manners knows you mean well, but relatives and friends will interpret it as evidence that your invitation is insincere, and you are hoping that they won't accept so that you can invite people you'd rather have in their place.

It is not the task of hosts to answer, as well as issue, invitations. That is up to the guests. If they must decline, they can easily do so without even having to cite reasons. Oddly enough, they believe they make their own decisions better than anyone else can do.

No, you don't have to provide hotel rooms for guests. However, if you really want them there and are worried about their expenses, doing so, or finding local friends who will put them up, would be a gracious way to help.

⌒Nervous Invitations⌒

DEAR MISS MANNERS:

My daughter is a lesbian, and she and her partner would like to plan a civil union ceremony. But we need to know approximately how many guests will be attending the reception, supplying a minimum but making sure that the maximum number of guests could be accommodated.

Most guests will need to drive about four hours to where the ceremony will be held. Short of calling all those that would be invited to see if they would even consider such an overnight trip, I'm not sure how to find this information.

Do you have any suggestions on how we can find out, without putting people in an awkward situation, if they support the couple enough to go?

GENTLE READER:

Yes. Suffer like all other hosts by issuing invitations at the proper time, waiting anxiously for replies, and extracting overdue answers through polite nagging. Probing people about whether they "support the couple" is a disastrous idea. You will embarrass people into thinking that they will be condemned if they do not want to travel, and shake those who disapprove out of the silence they have thus far kept.

No wedding could survive a referendum from the prospective guests. Genuine well-wishers harbor such notions as, "With her looks, you would have thought she could do better," and "I suppose he is after the money," and "I give it six months." This is why polite people do not say everything they think, and sensible people do not urge others to do so.

 *Free Passes*

DEAR MISS MANNERS:

My roommate has several family members whom he has either not kept in contact with or for whom traveling for the ceremony won't be feasible. You recommend inviting these types of guests so as not to hurt their feelings, however, I've always thought that doing so gave the appearance of begging for gifts. I wonder, would it be an appropriate compromise to send invitations to them without including information regarding the registry?

GENTLE READER:

Oh, so you think it is all right to beg for gifts from people who *are* likely to attend?

⌒Stay-Away Invitations⌒

DEAR MISS MANNERS:

My daughter and her fiancé have chosen a very small place for their wedding reception. As a result, the guest list has been painfully cut, and there will be hurt feelings on both sides of the family as well as among friends. Would it be impolite or presumptuous to send letters to those who will not be invited in order to explain the circumstances? Or would it be best left unmentioned, letting them wonder why they weren't invited and not addressing the situation at all?

GENTLE READER:

What is the letter going to say? "We had to choose between having the wedding in a charming little place without you, or in an ordinary place with you, and we decided to lose you."

If Miss Manners were you, she would not attempt to explain to the excluded guests that the location is more important than their presence. Rather, you might throw a party for the bridal couple upon their return from their wedding trip and invite those people to what you can still call a wedding reception.

⌒Repeat Invitations⌒

DEAR MISS MANNERS:

This will be our son's second marriage, his fiancée's first. My husband and I think it is up to the guests that attended his first wedding to decide whether or not they want to attend another wedding. The bride's mother thinks it is improper to invite people that have already attended his wedding. We want to do what is best for our son and future daughter-in-law without offending anyone, especially the bride's mother. What is the proper thing to do?

GENTLE READER:

Is there someone in particular that the bride's mother does not want to see there? Such as the previous bride? Or just your entire list?

The custom is to invite your relatives and friends and to let them decide whether they have had enough. Miss Manners does acknowledge, however, that anyone in the habit of marrying often would be kind to prevent wedding fatigue by having successively smaller weddings.

Open Invitations

DEAR MISS MANNERS:

At the small community church we attend with seventy to eighty people, a trend we find offensive has been started. One invitation is sent, addressed to the church congregation, and is read aloud from the pulpit to those in attendance and then posted at the back of the church. No one who attends our church is sent a personal invitation. This is even being done by our pastor's children.

What do you make of this, and what should our response be? We realize that invitations are expensive, but it doesn't seem like a good area to cut back on these expenses.

GENTLE READER:

Always looking for a kindly interpretation, Miss Manners is assuming that these invitations are not intended to replace individual ones sent to friends. Rather, she hopes, they are there to reinforce the traditional notion that public ceremonies are—well, public. Anyone in a congregation is therefore permitted to attend weddings or other ceremonies held in the church.

Bulletin-board invitations do not obligate unnamed people to observe the usual conventions, such as replying to invitations and sending presents. Nor should they entitle those anonymous people to attend anything but the ceremony itself.

Miss Manners would have very little sympathy for anyone who omitted the individual invitations to those expected to attend related festivities. She wouldn't quite snicker at the empty—or overcrowded—receptions that are likely to result, because she doesn't enjoy other people's discomfort even when it is deserved. But, for once, the failure of anyone to perform the duties of invited guests would be no fault of the guests.

⌐Self-Invitations⌐

DEAR MISS MANNERS:

A young lady that I worked with last year learned from mutual acquaintances that I am getting married in July. Though we worked closely together on the same project, we were never what I would call close friends. Since finding out about my out-of-state wedding she has come to me three times, reminding me to give her hotel information, etc., so she can make her flight arrangements.

Miss Manners, she is not invited to my wedding. How do I handle her assumption that she is? I really don't want to hurt her feelings.

GENTLE READER:

Here is a phrase that every prospective bride and bridegroom and everyone in both families should memorize: "Oh, dear, it's just going to be a small family wedding, with maybe a few old, intimate friends. You are so nice to take an interest."

Miss Manners doesn't care whether you are inviting half the state and putting the families involved into perpetual poverty thereafter; it is still a "small" wedding. Let us say that the word is used out of modesty, rather than crowd estimation.

⸻ Invalidating Invitations ⸻

DEAR MISS MANNERS:

Caught up in the spirit of family and goodwill, I sent my home-less, drug-addict, criminal cousin a save-the-date card for my wedding. I sent it to his mother's address, and she said, "Who knows if he'll get it? I'll try to pass it along."

I was relieved to hear that, because I already regretted sending it. The last time I saw him was at his sister's wedding five years ago, and he hit on me. It was disturbing and I get upset thinking about it.

Now my aunt tells me he is in good health and living with his fiancée and her parents. He received the save-the-date and wants to know why he never got an invitation. My aunt thinks he should. I'm glad to hear he's doing better, but I don't want to have a reunion with him on my wedding day. I am very shy, and the reception will already be challenging for me, without the added creepiness.

I don't want to offend my aunt, but she keeps changing her mind about whether her son matters to the family. She has not actually seen him since he resurfaced—only spoken to him by phone.

I am thinking of saying I know it is bad form to send a save-the-date and not an invitation, but he made me uncomfortable last time I saw him. I would suggest a family lunch after the honey-moon as a better occasion. He could meet my husband, we could meet his fiancée, etc.

Is this appropriate? And would I write a letter inviting him to lunch instead, and apologize that wedding arrangements were finalized before I was told that he could be contacted?

GENTLE READER:

Can you manage to rekindle that spirit of family and goodwill? "Save-the-date" being a recent addition to the social conventions, people seem confused about the obligations it entails. It is not binding on the guests, who need only answer the actual invitation when it appears. But it *is* binding on the host, who cannot ask someone to save a date and then declare, "Oh, never mind. You didn't make the final cut."

Anyway, your fears seem exaggerated. Both his present situation and his mother's word suggest that he is doing well. And the chances of his hitting on a bride in the presence of his fiancée are not great. If he does, you will have your new husband by your side to protect you.

DEAR MISS MANNERS:

My fiancé and I have a beautiful son together who has an important role in our wedding. We invited several people, mainly friends, who, since learning that our son will be participating, have become disagreeable. They have previously professed to adore our son even though they don't agree with the manner in which he was conceived.

They are now being so rude that we no longer want them to attend the wedding. They don't believe children under 18 should be in a wedding or even allowed to attend, especially one conceived outside of wedlock. They believed we should have married before our son was born.

Is there any way to politely un-invite them even though they have already sent in their response cards saying that they will be there? Since they have announced this view, we haven't spent much time with them as our son is so important to us.

GENTLE READER:

There may be extreme cases in which an invited guest has to be barred from the wedding, in which case the form is to say, "Considering how you feel, we don't think you would be happy attending."

But if this were said to all those holding opinions about the courtship and the ceremony, everyone would get married in isolation. Mind you, Miss Manners considers it dreadful to voice such opinions even, as often happens, when the couple seem to discuss their plans thoroughly enough to appear to invite comment. However, she would suggest letting this go. They are unlikely to critique the wedding while it is going on, and may well revert afterward to saying how adorable your son is.

PROBLEMATIC CASES

⌒ Old Ties ⌒

DEAR MISS MANNERS:

I imagine many women in their thirties are grappling with my problem about wedding invitations. The older you are, the more friends you've accumulated over the years. In deciding whom to invite, I go back to circles of friends from graduate school and college—circles where I've kept in touch with perhaps half of each group, yet attended all of their weddings. I'm wondering where to draw the line. Do I send invitations to the people I'm still close with and only announcements to my fading friends (who will inevitably hear through the grapevine that I'm getting married)? Or invitations to everyone and just hope there's a natural attrition rate?

GENTLE READER:

Miss Manners cannot claim that it is rude to invite only close friends to one's wedding and send announcements to those now more distant. That is the correct distinction to make. But she would like to persuade you to issue invitations all around anyway.

There is a sequel to that "older you get" formula that applies to late middle age: The older you get, the more you value the friends of your youth. Your now-fading friends will, of course, remember that you attended their weddings and may therefore feel slightly miffed not to be invited to yours. It is, indeed, likely that they would not rush to attend, but the omission of an invitation could stick in their minds and might act as a barrier when you reach the stage of wanting to renew old ties.

⌐Bad Attitudes⌐

DEAR MISS MANNERS:

My parents are both very conservative, with old-fashioned values. My fiancé's grandparents are also very conservative and religious. I know that being around gay couples makes them extremely uncomfortable. But some of my closest friends are gay.

I am not worried that my gay friends will be engaging in inappropriate displays of affection. But just simple things like holding hands or slow dancing might make my parents and my fiancé's grandparents extremely uncomfortable and offended.

I don't want to offend them. But I also don't want to offend my gay friends by singling them out and telling them they are not allowed to hold hands or slow dance with their date!!! I could ask *all* of my friends to refrain from holding hands and slow dancing, but at the same time, these are my guests and I want to make sure *everyone* is enjoying themselves and having a good time. Who do I offend—my family, whose values I understand are different and whose values I respect, even though I do not agree at all with those values, or my friends, whose lifestyle I fully support?

GENTLE READER:

Never mind about values and lifestyles—just tell the band to play fast.

For parties, the guest list is composed with known or likely compatibility in mind, but ceremonial occasions are different. That is when you invite relatives and friends simply because they are close to you—and then you hope for the best.

Miss Manners is glad that you understand that you cannot restrict polite guests because they may be the targets of impolite ones. But she trusts that the grandparents, who have surely been in the world long enough to see gay people, will have the courtesy to suppress any discomfort they may feel.

⌒Neighbors⌒

DEAR MISS MANNERS:

Should my wife and I invite close neighborhood friends who have never met my daughter to her wedding? The wedding will be held in a neighborhood venue.

GENTLE READER:

If they are close friends, they should be invited for that reason alone. But if they are simply close neighbors, Miss Manners still suggests considering inviting them on the grounds that they might otherwise complain about the traffic congestion.

AUXILLIARY GUESTS

A stranger is stalking wedding guest lists: The Guest Once Removed. This is not someone whom the bridal couple or their families thought to invite or who is likely to have any emotional attachment to the occasion. Pressure from people who regard a wedding as being a sort of prom that would be no fun without a date has created the expectation that single guests are entitled to bring their own guests.

Miss Manners is all for inviting coupled wedding guests as couples—indeed, there is a new rudeness, which she is trying to stamp out, of inviting only half of an established couple. Those who are married, engaged, or otherwise firmly attached must be asked in tandem to social events (as opposed to office gatherings, which are still office gatherings, no matter how many drinks are served). This is not the same as being expected to surrender control of a guest list to the guests themselves.

If the hosts are feeling generous, they can ask their unattached guests if there is someone they would like to bring, extract that person's name, and use it to issue another invitation. The considerate way to do this is individually, so that no guest feels pressured to bring a date or is embarrassed about suggesting a non-date, such as a friend, local host, or caretaker.

Such people must then be treated with the courtesies due to all guests. Miss Manners has been told dreadful stories of guests' guests being told they cannot fully partake in the festivities. One young lady was told by the bride that she would be allowed to attend the reception only if one of the A-list guests failed to show up—and was yanked when one came late. Another was criticized first for unintentionally catching the bridal bouquet when it came her way, and then for not turning it over to a "real" guest.

For their own sakes, those who have been invited by guests, rather than by hosts, should make sure that their benefactors were authorized to do this. Even then, it would be wise to write a note to the bride along the lines of "Ethan has asked me to accompany him to your wedding. I would consider it a great honor to attend, but I would also understand if his enthusiasm has over-run any boundaries. In any case, I send you my very best wishes for your happiness."

Such a gesture establishes that you do not regard the wedding as a public event at which you can amuse yourself without having an interest in the marriage taking place. And when a bride considers how many people on her list did not even respond to her invitation, she is likely to appreciate someone who took the trouble to write such a letter.

⌒ Responding to Requests ⌒

DEAR MISS MANNERS:

I am from a small, midwestern town, where we invite friends to weddings—not friend 'n' escorts or escortees. Where I live now, it is different. Persons who attend weddings are assumed to need the security of a partner in order to celebrate the event—even if that person is a complete stranger to the bride and groom.

This is repulsive to me. I do not want outsiders at my wedding. I consider it an intimate ceremony, which is not to be thrown open to casual inspection. How can I get around the trend? I don't want to offend my friends or have them think my motivation is financial. Can we get away with leaving "and guest" off invitations?

GENTLE READER:

Miss Manners knew you and she would get along when she saw that "'n,'" which not only acknowledges that letters are missing on both sides of the N, but seems to hold that mutilated conjunction with pincers. So of course you also understand how outrageous it is for wedding guests to expect to be able to bring casual dates to such a momentous occasion.

The offense to guests, as well as to hosts, is in that phrase "and guest," which may be translated as, "oh, just anyone." Spouses, fiancés, or whatever passes for such if one doesn't inquire too closely are different; those people are prospective friends. So you should ask those guests of whose personal lives you have lost track if they are attached, and if so, to whom, so that you can invite by name.

What do you say if a guest asks to bring a friend? Well, you have a choice:

1. "How delightful. We'd love to meet him," or
2. "I'm so sorry, we're only asking people we know to our wedding, but we'd be delighted to meet him on another occasion."

⌒ Making Exceptions ⌒

DEAR MISS MANNERS:

Initially we decided that invited guests at our daughter's destination wedding in Las Vegas could invite a guest if they were a spouse, engaged, significant other or living together. Should this change for her attendants if there is no significant other in their life? She was confronted by one bridesmaid who didn't want to be left out, even though the majority of other singles (and one other attendant) are coming alone. Since they are spending money to travel, a dress, etc., should they be allowed a guest?

GENTLE READER:

Under ordinary circumstances, Miss Manners has little patience with single people who claim they would not enjoy weddings without companionship of their own choosing. If they have no pleasure in seeing their friends married and meeting their families and other friends, why attend at all?

Destination weddings are another matter. If guests are to devote days instead of hours to the event, it is different. Even Miss Manners does not expect them to vacation alone.

~Refusing Exceptions~

DEAR MISS MANNERS:

I know columnists receive gag letters, but believe me, this is not one! The parents of one of our daughter's bridesmaids have a monkey which they are training to help care for a paraplegic. They take the animal with them when they go out. They have threatened not to attend the wedding because we did not include the monkey on their invitation.

I do not feel that a monkey belongs at as solemn an occasion as a wedding. It chatters continually and bangs around its cage. Also, there will be children in attendance, and I fear they will be bitten. I think what they are doing is admirable, but is it unreasonable to ask them to leave the monkey in the care of others on this special day? My daughter does not want it either, but is reluctant to press the point because she wants to continue to be friends with the daughter and will have to see the parents on occasion. How can we graciously let them know our concerns?

GENTLE READER:

Well, let's see. Miss Manners has been riffling through the files she keeps right behind her august forehead and has not succeeded in finding anything under Monkeys, Undesirable as Guests. But let's do a bit of cross-file checking here. How about the rule saying that wedding guests may not bring along their own, uninvited guests? That should take care of it.

No?

All right, here's one under Animals, Working. It says that trained assistance animals, such as Seeing Eye dogs, may go anywhere their owners do. But this monkey is not yet trained and, not being in attendance on one of the guests, would be there in a social and not a working capacity.

You are quite right to suspect that monkeys who are solely out for a good time do not make ideal guests, although Miss Manners wouldn't count on the children's not having a better time than they suspected possible. To inform the guests of your decision, you might adapt the general rule formed for excluding children—"We are so sorry that we can't have your darling monkey, who would undoubtedly behave beautifully, but we feel we just can't make an exception because other people might want to bring theirs, who might not behave as well."

⸺ A Sensible Request ⸺

DEAR MISS MANNERS:

Unfortunately I am currently unattached and would not want to attend a wedding with a lady I was not serious with. It's just too romantic an occasion. Is it okay to attend a wedding without a date?

GENTLE READER:

Are you suggesting enjoying the wedding for its own sake and then mixing with the other guests?

Radical as that may seem, it is the correct attitude to take—and one, Miss Manners notes, which was often its own reward. Before everyone complained that they could never meet anyone eligible, weddings were considered a major venue for doing so. And being free to become acquainted with a bridesmaid or the bridegroom's cousin has more romantic potential than sitting next to a casual date who is bound to be thinking whether or not she would like to be standing at an altar with you.

⟿Children⟾

DEAR MISS MANNERS:

I've been told that children should not attend a formal wedding reception, but I've been to several where children were present. I have many young cousins and a niece and nephew and am unsure how to handle this situation when I get married.

GENTLE READER:

There are two schools of thought about children attending weddings—one that holds that they are adorable and add to the spirit of the occasion, and the other that they are unruly and bound to be a nuisance.

Miss Manners belongs to the former. It seems to her that weddings being the joining of two families, as well as of two individuals who happen to have a yen for each other, children are an appropriate part. Of course, she is assuming reasonably polite children, which may be rather a leap these days.

She does not therefore condemn those who take the other view. But children must then be excluded as a category, the good with the bad. Pointing out who behaves like a piggy is just not good for family relations.

⟿Expecting Children⟾

DEAR MISS MANNERS:

Two friends of ours are expecting a baby about a month before the date of our marriage. I want to make it clear that their child is welcome at our wedding, if they want to bring him/her.

I know the correct way to do this is to address the envelope to both parents and child, but since we don't know the gender or (obviously) the name of the expected baby, I ended up just writing "Mr. and Mrs. X and family," which seemed wrong. They did RSVP for all three of them, so obviously understood what I was trying to express; but is there a less impersonal way I could have addressed the envelope?

GENTLE READER:

It is difficult to get personal with someone who has not yet made an appearance in this world. Miss Manners is glad you did not succeed too well in your effort at being inclusive, and lead your friends to believe that the entire extended family was encouraged to show up. However, you might have waited until the baby showed up, and then added to your congratulatory letter "and we do hope you will bring little Zoe to the wedding."

⟿ Reversing Attitudes ⟿

DEAR MISS MANNERS:

When my daughter got married eight years ago, my brother, his wife, and five children came cross-country to be at the wedding. My daughter had wanted an evening, formal reception with no children invited. I thought it rude, however, that after the sacrifice of time and much money to be at her wedding, she would not consider having my nieces and nephews there. So my daughter conceded to my wishes and allowed the five children to attend the reception.

This May, one of those children is getting married. My daughter, her husband, and three children were planning to attend the wedding. Then we found out that no children are invited to the reception—because if all the children of the guests were invited, it would be chaos and expensive.

These are the same reasons my daughter didn't want children at her wedding. She had to explain to wedding guests why there were five children at the reception when all other children were not allowed to attend.

My daughter feels that her three children should be allowed to attend the reception simply to reciprocate the goodwill my daughter showed her family. After all, how many other guests will be traveling 3,000 miles and purchasing five airline tickets and a week's hotel stay to attend the wedding? Babysitting will also be a problem since my daughter's policy is not to leave her children with people they don't know. AND, my son-in-law is not happy about spending this kind of money to sit in a hotel room with his children during the reception!

GENTLE READER:

As Miss Manners understands this, your daughter had specific reasons for not wanting children at her wedding reception, and was embarrassed afterward because some were allowed and others not. So she discounts her cousin's having the same reasons and feels that she should risk the same embarrassment. (Miss Manners, in turn, discounts your argument that no other children would be eligible, unless you heard this from the hosts.)

There are arguments to be made both for and against the presence of children at weddings. However, Miss Manners does not care for the argument that the bride's childhood appearance created a debt that must now be paid. If your daughter is going to plead for an exception, she would be better advised to gush to the bride about how delightful it was to have children at her wedding and reminisce about how beautiful and well-mannered her little cousin was.

⁓An Obligation⁓

DEAR MISS MANNERS:

Do the bride and groom have any obligation to provide or help find babysitters for out-of-town guests?

My family (including my three-year-old son) is traveling to participate in a wedding where I am the best man, however, the wedding does not allow children. I am really distressed over what I will do with my son during the wedding and reception. I called the bride and asked her about possible babysitters, and she just said that she didn't know any.

This situation has really dampened my enthusiasm for this wedding—am I just being petty?

GENTLE READER:

The bride and the bridegroom do not have an obligation to provide or help find babysitters. It is thoughtful if they try to anticipate what would make their guests' stay easy and pleasant, and some go to the trouble of hiring a babysitter to look after all their guests' children, but Miss Manners is afraid that concierge service is not on the required list.

However, your best friend has an obligation to help you out, most especially when you run into difficulty in the course of performing honorable service for him. His fiancée ought to be willing to share responsibility for someone with whom she can expect to become close. Oh, whoops—those are the bride and bridegroom, aren't they?

⁓A Gracious Alternative⁓

DEAR MISS MANNERS:

I want my wedding to be for adults, but I have guests coming in from out of town with children. I have arranged for a child-care room at my site, complete with children's food, games, toys, movies, and paid child care. I feel that by providing this, it will help those who cannot get child care, cannot afford it, or simply live out of town. By providing this, free of charge of course, I feel it would not be rude to let the guests know it's an adults-only party and that if they bring their children the child-care room would be *mandatory* for them.

How do I word this clearly enough so they know children are not allowed in the event, but cordially enough so they feel the provided care is a generous alternative gesture?

GENTLE READER:

Mandatory is not an enticing word to put on an invitation. Nor is it a good spirit in which to issue an invitation. Hospitality requires that you tell people what you are offering them to enjoy, not what you are ordering them to obey.

Miss Manners hastens to add that she does not mean that you must have children attend the wedding, charming as she happens to think that is. Technically, all you need do is to issue your invitations in the names of the parents only; that should be enough for them to understand that their children are not included.

Ha. You know those people, and they will bring them anyway. Or they will wheedle to do so.

So here is what you do: You send separate formal invitations in the names of the children only, inviting them to a children's wedding party that takes place at the same time as the wedding itself.

Note that Miss Manners specified that the invitations were to be formal. No balloons or circus animals, for once. They should be somewhat in the style of the wedding invitations and should ask for the favor of a response. On the families' arrivals, the person in charge of the children should stand at the door to greet the children and bear them off, saying, "I believe you are one of my special guests."

⁓A Warning⁓

DEAR MISS MANNERS:

My husband and I have been invited to the wedding of a childhood friend. We have a young child and inquired of the mother of the groom months ago if children would be welcome at the festivities. She told us that the bride did not want children and child care would be provided.

I thought this was a perfectly acceptable compromise. However, we just received the invitation and the reception card says "Adult Reception."

We were planning on going to great lengths to attend, but now we are so offended by the wording on the card that we no longer want to go. Is this acceptable? Was word of mouth not enough?

GENTLE READER:

Not if they want to warn you that the content of their reception is—well, whatever the content is in adult videos. Miss Manners wouldn't know.

⌁ Parental Discretion ⌁

DEAR MISS MANNERS:

My cousin's wedding invitation is addressed to my husband, myself, and our four children, ages nine to one-and-a-half. My aunt, the mother of the bride, told my father that she was upset when she heard I was thinking of hiring a babysitter, at least for the two youngest, because she desired all my children to attend. She loves children, especially tots, no matter how rambunctious they are. I know she wouldn't bat an eye if a youngster ran up the aisle or cried through the service.

On the whole, my children are sweet and well behaved, and many enjoy their company. However, most times they are typical children and behave as such. I'm afraid the scene might be this:

The four-year-old will talk loudly through the whole service, the two-year-old will flirt with the people behind him, and the one-year-old will want to get down and go off to observe on his own. My husband will not be able to attend and help me. Although my dad would lean over backward to assist me, I don't want to put him in the position of parenting my children at an affair at which he should be enjoying himself. And, quite frankly, if I had to spend time in the back of the church, outside, or running after them during the reception, I'd just as soon stay home.

Miss Manners, I want to honor my aunt's wishes. I know she will be disappointed if I only bring part of my brood, but the thought exhausts me.

GENTLE READER:

You have no idea how refreshing Miss Manners found your letter. To understand that, you would have to see the piles of correspondence she has from people who are vehemently opposed to having any children at family occasions, and from their relatives who are equally vehement about bringing theirs, whether it is appropriate or not.

How nice of your aunt to take such a warm interest in your children, above the technical perfection of the occasion. And how nice of you to take such a warm interest in the occasion, above the natural limitations of your children. While hosts are within the bounds of politeness to invite adults-only to a wedding, the parent of invited children is the one to make the decision. (Miss Manners' awkward wording is to head off any misinterpretation that a parent can make the decision about the attendance of children who were not invited.)

You make a strong case for not bringing yours. The polite way to say so, given the hospitality of your aunt, is "You are so sweet to include them, but, really, they're not old enough to appreciate and enjoy it. They'll be happier hearing about it and meeting the couple on an occasion when they can really enjoy their attention."

Colleagues

DEAR MISS MANNERS:

How can I explain to co-workers I do not socialize with that they are not invited to my wedding? Several people have mistakenly assumed they are invited, although I have never given them any indication that they would be, and my guest list is above and beyond what I had hoped for. I really do not want to hurt their feelings, but I am put on the spot when they make these comments.

GENTLE READER:

Rude as it is for people to let on that they expect to be invited to a wedding—especially people who are not in your social circle— you are right to handle them delicately. It is a rough desire to wish you well that leads them into this awkward error.

Your reply must be that you are having a very small wedding, only for your family and immediate circle of close friends. Never mind that other co-workers will be invited—you are quite right to count people only by whether you see them socially and not by what jobs they hold.

A wedding is not a professional occasion. And a small wedding is not necessarily one to which very few people are invited. It is one to which the person you are addressing is not invited.

⌐The Unprofessional Invitation⌐

DEAR MISS MANNERS:

A colleague of my husband's handed him an unaddressed wedding invitation and said something unclear about inviting him "for professional reasons." He told her he would like to attend the wedding, at which point she made it clear that the invitation did not extend to his wife. My husband plans to attend the wedding, because he genuinely wishes her well. It is of no emotional consequence to me whether I attend, and of course I won't, as per the bride's wishes.

But has the bride been rude by inviting one member of a couple but not the other? If it is a rudeness, against whom has it been committed—my husband, who was discomfited to explain the situation to me, or me, who was excluded but feel no pain thereby?

GENTLE READER:

Against Miss Manners, who was neither discomfited by nor interested in the wedding, but who must guard the world against crimes of etiquette.

To invite someone to one's wedding "for professional reasons" is an unspeakable idea, which was only emphasized by not inviting you both as a couple, which is the way married people are treated in social life. Whatever career advantage the bride hopes to gain by treating your husband in this insulting fashion, Miss Manners cannot imagine what advantage he hopes to obtain by accepting. Probably none—probably he was just naïve enough not to be outraged.

If you don't have the heart to explain to him that the bride obviously did not want him to accept, Miss Manners doesn't either.

A Reply

DEAR MISS MANNERS:

Surely you do not cling to the quaint notion that all wedding guests are intimates of the bride or groom. That may have been true once, but today many invited guests have never met either of them.

Consider the situation my husband and I have encountered, not once but twice. The president of a small company has a son or daughter who is getting married, and he thinks it would be jolly if he invited the whole management team. We could hardly not accept, although I resented being forced to buy a gift for someone I did not know. We attended the weddings, even though one was a hundred miles away.

Like you, I do not condone rudeness. If I accept an invitation, I do my utmost to fulfill the obligation. However, I can understand someone in the situations I described who finds something more enjoyable to do than get dressed up to watch two strangers get married, and then stand in line with a couple hundred others for the standard hotel fare of fried chicken, ham, and overcooked vegetables. So they figure if they are on record as having accepted and sent the required gift, they can safely spend the day as they wish.

GENTLE READER:

Miss Manners assures you that the hosts would rather have their guests safely on record as having declined the invitation than prepare for the comfort of those who do not show up. Not that she is in great sympathy with people who invite their business associates to a private occasion in which these people can have no genuine interest. It is almost asking them to treat it as a business meeting—one attends if one can, but not if something more important comes up.

Nevertheless, a civilized person should resist that temptation. Spoiling someone's wedding reception—as would happen if the entire management team failed to arrive to take their designated places—is not the way to teach one's boss a lesson.

TROUBLESHOOTING

⁓Dis-inviting the Uninvited⁓

DEAR MISS MANNERS:

I find myself in the awkward position of receiving insistent correspondence from someone who has determined, despite the lack of an invitation, that he is invited to my very-soon-to-occur wedding. I made the apparent mistake, in responding to a great deal of kind affection from the person over the years, of mentioning quite vaguely but happily that I'm getting married (some time ago), and since then this person has asked over and over again for the specific details so that he can arrange for travel to come.

I'm convinced that this insistence comes not from malicious or otherwise unpleasant intentions but purely from social incompetence and excess of enthusiasm. But I confess, I had never the intention myself of inviting this person to my wedding, and indeed there are several reasons why his presence would cause discomfort, and probably acute discomfort, to my fiancé. (This is not an ex of mine, but a cleric with certain opinions and evangelizing tendencies.)

Without desiring to injure this person, I tried as politely as possible to explain that it will be a very small party, and though under other circumstances it would have been lovely to have him, in this case it isn't to be. This was mysteriously misunderstood to be a confirmation of the invitation never sent.

Is there any way without causing pain that I can dis-invite him?

Even the Almighty has been invoked as clearly blessing his presence! How can I argue against that? What do I do now? (Besides sever the friendship forever . . .)

GENTLE READER:

This letter begs more questions than answers. Indeed, how do you dis-invite someone you never invited? Why exactly is this person a friend of yours whose friendship you fear severing?

And why is the Almighty encouraging his followers to crash weddings? It seems, perhaps, that it is this fear of the Almighty that is clouding your fortitude. One more firm, but polite, attempt to explain that it was not, in fact meant to be, and then we're afraid, the rest is up to him. Or Him, as the case may be.

⁓Tolerating the Uninvited⁓

DEAR MISS MANNERS:

The damage is already done for me, but I'm hoping you will still reply to afford me some peace of mind. When I was addressing invitations, I was careful to put exact names on the envelopes, such as John and Jane Smith. My fiancé and I were eager for a smallish, intimate wedding.

What happened in several instances (grr!) was that invitees sent back the reply cards with additional names listed (in two cases, four additional people). Granted, these were relatives in most cases, but I had been specific in inviting those persons with whom I have a relationship (or at least could not avoid inviting), *not* all of their evil adult children!

Was there something I could have done other than grin and bear it (and strategically seat these offenders in punishing ways)? May I also mention that these adult uninvited guests also had the gall to bring unannounced guests of their own (disaster with place cards) and never once came to congratulate my new husband and me during the reception. Still steaming, but happily married.

GENTLE READER:

Glad to hear that you did not let your anger and evil relatives (grr!) get the better of your marriage—and that your revenge was within the legitimate bounds of etiquette. (Although what constitutes seating punishment? At the children's table? Among the centerpieces?). Clearly, your guests behaved badly. A phone call politely reiterating your specific invitation upon receiving the offending replies would have been well within your rights.

⌒Substitutes⌒

DEAR MISS MANNERS:

My fiancé and I have planned a lavish wedding, owing much to the generosity of our parents. All married couples and those in serious relationships were invited as a couple. We have, however, received a handful of responses where one person in the couple cannot attend and the other person has approached us to ask if they can "substitute" another guest.

We were baffled by the behavior and caught totally off guard. When the first person asked I explained that we weren't planning on inviting the newly suggested guest, and we do have other people we would like to invite if/when there are more spots available. I assumed the matter would be settled right then and there! The guest actually had the nerve to argue that it's still the original number invited (missing our point entirely) so we backed down rather than making a big fuss about it. We have since had several other "place takers" come forward. Our wedding dinner is expensive, so we resent asking our parents to pay for guests we never invited in the first place. What is the best way to decline this request?

GENTLE READER:

That this happened once is odd. Several times and we begin to think you are either a celebrity or a heck of a party thrower. It is not often that people are clamoring to get into a stranger's wedding. That said, if both you and your guests could manage to refrain from thinking of your guests as "spots" filled, this whole conflict would garner a lot more sympathy and a lot less confusion. A firm "We would just like to have people we know and love with us on this important occasion, but we would love to meet your friends another time" with no further explanation or backing down, should suffice. And if you must have a B-list to replace missing guests, at least have the decency to keep quiet about it.

CHAPTER SIX

The Paper (and Electronic) Work

SHOUTING FROM THE HOUSETOPS now strikes Miss Manners as an admirably restrained way of reminding the world that you are getting married. Couples have taken to firing off barrages of personal revelations, photographs, videos, computer icons and animations, novelty items, instructions and requests into the inboxes and mailboxes of everyone they know and many they do not.

First come the mass e-mails, which are linked to the Web site. That contains the announcement of the engagement, biographies of the couple, and the story of their courtship, all accompanied by pictures that go from their own baby pictures to romantic pictures to, in some cases, pictures of their babies. Wedding plans are gradually added, with commentary about their choices and decisions. Then comes the all-important gift registry.

Meanwhile, paper is also being distributed. There may be a so-called formal engagement announcement (etiquette recognizes no such thing). There is almost certainly a save-the-date card or gimmick followed by numerous invitations to showers, each with its own gift registry.

The actual wedding invitation therefore surprises only those who didn't get one. But its envelope is jammed with cards containing information that appears on the Web site (in case Grandmamma has managed to crash her hard drive yet again): flight schedules, group rates at hotels, babysitting services, valet parking validation; admonitions about not smoking, not arriving late, and not wearing colors that conflict with the wedding theme color; directions on how to get there; weather predictions; a fill-in-the-blanks response card with a mysterious M——— and a line on which apparently to indicate one's entourage; a deadline for answering the invitation, possibly with a threat for failure to comply; a menu from which to select dinner, or an order to bring a dish for everyone to eat, or a warning that there will be a charge for drinks; and the cards of stores where the couple wants you to shop for them.

Nevertheless, the Web site continues to be updated, enabling everyone to see who has responded and what has been purchased. Even after the wedding, it continues. Wedding pictures are posted, comments are solicited from guests, honeymoon pictures are posted, and the gift registry lives on. So does the saga, as it is likely to be followed by the first home, the baby, and the baby's entire life. Each with its own gift registry.

Miss Manners does not mean to suggest that none of the wedding material is useful or endearing. Guests do need to know where to go when, and might find it convenient to get the answers to nosy questions without the embarrassment of asking.

But they soon come down with wedding fatigue. People who are deluged with information on a subject in which they have limited interest (apologies to the couple, but such is life) do not become increasingly informed. Quite the opposite. They tune out. This may explain why guests who claim to have read everything keep asking the bridegroom where he is from and the bride whether she is changing her name and both of them where they are going on their wedding trip.

All that was covered at length on the Web site. Weren't they paying attention?

No, not really. So couples could save themselves the trouble of putting out all that background material. But at least they can know that it will be there some day for their children. That is, if the technology hasn't changed ten times over and it can no longer be read.

DEAR MISS MANNERS:

I work in a medical office with a woman whose son is to be married this summer, and everyone who comes to the desk is told about the wedding and shower. I hear about them numerous times a day. When I'm asked if I heard the "story of the day" I am told it again, no matter what my answer is. I don't care about this wedding and shower, but I am polite and listen.

Am I obligated to go to the wedding or send a shower gift since I have been invited to both? Everyone at work is going, but I don't feel I have to since I don't know the couple personally, only the mother (who has filled me in on every intimate detail of the couple).

GENTLE READER:

No, you don't have to go as long as you decline politely. But Miss Manners suspects that the problem is rather that you feel as if you know them only too well.

DEAR MISS MANNERS:

Further evidence of the degeneration of the wedding invitation: a small, very fat envelope arrived by mail; the invitation inside (a piece of paper folded like a wallet) was so bulging that the senders had jury-rigged a closure by gluing a ribbon tie to hold it closed; when the tie was released, the invitation literally exploded, showering little cards all over the room—not just Rsvp cards, but many business cards from (I assume) the establishments where I was expected to purchase the gift. Is this a new ploy on the part of business establishments?

GENTLE READER:

And a new ploy on the part of the couple to capture your wandering attention?

THE WEB SITE

Dear Miss Manners:

A friend recently sent me a link to a Web site with information about her niece's wedding six months from now. The backfield was crimson. The print and wedding-theme logos were white. There was a grid of nine boxes to click, pulling up different windows listing dates, events, accommodations, attendants, guest book, and bridal registries.

There was a box marked PHOTO ALBUM, which pulled up a slide show of family photos. There was a box ABOUT US, which pulled up a photo of the couple and prose about who they are and how they met.

I thought it vulgar—so high tech as to seem like a promo for an upcoming theatrical release, perhaps a bad joke. Is the romance gone from weddings in the name of slick merchandizing of the couple hoping to take in a truckload of gifts? It is all so show-biz.

Gentle Reader:

Of course the couple is influenced by show business. Do you think they are spending their engagement gazing at each other? They are working on the set, the costumes, the makeup, the props, and the extras (that's you, the wedding guests). So they not only created the promo, but included an illustrated fan magazine story about themselves.

Yet the wedding Web site, which has been commonplace for a long time now, does serve a purpose in conveying logistical information to the guests. Too bad that unlimited space on the Internet seems to have turned everyone into the person no one wants to sit next to on the airplane. Beyond the widespread general desire to pour out their lives and thoughts to all and sundry, lovers are notoriously susceptible to believing that they are the center of the universe and the envy of all.

True, this is not in the best of taste. But kindhearted people are inclined to indulge them in this on the grounds that they are not, at this moment of their lives, in their right minds.

DEAR MISS MANNERS:

My fiancé and I are spending a considerable amount of money to have a nice day for our guests. Would it be inappropriate for the invitation to ask guests to RSVP on our Web site? This would save us significantly on invitations and postage.

GENTLE READER:

If you mean that you would use an e-vite for your wedding, yes, it would save money, but if you mean to mail paper invitations asking for a Web site response, there would be no saving to you. Responding is your guests' responsibility, paper, postage, and all.

You should be aware, however, that the Internet is not a medium that inspires a firm sense of commitment. Granted that guest commitment is a scarce commodity these days and even the most formal invitations do not always have the invited rushing to take up pen and paper. The difference here would be that if you require only a casual response, your guests will feel justified in treating all their responsibilities casually.

THE SAVE-THE-DATE CARD

DEAR MISS MANNERS:

I am feeling both incorrect and unhappy about save-the-date cards. It would seem to me that friends and family of the bridal pair are generally well aware of the date, which is usually several months hence. With such cards, the guests are, essentially, being denied the opportunity to decline graciously when the actual invitation arrives; the save-the-date card somehow demands attendance and precludes the possibility of other plans or, heaven forbid, a desire to skip the event.

Is it possible these cards have become another of the bizarre "traditions" that threaten to overwhelm the modern wedding (programs! matching manicures! goodie bags! choreographed first dances! favors! extreme costumes!)? Are they another piece of expensive, unnecessary clutter that timid brides and their mothers now feel bullied into producing? Or am I a grumpy old sourpuss, refusing to acknowledge that these cards serve a useful and appreciated purpose?

GENTLE READER:

Whether you are a grumpy old sourpuss, Miss Manners cannot say. But save-the-date cards are indeed useful to those who want to attend the wedding, and appreciated by those watching the fluctuation of airline prices.

It is those who do not want to attend who feel resentment. But they should know that such notices are merely an advance warning and carry none of the obligations of an actual invitation. When that is received, at the proper time, it may be declined with regret without offering an excuse or, if one is cornered in person, with apologetic mumblings about calendar mix-ups.

THE INVITATION (AND NON-INVITATION)

What do you want your wedding guests to do with your invitations after they receive them?

Well, yes, it might be a nice idea if they answered them. Perhaps they might also want to carry them around, in order to have the address handy when they spot a jumbo entertainment center that would look darling in your new studio apartment. They could then file the invitation in the household calendar, so that they showed up at the right time and place. After that—okay, they're probably not going to have them bronzed.

What you don't want them to do is to forward them to Miss Manners with the indignant notation "Will you look at THAT!?!" written across your lovingly joined names. Yet people do. And these are not finicky cranks like Miss Manners. By far the largest category of invitations submitted for her disapproval are actually attempts to shake down the wedding guests, either by charging them or suggesting donations, or to make them feel like guests while not actually inviting them. So much for the idea that rudeness is just an unfortunate symptom of unhappiness, while bliss inspires courtesy.

The most original example sent Miss Manners (and "original," in the etiquette trade, is seldom a compliment) was a formally worded one from a couple who gave themselves "the distinct pleasure of announcing our marriage. Our life together began in a private church ceremony consisting of just the two of us. Although your presence would have been a blessing and an honour, we ask for your continued thoughts and prayers."

Now, a wedding announcement is a perfectly respectable item of social correspondence. No apologies are made for not including the person at the wedding; the fact of the marriage is simply conveyed, after it has happened, and it calls for nothing more in response than a note of congratulation. This, with its unconvincing insinuation that the couple was somehow forcibly prevented from inviting guests, is a non-invitation rather than an announcement. The person who received it reported "a distinct lack of pleasure" in reading it.

Then there was the lady who wanted wedding guests, only providing she didn't have to get married:

> My granddaughter, a twenty-five-year-old schoolteacher, has been living with a man sixteen years her senior, who has a son twelve years old. He has just closed a bar he operated and is apparently heavily in debt. They are planning a large fake wedding— nothing legal, everything as if it were the real thing—because she wants to have a baby, but thinks if she is legally married to him, she will become responsible for his debts. Maybe I am too old-fashioned, but my husband and I refuse to go.

Yes, you two and Miss Manners are hopelessly old-fashioned in believing that wedding guests ought to be genuine guests invited to a genuine wedding. She suspects that the rest of the world has not progressed either to the point of enjoying being socially duped.

⁓ A "Will You Look at THAT!?!" ⁓

DEAR MISS MANNERS:

I received the following in the mail last week and I'm not sure what I'm to do. (The names are changed for privacy, the rest is word for word.)

> *Lisa Ann along with the memory of*
> *the late Christopher Luke Castle*
> *and Cathy R. and Hamilton Fenton*
> *are proud to finally announce*
> *the marriage of*
> *Louisa Anne Castle*
> *To*
> *Stanley Sean Fenton*
>
> *
>
> *Luanne and Stan will unite*
> *their devoted love and affection*
> *which began twenty years ago*
> *in a private ceremony*
> *on June 21*
>
> *
>
> *Because you are so far away*
> *and can not be with us to celebrate our union,*
> *we wanted you to know of our marriage and*
> *hope you will wish us well and think of us*
> *on our happy day!*

It arrived in a single envelope about five weeks before the event. Don't you usually send out announcements after the event? I'm so confused. Is this just a request for a gift?

GENTLE READER:

It is hard to say just what this is. A sigh of relief, from beyond the grave, from a father who can now stop spinning because his daughter's twenty-year courtship has progressed to marriage? A presumptuous refusal, by the hosts on behalf of the recipients, in response to an invitation that has not been issued?

And what went on in that private ceremony twenty years ago?

Miss Manners is at least sure that this is not either a proper formal communication or a proper informal one, since it uses the formal third-person style without honorifics and with informal nicknames. But that revealing, if split, infinitive, "to finally announce," certainly provides more emotional information than can be found in the usual bland forms.

She would not, however, assume that it is a request for a present, even though many people assume that to be the prime motivation for marriage. Nowadays, the greedy express themselves explicitly, enclosing written demands for cash or specific dry goods. Let us assume, instead, that the timing was simply as misguided as the wording. You need send the couple only your good wishes.

⟶ A Host-Yourself Invitation ⟵

DEAR MISS MANNERS:

We are having a wedding for my daughter and her fiancé at 3:30, with a reception afterward at the church with finger food, cake, and punch. That night, we plan to go to a restaurant where a band plays and the bride and groom can dance.

How can we correctly invite guests to come join us there for eating or dancing, to watch the bride and groom dancing, and let them know that any expenses will be theirs? We would like many of them to come join in the celebration, but cannot afford to pay the bill for everyone to eat or drink.

GENTLE READER:

There is no correct way to issue an invitation for people to take themselves out to dinner. Miss Manners is afraid that providing entertainment in the form of allowing them to watch a newly married couple dancing doesn't change that.

You can try to instill in them a desire to keep partying after the reception is over by running around the reception telling them, breathlessly, where you are all going later, and adding, as if spontaneously, "It would be fun if you went, too." Just don't blame Miss Manners if they have so much fun that they all decide to go along for the next stop, as well.

⌒A Handwritten Invitation⌒

DEAR MISS MANNERS:

I am planning a wedding for this spring and since my budget is not unlimited, I would like to know if hand-printed invitations (calligraphy) would be acceptable. I would still use formal style— the cards just wouldn't be professionally engraved. Would this upset people who received them?

GENTLE READER:

Miss Manners hesitates to say what would upset some people nowadays, but anyone who took your plan amiss would have an upside-down sense of propriety. Engraving is the proper way of imitating handwriting for the convenience of large mailings of formal invitations. A bride who did have an unlimited budget might well consider having her invitations done by hand instead.

⌒A Criticized Invitation⌒

DEAR MISS MANNERS:

I appear to have committed a *faux pas*. My fiancé and I are getting married in a concert hall at six o'clock in the evening. He's excited to don a tux, and the bridesmaids are wearing dresses of their choice (so some of them are floor length and some are shorter).

I guess this means we're having a formal wedding, but we picked out colorful, modern-looking invitations. Now people are admonishing us for choosing informal invitations for a formal event. Is there any way to respond to their criticism? Is there any way to redress our error?

GENTLE READER:

Since the invitations have already gone out, it is unfortunately too late for you to re-do the chief part you did wrong—the guest list.

⌒Naming the Hosts⌒

DEAR MISS MANNERS:

My parents have generously offered to pay for our wedding. My mother, who selected wonderful, tasteful invitations, also offered to take on the job of preparing them, about 200, for which I am very grateful.

However, my mother-in-law saw the invitations and erupted in tears. The invitations stated: Mr. and Mrs. Bride's Parents invite you to attend the wedding of daughter and fiancé.

My mother-in-law has been divorced twice, and she told my fiancé and his brother that she believed that my parents did not list her name because of her divorced status.

I am furious. My parents would never do such a thing.

I am certain that my mother consulted etiquette guidelines when she selected the language and form for the invitations. Were the invitations properly drafted, given that my parents are paying for the wedding? How shall I handle this personally with my future mother-in-law? Right now, I feel angry and insulted that she would accuse my parents of such an action.

GENTLE READER:

Your prospective mother-in-law's notion that her name was omitted because of her divorces is only pathetic. What is insulting to your mother is your own notion that she might think she has bought exclusive rights to be on the invitation by paying for the wedding.

The fact is that this is a simple misunderstanding about the traditional wording of a bridal invitation and a common, practical variation of it. The form dates from when a young lady was married from her parents' roof and protection, so they—not the couple, and not both sets of parents—did the inviting as the hosts of the wedding. The bridegroom did not need family identification, because he had conducted the courtship under the eyes of all who were likely to be wedding guests. All of them had long since inquired, "Who are his people?"

Now that brides live and choose husbands where they please, the bridegroom's family's guests may be puzzled to receive an invitation from people they don't know. So his parents' names are sometimes included. Or they may include a personal card with the invitations.

Miss Manners recommends that you and your mother gently explain the misunderstanding to your prospective mother-in-law and suggest that she include her card. Or you could turn this into a full-fledged family feud that poisons your wedding, not to mention your married life.

⌒Multiple Parents⌒

DEAR MISS MANNERS:

When the parents of a child are divorced and one or both has remarried, does the child now have three or four parents, or does he continue to have only the original two? I have read many announcements where the parents are listed as: "Mr. and Mrs. John Jones and Mrs. Mary Jones" (where mother has not remarried); "Mr. and Mrs. John Jones and Mr. and Mrs. James Smith"; or "Mr. John Jones and Mrs. Mary Smith."

With all the remarrying of today, doesn't the child still have only two parents? (Deceased parents are a totally different issue.)

GENTLE READER:

When it comes to distributing parents among children, Miss Manners is inclined to be generous. Her own dear mother—she only had one—was a teacher, and she used to be pleased when all sorts of adults, including former stepparents no longer married to a parent of origin, continued to take an interest in a child. So while the announcements you mention are socially cumbersome, Miss Manners is not going to condemn them.

⌒ The Invitation from Beyond ⌒

DEAR MISS MANNERS:

I received an invitation that read: "Janet Smith and Dr. John Jones, deceased, request the honor of your presence at the wedding of their daughter . . ." (Incidentally, the mother has remarried since the death of Dr. Jones.)

GENTLE READER:

It is not an uncommon impulse to want to treat the dead as if they were alive, and this particular kind of attempt to resurrect a parent for a wedding always breaks Miss Manners' heart.

However, less tenderhearted people only break up with laughter. "He's dead!" they exclaim; "so just exactly where does he want our presence?" It is no honor to subject one's parent's name to such creepy usage. Only the living can issue invitations. This one should have been from "Ms. Janet Smith" or "Mr. and Mrs. Jeremiah Newhusband" requesting "the honor of your presence at the marriage of her daughter, Petunia Smith . . ." and left memorializing the father to the service or the toasts.

⌒ Honorifics ⌒

DEAR MISS MANNERS:

I want to word my wedding invitations so as to include the women's names in an acceptable way without bowing down too much to tradition. It is important to me that women are not referred to as "Mrs. His Name" (first and last) because I believe that such wording, no matter how formal, implies not only that married women are unequal to their husbands, but also that married women are not important in their own right—that their identities are subsumed by the identity of the husband.

I have in mind having the names of both my parents and my stepparents at the top as "Adam Ray and Sharon Magnum with John Wesley and Susan Hearn Doe." I would prefer not to use the phrase "the parents of" as a way of avoiding the issue, because all of the people to be mentioned on the invitation are important to me, will be paying substantially for the wedding, and deserve to have their full names acknowledged.

GENTLE READER:

Please allow Miss Manners gently to suggest that before one attempts to improve upon tradition, perhaps one should find out what that tradition is. Two points that you seem to have missed are that honorifics are used on formal invitations (but not "parents of") and that people should be consulted about how they wish to style themselves.

Never mind your arguments about how you think other people should be addressed, unless the ladies in question share them. If they do, the correct formal honorific before their full names is "Ms." If they do not, they should be styled "Mr. and Mrs." In so personal a matter as a name, your convictions do not properly apply to people who do not share them.

Genders

DEAR MISS MANNERS:

I know we will have a dilemma with both invitations and etiquette for my daughter's wedding. Her father had a sex change and is now a woman.

My daughter has had some difficulty figuring out what to call her former father and dealing with his newly acquired expertise in being a woman. He/she has a new female first name and new surname (so our daughter's name matches none of ours) but has not come up with a new familial name for herself. Our daughter was adamant that he/she not call herself "mother" when he/she used that once. (Please forgive me, Miss Manners, but using proper grammar here gets really difficult in this uncharted territory!)

My husband, the stepfather, has been much more distressed with this sex change than I. Though it's been almost five years and our paths with the former father occasionally overlap socially, out of respect for my husband's feelings, not all of our friends know what has happened. We have still referred to the former father as a male.

Can you please give me any advice on how to handle the wordings, both for a formal invitation and, if there is a correct etiquette, for a less formal wedding invitation? Also, advice on pre-parties as well as the wedding ceremonies and reception.

We really hope that the former father can participate in this joyous event, but there is a real concern about the shock factor for people who don't know, and that her/his loving to be the center of attention will overshadow what this celebration should really be about.

GENTLE READER:

Uh, people are going to notice anyway. You might consider taking your former husband around the pre-parties and reintroducing her to your circle, so that the guests can get over the surprise before the ceremony and focus on that event, rather than its provenance.

The rest of it is not difficult, Miss Manners promises. You should treat your daughter's father—and that this person did father her does not change retroactively—with dignity, but you needn't offer explanations. Any invitation should come from "Mr. and Mrs. Clive Carvington and Ms. Catherine Tyson."

ANNOYING FLOTSAM

⌒ The Response Card ⌒

Guests ought to be insulted by response cards. Decent people already know (yes? yes?) that they must always reply to all invitations, even the most casual ones. Does anyone think it all right to stand there speechless in response to "Do you want to take in a movie tonight?" unable to realize that a decision, one way or the other, must be made and conveyed immediately?

For formal invitations, a quick and clear response is even more important, and not only because the caterer needs to know how much food to prepare. That is reasonable enough, but it skips the fact that ignoring an invitation is a major insult to the hosts.

There seem to be a great many indecent people who don't mind issuing such insults, and the notion has taken hold that it is at least partially the host's responsibility to ensure that the invitation is answered.

First it was the addition of "R.s.v.p." or "The favor of a reply is requested" to invitations that traditionally assumed the guests would not need to be prompted to do the obvious. Even that didn't help. Then closing dates were added, with an increasing lack of success. Desperate hosts started supplying paper and envelopes, and even tried to guide their guests' hands by the peculiar method of providing an M to start them off writing "Mr. and Mrs. Dominick Applewaithe . . ."

No go. It only led cheeky people to claim that the absence of such help indicated that no response was wanted. One lady wrote plaintively to Miss Manners that she did receive a response card and envelope, but that since the envelope was not stamped, she was at a loss to know what she was expected to do.

The sad fact is that for indecent people, response cards are not going to help. Just as many cases of unmailed response cards are reported as other unanswered invitations. You might as well save the expense and trouble of enclosing them.

⌒ Responses to the Response Card ⌒

DEAR MISS MANNERS:

In a wedding invitation from a very influential family I looked for a response card, but there was none. On the invitation itself, on the lower left-hand corner, were the initials "R.s.v.p." with no date to return a response by.

Since I thought this was odd, I asked my sister, who replied that this is now the proper way and that we were supposed to buy our own response cards to send back. I disagree and think the party involved should send response cards. Who is right?

GENTLE READER:

Has it come to this? That people who refrain from doing something incorrect are now being thought rude by the very people who violate the rule themselves? Allow Miss Manners a minute to sit down and search for her vinaigrette.

Response cards were never correct. They are a desperate, and not particularly successful, way to make up for the extreme rudeness of people who think it too much trouble to inform their hosts whether or not they will attend an occasion to which they have been kindly bidden.

DEAR MISS MANNERS:

My husband and I received a formal invitation to a distant relation's black-tie evening wedding, but, unable to afford the attire for such an event, we chose not to attend. However, the invitation's response card had only selections for what we would like to eat at the reception, and no place where we could let the couple know that we would not be attending. We were under the impression that when there is no option on the invitation to decline the event, then not returning the card tells the couple that we will not be attending.

Later I received a frantic call from the bride's mother asking whether we would be attending and what we wanted to eat. My husband's family thought we were wrong not to respond immediately to say we wouldn't be attending.

Should I have written a note on the response card declining, but offering our best wishes? Or were my husband and I correct that in such a situation no response is a "No, thank you"? This type of invitation (without a means to decline) is common for this branch of the family, and it is not the first phone call to confirm events.

I know I am supposed to respond with the same method as the invitation, but since they generally do not provide a means to decline, and do not agree that no response means "No, thank you," should I telephone them instead? I do not wish to appear like I am snubbing them.

GENTLE READER:

May a despairing Miss Manners plead that you, and the many others who declare themselves baffled by formal invitations, apply a modicum of common sense to the situation?

If so, you would surely realize that silence is both uninformative and, as you have guessed, a snub.

Responding in kind means that a written invitation is answered in writing, a telephoned invitation by telephone, and so on. So unless you are unable to put your hands on a pen, a piece of paper, and a stamp, you do not lack the means of responding. Even then, some response, say by telephone, would be better than none at all.

DEAR MISS MANNERS:

How can one decline an invitation including an engraved response card that has a blank space indicating the number of guests attending? Placing a zero on the blank with no explanation seems ridiculous.

GENTLE READER:

Writing a zero on the card provided is, Miss Manners agrees, unspeakable. But you could put a dash there, and write a brief

statement of regret ("So sorry I can't be there—very best wishes")
after it.

DEAR MISS MANNERS:

What a bummer to see those silly reply cards, to wit: "M
_____ will ____ attend." What does this mean? What are
they thinking? My custom has been to write on the back of the
enclosed card, "Mr. and Mrs. Lovely Neighbor accept with pleasure your kind invitation for the 4th of September." But it occurs
to me that this may be the moral equivalent of writing, "You twit!
Please expect that I know how to respond to an invitation."

GENTLE READER:

So?

⌒ The Registry Card ⌒

DEAR MISS MANNERS:

The department store where my sister is registered gave her 600
registry cards to put in all 600 formal wedding invitations. When I
was married, it was my understanding that the proper etiquette was
to place bridal registry cards in bridal shower invitations only.

Has etiquette changed, as my sister states? She is having four
bridal showers and is inviting fifty women to each—200 people.
Should she include the cards both in their shower and wedding
invitations?

GENTLE READER:

Where is your family getting its information? Etiquette hadn't
even changed to what you thought it was when you got married,
let alone to what your sister claims. It has always been rude to
notify guests what you want to receive as a present or where you
want them to buy it, and it always will be. The only use of bridal
registry cards that Miss Manners authorizes is as scratch paper for
the bride.

⌒The Assignment Card⌒

DEAR MISS MANNERS:

This wedding invitation enclosure card [which reads, "Miss Manners says it's okay if you would like to help with donations of food for the reception"] left me and other recipients speechless. Since you never seem at a loss for words, would you please comment?

GENTLE READER:

Miss Manners is speechless, too, and you will have to excuse her, because when she recovers, the first person she wants to talk to will be her lawyer. Not only did Miss Manners never say any such thing, but she is on record as being violently opposed to the notion of issuing nonhospitable invitations.

Guests (as opposed to those who may volunteer to help, or who respond to a suggestion that everyone pitch in on a cooperative event with no particular host) are not expected to supply their own hospitality. "We're getting married and we expect you to cater the reception" is not an acceptable way to entertain.

⌒The Warning⌒

DEAR MISS MANNERS:

Living in Miami, we are surrounded by both Spanish and English. My husband and I attended a wedding where the entire hour-and-a-half ceremony was in Spanish. Unfortunately, I am not fluent in Spanish, and my attention span did not last ninety minutes. Should a couple inform the guests on the invitation if a wedding is to be in Spanish, so each can choose whether or not to attend?

GENTLE READER:

You certainly have a peculiar way of choosing whether to attend a wedding. It is Miss Manners' understanding that wedding guests are there out of affection for the bridal couple, not in the expectation of riveting entertainment adjusted to whatever their attention spans happen to be. Unfortunately, there is no way to indicate on a wedding invitation that unsuitable people should decline. If there were, it would read, "If you don't care about us, don't bother to attend."

ASSEMBLING THE INVITATION

~The Tissue Paper~

DEAR MISS MANNERS:

When sending wedding invitations, what is the explanation of the white silk paper inside the card? When we received the invitation cards that we ordered, there was no silk paper.

GENTLE READER:

Silk? Did the bride get her veil caught in the invitations?

Oh, you mean the tissue paper. That was there so that the engraving didn't get smudged when it was fresh. By the time you get all those addresses written, this will not be a problem. Nevertheless, some engraving companies send separate bundles of tissues to be inserted, just to prove that the invitations are really engraved. If it were true that no one can tell the difference between engraving and raised printing (Miss Manners can easily, but she is too overcome with pleasure at others' happiness to indulge in a sneer), they would be out of business.

~The Envelopes~

DEAR MISS MANNERS:

Why do wedding invitations come inside two envelopes? Wouldn't one be sufficient?

GENTLE READER:

Well, a postcard would be sufficient to convey the information, if it comes to that. The tradition of using two envelopes simulates the old hand-delivered message, combining it with the utilitarian necessity of its being sent by mail.

Miss Manners is making that up. Rational explanations of old customs are always supplied after the fact, not so much to explain what has been lost in time as to disguise the fact that customs are rarely logical. But arguments of paper waste have penetrated this custom before. During World War II, a small, unfolded wedding invitation was used in a single envelope, and you could take advantage of this less venerable tradition.

⌒ The Address ⌒

DEAR MISS MANNERS:

I am a calligrapher and have been asked to address wedding invitations, both outside and inside envelopes. What is the proper way to word the various situations that arise? There are so many different ways of living together, and of each person having different titles.

GENTLE READER:

There sure are different ways of living together these days, and Miss Manners doesn't want to hear about some of them. All that concerns her, and you, is that people who live in the same household may be sent joint invitations, but may need to have separate lines for their names. If, for any reason, simple joint honorifics ("Mr. and Mrs.," "The Misses Doe," "The Doctors Roe") cannot be used, then put each full name with its proper honorific on a separate line on the outside envelope, and each honorific and surname on a separate line on the inside envelope.

DEAR MISS MANNERS:

In addressing my formal wedding invitations I have come across at least two sets of married couples who fall into a new category. The husband and wife share the same last name, but get very upset at being referred to as Mr. and Mrs. John Doe. (Their objection is over the woman being labeled as Mrs. Man's First and Last Name.)

As etiquette should make others comfortable, I should not use the standard formal outer envelope format. However, that leaves me in a quandary about how to address these invitations. Should I use Mr. and Mrs. John and Jane Doe, Mrs. Jane Doe and Mr. John Doe (on separate lines), or simply Mr. and Mrs. Doe? Or is there another option that would suit the situation?

GENTLE READER:

Count yourself lucky that you at least know what they prefer. To Miss Manners' dismay, we have no generally recognized standard for addressing, and, to her despair, people get furious at those who don't happen to choose their preference. Use the two lines on the outer envelope and "Mr. and Mrs. Doe" on the inner envelope, where it is correct to omit first names.

The Mailing

DEAR MISS MANNERS:

Is it permissible to send out wedding invitations six weeks before? This would permit family and friends to respond, make travel plans, and somewhat compensate for poor mail service.

GENTLE READER:

Indeed, Miss Manners has decreed that four to six weeks prior to the wedding is proper in this age of scattered families and erratically discounted air fares. The traditionally shorter period assumed that the bride and bridegroom met across the fence between their houses, and the neighbors had been watching the whole courtship from the porch.

THE WEDDING ANNOUNCEMENT

DEAR MISS MANNERS:

A few years ago, I had a rather nasty breakup with a young man to whom I had briefly been engaged. I am now engaged again, to a wonderful man. Could I send an announcement of my marriage this winter to the previous man? Would that be perceived as petty and unforgivable, or is it within etiquette's definition of revenge? I would not want to step outside the bounds of propriety.

GENTLE READER:

What you are proposing to do is within etiquette's definition of propriety, never mind revenge. Wedding announcements are intended to be sent to anyone you think might be interested to hear of the marriage.

That settled, Miss Manners would like to discuss your motive—not so much whether it is pleasant, but whether it has a chance of producing the effect you wish. She asks you to consider that the gentleman on whom you wish to wreak revenge would be perfectly within the bounds of propriety to send you a letter in which he expressed nothing but delight at your marriage—and that he might even mean it. She therefore believes that you would be better advised to concentrate your emotional attentions on the wonderful gentleman to whom you are now engaged.

⁓ The Overdue Announcement ⁓

DEAR MISS MANNERS:

My daughter just informed me that she was married a year ago. Do I send announcements now? Do I give her a reception now? Please advise me as soon as possible.

GENTLE READER:

Miss Manners sees that you expect higher standards of promptness from her than you do from your daughter. A year is late to send formal wedding announcements, which are correctly mailed on the day of the wedding. Nor should you exactly give them a wedding reception. But by all means inform everyone who might be interested, through letters and telephone calls. It would also be nice to give a reception in honor of the couple, informing guests in a toast (rather than ahead of time on the invitations) of the union.

The At-Home Card

DEAR MISS MANNERS:

I am a born feminist soon to marry into a family with very traditional attitudes and a large, like-minded social group. My fiancé and I were introduced at a party as "This is John Doe and the future Jane Doe."

In a flash of annoyance at the presumption that I would carry on a tradition deeply rooted in sexism, I responded tersely, "No, the forever-to-remain Jane Smith!" This exchange upset my future mother-in-law, who directed the question "Why are you getting married if she's not going to take your name?" to my fiancé out of my hearing.

I do not wish to offend my future family and their friends, but it is difficult for me to keep my zeal in check. How might I gracefully correct others who might make the error? I would also like them to know that I am open for a discussion of the subject at another time.

GENTLE READER:

It is not that Miss Manners does not sympathize with your desire to be addressed, in your future married life, as you wish to be. It's just that she has more sympathy for the poor lady who is about to acquire a zealous daughter-in-law in search of forums to debate a personal decision.

A graceful way to let people know what your name will be after marriage is to enclose at-home cards with your wedding announcements with your and your husband's names on a line each, instead of as Mr. and Mrs., and to have paper made with your name, on which to write letters of thanks for wedding presents and all the rest of your correspondence.

An ungraceful way is tersely to correct people who make a simple mistake, based on years of tradition, and to tax them with sexism for following social custom. Miss Manners fails to see why you need open the matter for discussion. Are you not prepared to be as tolerant of other ladies' choices as of your own?

⌒Responses to Announcements⌒

DEAR MISS MANNERS:

My husband and I were married in a foreign country. When we returned home, we sent out announcements but did not have a reception. The responses we got were varied. Could you please tell me what an appropriate response would have been (i.e., gift, cash, card, or a combination)? We were not registered.

GENTLE READER:

You got varied responses because you sent your announcements to a variety of people. That is as it should be, and Miss Manners is not going to deal with any subtexts about feeling cheated out of loot. A wedding announcement requires only a letter of congratulation. However, people who are particularly fond of the couple often take that opportunity to send a symbolic representation of their affection.

DEAR MISS MANNERS:

I recently married my partner in a state that permits same-sex weddings. It was a small civil ceremony with only two witnesses; we didn't even tell anyone we were going to do it. Later that week, I sent about fifty handwritten announcements to friends and family.

Out of all those people, we received almost no acknowledgment: one phone call and one card, and that's it. Even some people we see fairly regularly did not take a moment to congratulate us.

I understand that what we did is, for some reason, considered controversial and even terribly shocking by some. But these are people I've known, in many cases, for my entire life, people whose elaborate weddings I've attended and participated in, people for whom I've purchased lavish wedding presents even if I could not attend their ceremonies.

Not that I expect any gifts in return ... far from it, we didn't even register. But I take great offense at the lack of acknowledgment, as if I've done something so terribly shameful it must be forever ignored.

I must point out that my homosexuality itself is not the issue. I've been "out" to everyone I know for over ten years, and everyone has always liked my partner very much. Am I being petty for begrudging people the time to "get used to" this new development?

I tell myself that since I eloped and didn't make a big deal about getting married, my friends and family feel they don't need to make a big deal, either. But even "best wishes" e-mails would have been nice.

How do I go forward in dealing with these people? Do I allow my marriage to become some great, unspoken tension between me and the people I once considered close? Am I now free to ignore any future announcements sent by those who are snubbing me?

GENTLE READER:

Miss Manners has some information that will be as reassuring for you as it is discouraging for her. It is that people routinely ignore wedding announcements, shockingly rude as that is.

They know that they are supposed to send presents when they

receive invitations to weddings, although it rarely occurs to them that they are also obligated to answer those invitations. But they fail to understand that when friends make an announcement—whether formally or face to face—it should elicit congratulations.

RESPONDING TO A WEDDING INVITATION

Accepting

DEAR MISS MANNERS:

Back in the olden days, one replied to a wedding invitation by writing an abbreviated copy of it, starting with one's own name:

> *Mr. and Mrs. John Jones*
> *accept with pleasure*
> *the kind invitation of*
> *Mr. and Mrs. Roberts*
> *for Saturday, the tenth of June*
> *at half after seven o'clock*
> *City Club*

Is this form of reply passé? What is currently the proper method of replying?

GENTLE READER:

Passé in what sense? There is no need to update this form, as it is succinct and correct. It is not for guests to treat the style of the occasion with less formality than the hosts do.

Miss Manners does not deny that an awful lot of people have declared the necessity of answering invitations at all to be out of fashion. Since they are not the hosts, they have kindly taken it upon themselves to declare that hosts "don't care anymore" to know who is attending their events.

This is a shameless falsehood. Ask anyone connected with giving a wedding. Therefore, the olden days, as you call them, are still upon us and will be forever, or at least until such time as people get fed up entertaining ingrates and stop issuing invitations.

⌒ Declining ⌒

DEAR MISS MANNERS:

I am a single, middle-aged man with no intent of marriage. I have celebrated many weddings of friends, relatives, and colleagues, as either guest or groomsman. Now I'm receiving invitations to the many more weddings for the children of these couples. Though they have my best wishes, I have no desire to participate either with my attendance or by providing gifts. How may I politely express my position?

GENTLE READER:

You are in luck. Etiquette has taken the precaution of supplying the exact words you need; you have only to fill in your name at the top, neatly centered.

Mr. Algernon Asquith
regrets exceedingly that he is unable to accept
the very kind invitation of
Mr. and Mrs. Quiverful
for Saturday, the eleventh of June

Miss Manners only asks that you do not fool with this wording in the disastrous hope of personalizing it to your situation. There is no polite way to say that a gentleman thinks he has gone quite far enough in enduring the nuptial festivities of his friends without boring himself senseless at those of their children.

DEAR MISS MANNERS:

Desperate male in his 40s finds equally desperate woman online. They meet, and after two dates decide to get married. He is eager to lose his virginity, and she is about to lose her welfare benefits. They decide to get married at city hall.

Invitations are sent for their reception. Printed on a home printer, the ink is smeared, making it hard to read. In it is a list of all the stores they registered at, including Web sites. The reception was for two hours at the home of his parents. Neither has a job, and they were banking on a lot of gifts so they could return them to finance a honeymoon trip.

I did not attend, but I sent a congratulations card. I take marriage vows very seriously and didn't feel like being taken advantage of. Several co-workers felt the same way and chose not to attend or send a gift. Your opinion, please.

GENTLE READER:

That you do not like these people. Miss Manners hopes it will not disappoint you to learn that there is nothing rude about declining the invitation and sending only your congratulations.

DEAR MISS MANNERS:

My ex-boyfriend and I did not part ways amicably, primarily because he cheated. Unfortunately, our social and professional circles overlap to such an extent that it has been impossible to completely avoid contact with him in the three years since we broke up. Our relationship is polite but not friendly, and it would not bother me in the least if I never saw him again.

He is now engaged to be married, and for unfathomable reasons he and his fiancée (who knows nothing of our relationship) sent me a wedding invitation. Am I obliged to send a gift?

GENTLE READER:

No, and you didn't even need to supply the interesting backstory. If everyone who received and declined a wedding invitation were obligated to send a present, greedy couples would be blanketing society with invitations to people they hardly know.

Come to think of it, some of them are. The recipient's basic obligation is simply to respond quickly. Nevertheless, Miss Manners hopes you can find it in your heart to do the additionally charming thing and write the bride, if not the couple, a note wishing them well.

⌒Hesitating⌒

DEAR MISS MANNERS:

The man with whom I have had an "affair" for the last fifteen years is getting married. Technically, I guess it hasn't been an affair, since neither of us was married or in a significant monogamous relationship. However, the sexual aspects of our relationship were quite important and were hidden from our various other friends.

He plans to invite me to the wedding. After all, I am one of his closer and longer friends and to not invite me would raise suspicions, he says.

Should I go? Any particular presents that should be avoided or that you would recommend? We have stopped our sexual encounters, however, he continues to visit me occasionally alone, as well as sometimes with his fiancée. Would it be proper for us (or him) to let her know our history?

GENTLE READER:

Let us take that last question first; Miss Manners has the feeling it is the key to the rest.

What, pray, did you have in mind? A luncheon with the lady during which you wait until she has a mouthful of chef's salad before murmuring, "I don't know if Jeremy happened to mention this to you, but . . ."? Warning the gentleman that the next time they pay one of their visits, you expect him to sit with you on the sofa, facing her, and to say, after simultaneously clearing your throats, "By the way, there is something we think you should know"?

Surely the gentleman's history is his to confide or not, as he sees fit, and in a manner of his own choosing. To suggest otherwise is something very close to blackmail. You would not care to have him coming around in the future, should you form a serious attachment, with an offer to enlighten the gentleman.

Your quibble about what does or does not constitute an affair suggests that you believe that the only legitimate hurt one can inflict is deception. In his remark about not arousing suspicion, the gentleman has indicated that he disagrees.

The answer to your questions about attending his wedding and choosing a present is to continue the discretion you showed, when it was presumably in your own interest, now that it is no longer your concern. As the visits seem to have worked, Miss Manners presumes you are enough under control of your behavior to attend the wedding under the guise of innocent friendship. Your present, also, should be in keeping with that relationship. A photograph album of your last trip with him would, for example, be in bad taste.

DEAR MISS MANNERS:

Is it acceptable to turn down a wedding invitation because of the sheer cost to get there?

I have a friend who is getting married next summer in a remote location. It would take a few hours to fly there and five hours to drive from the airport, and the monetary cost is very high. This is a friend we rarely see and are not close to. If we send a nice (possibly expensive) gift and send our regrets, is that okay?

GENTLE READER:

A wedding invitation is not a summons with the fine already attached. You may turn one down for whatever reason—that you are not particularly close to the person being married, that you cannot easily afford the trip and the time, or that you just don't feel like going.

All Miss Manners requires is that you answer the invitation without any such explanation (none is needed) and wish the couple well. You don't even have to send a present, but if you want to do so, you needn't feel that its worth has to make up for your absence.

⌒Reneging⌒

DEAR MISS MANNERS:

I sent an RSVP for a friend's wedding and was not able to go at the last minute. I was trying to meet a crucial deadline for work, but I don't want her to think that I did it on purpose or that I didn't think her wedding was important. How can I handle this, and should I offer to pay for my plate cost since I didn't attend?

GENTLE READER:

How can you expect to convince your friend that you thought her wedding was important when your actions clearly demonstrated that you did not?

Work is not the trump you seem to think. Miss Manners doubts that your employer locked you up against your will. You planned badly, or you accepted a last-minute assignment you should have refused, or you knew you might not be able to show and should have declined the invitation. Whichever it was, you decided that the wedding was less important.

The bride may well focus on the money angle; people often do when they are insulted. Sending her a check would be a crude way of covering that. It would not cover the empty place you left, physically and emotionally.

Since you are conspicuously in the wrong, your only hope of mending things is first to grovel and then to make a major counterdemonstration of your affection and interest. For example, you might throw a party in honor of the newly married couple. And of course you will understand if they don't show up because something came up at the last minute.

TROUBLESHOOTING

DEAR MISS MANNERS:

For my niece's wedding we are trying to avoid a situation that we witnessed at a friend's wedding reception. It was a sit-down, plated dinner, and the venue could accommodate 220, including the wedding party.

Of the 200 invited guests, 120 responded with acceptance or regrets within the time frame requested. The remaining 80 were asked by phone if they would attend. More often than not, the messages were left on voice-mail at their respective homes. Of these, 40 responded rather quickly. The remaining 40 were called again, and there were about 10 responses before the final count was given to the caterer. Not knowing whether the remaining 30 people would attend, the hosts decided to hold open three tables of eight (24 seats).

Four of those who had not responded did attend, leaving 20 empty places at the two tables. There were also some who accepted but did not attend.

Is there a way that a host can avoid such waste? After making such efforts, must a host still make accommodations for guests who do not respond? It would be an embarrassing situation for all if those who had not responded appeared and there was no place for them.

May a host advise those who have failed to respond that "We are so very sorry that you will be unable to attend and hope to share our joy of the occasion with you in the future"? I would not have dreamed of doing this many years ago when I was married.

GENTLE READER:

Whew. There's a lot of math involved in cleaning up other people's rudeness. The hosts of your friend's wedding have gone far beyond the call of duty in sparing their guests from the very thing they should be indulged in: embarrassment. Your solution is less taxing to the hosts and with just the right amount of shame, which, done within the confines of polite wording, is perfectly justified.

DEAR MISS MANNERS:

As the maid of honor in my best friend's wedding, I was charged with arranging a bridal shower and bachelorette party. Because the bride had moved across the country and was in town for only a short time, I had to plan all the festivities in one weekend. I notified all our friends to save the date for these events, then I promptly sent out the invitations.

No one showed up for either event. I was devastated, but not as much as the bride. I now look like an incompetent fool to her and her family.

The following week, I made one last attempt to contact people. I sent out an e-mail with the bride's contact info. "for anyone who missed the festivities and still wanted to wish the bride well." The bride did not receive one response, best wishes, or apology.

I have never in my life experienced such blatant rudeness, particularly from "friends." I am so upset that I do not know how to deal with these people. I am tired of apologizing to the bride. I will likely have to deal with them again at the next social gathering. Is there any way I can address this situation and let them know just how rude and inconsiderate they were? I really don't think I can just pretend nothing happened.

GENTLE READER:

Rather than being a bad friend, you may be the only friend to this hapless bride. We hate to say it, but the fact that no one showed up, responded, or apologized seems like more than a coincidence—unless the coincidence is that you both have a taste for exceptionally rude friends.

Is it possible that no one wanted to devote her entire weekend to this bride for some other reason? If there is a somewhat trusted person in this dreadful lot, you might ask her if there is something that you or the bride did to offend *everyone*. Clearly, repeated reminders and reproaches are not effective. You are more likely to get a sympathetic response with a diffident approach.

DEAR MISS MANNERS:

I'm concerned that some of our daughter's young, hip friends may wear "dress denim" (you know, a great shoe and a fancy top with your good jeans) to her upcoming wedding and reception. The country club, where the reception is being held, has a no-denim policy. How do I say this on the invitation without sounding snotty or rude?

GENTLE READER:

We're afraid that unless you are having a formal evening wedding (in which case you may put "Black tie" on the lower left corner of the invitation), there is no way to guard against the oxymoron that is "dress denim," if that is what your daughter's friends deem formal wear. Presumably there will be much discussion of great shoes and fancy tops in the ensuing weeks before the wedding, and your daughter and some like-minded friends and relatives should spread the word about proper attire. You have the perfect polite out in that it's not your snotty rule, but the club's.

DEAR MISS MANNERS:

I tend to agree with you that reply cards are better left out. However, I have since discovered that I seem to be the *only* person who agrees with you—my friends, my family, even my fiancé all think that they are for the convenience of your guests and that it would indeed be rude to not include them.

They point out that they have never seen an invitation without one, so perhaps what was once a slight has now become the accepted way of doing things. If I were to leave them out, I would have to field questions from just about everyone on our guest list regarding why, and I can't exactly tell them "because they are rude and insulting," as that would imply that my friends and family were in error in including reply cards in their own invitations. I'm tired of arguing over this; would Miss Manners be so kind as to release me from this restriction?

GENTLE READER:

Release you from not doing it or from explanations of why you're not doing it?

You might as well develop your polite response patter now. "I know that people find them convenient, but we were so looking forward to getting your correspondence," may sound high maintenance, but is at least gracious. Or you could cite the extra paper waste—mentioning the environment usually accomplishes the task of closing the discussion.

DEAR MISS MANNERS:

We are ordering invitations for our daughter's wedding and reception, and I am dismayed at all the cards and envelopes that apparently need to be sent to guests. Everyone seems to think that, today, no one knows how to R.s.v.p. other than to check a YES or NO on a response card and stick it into the pre-stamped, pre-addressed envelope. A lot of work for me, not to mention expense. My solution is to put R.s.v.p. at the bottom of the invitation to the reception and include an e-mail address, since this is how young people communicate anyway. Perhaps I should add a phone number for older guests who may not own a computer. What do you think of this idea?

GENTLE READER:

Have you considered that you might not have lowered your standards far enough? Many E-vites go unanswered, too. It may just be that your guests don't want to make the commitment. For any among them who might be polite, you should give the address, as usual, penning in simpler methods for those who are not, and hoping for the best.

Dear Miss Manners:

I have replied to formal invitations for many years by writing out a correspondingly formal response on cream vellum stationery with a black fountain pen, as my mother taught me to do many years ago. Now that so many feel it is necessary to enclose a response card and envelope with an invitation, I wonder if I may continue to respond as I have, or whether not using the response card might be considered a rebuke to the manners of those sending the invitation. Further, having been provided with the card, is it wasteful not to use it and its postage? I would much prefer to continue to write out my responses, but I certainly don't want to create the impression that I'm being in any way instructive or insulting to those who have so kindly sent me an invitation, and I would wish never to be wasteful. I am in a quandry, and look forward to your guidance.

Gentle Reader:

An acceptable compromise is to use your own writing paper with the provided envelope and postage. Stuffing your beautiful cream vellum into the inevitably tiny envelope may offend your sensibilities, but it should also produce the desired awkwardness without being directly instructive or insulting.

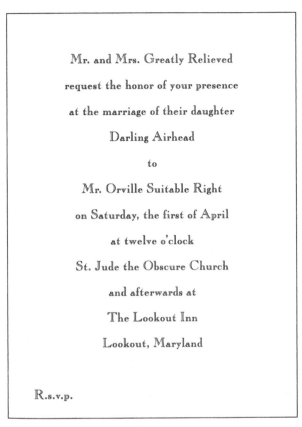

Mr. and Mrs. Greatly Relieved

request the honor of your presence

at the marriage of their daughter

Darling Airhead

to

Mr. Orville Suitable Right

on Saturday, the first of April

at twelve o'clock

St. Jude the Obscure Church

and afterwards at

The Lookout Inn

Lookout, Maryland

R.s.v.p.

Now that we consider it outrageous to invite some people to depart after the ceremony while inviting others to stay for the wedding cake and champagne, this is the standard invitation to a wedding and a wedding breakfast, reception, or dinner. A separate reception card could be used with an invitation to the ceremony, the letter "u" could be inserted in "honor," but this is not necessary.

It is no accident that there is no form for that abomination, the response card. "R.s.v.p." is quite enough of a concession. It should not be necessary to alert anyone of sense and goodwill that it is obligatory to answer such an invitation, and if the guests can't figure out where to write, they can check the return address on the envelope.

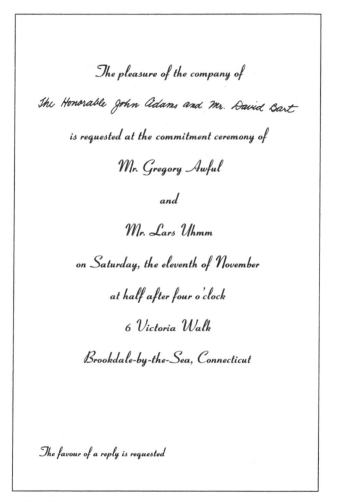

The pleasure of the company of

The Honorable John Adams and Mr. David Bart

is requested at the commitment ceremony of

Mr. Gregory Awful

and

Mr. Lars Uhmm

on Saturday, the eleventh of November

at half after four o'clock

6 Victoria Walk

Brookdale-by-the-Sea, Connecticut

The favour of a reply is requested

Although it is not actually a wedding invitation, it follows an optional but particularly flattering traditional form, in which the guests' names are written by hand.

Mr. and Mrs. Frank Lee Baffled

request the honour of your presence

at the marriage of their daughter

Camilla Madeline

Captain, United States Army

to

Duong Tran Awful-Nuisance

Lieutenant, United States Army

on Saturday, the twentieth of December

at two o'clock

Old Post Chapel

Camp Dusseldorf, Germany

Reception

immediately following the ceremony

Camp Dusseldorf Officers Club

R.s.v.p.
APO 1234
New York, New York

> *Admiral Stacey Awful-Nuisance*
>
> *Major General Trevor Nuisance*
>
> *request the honour of your presence*
>
> *at the marriage of*
>
> *Camilla Madeline Baffled*
>
> *Captain, United States Army*
>
> *to their son*
>
> *Duong Tran*
>
> *Lieutenant, United States Army*
>
> *on Saturday, the twentieth of December*
>
> *at two o'clock*
>
> *Old Post Chapel*
>
> *Camp Dusseldorf, Germany*

The European-style invitation is another solution to the complaint that the bridegroom's parents are omitted from the traditional invitation (because they weren't the hosts, because everybody knows them, because they lived next door to the bride's parents, and because nobody much cared about the male side of the event).

Mr. and Mrs. Samuel McGee

1 Marge Drive
Lake Lebarge, Alaska 78877

Ms. Heidi Megabyte

Mr. and Mrs. Theodore Bishop Right

request the honour of your presence

at the marriage of their daughters

Lauren Whitney

to

Mr. Maxwell Scott Nicely

and

Heather Brittany

to

Mr. Daniel Service McGee

on Saturday, the second of June

at six o'clock

Our Lady of Propriety Church

and at a reception

following the ceremony

The Bideawhile Hotel

Brookdale, Connecticut

R.s.v.p.
129 Primrose Path
Brookdale, Connecticut 01110

Complications in the marital lives of the parental generation have been handled in this double-wedding invitation by having the mother, father, and stepmother of the two brides as hosts, while the parents of one of the bridegrooms have slipped their own card into the invitations sent to their side of the family to avoid their friends' exclaiming, "Who on earth are these people?"

The pleasure of your company

is requested at the marriage of

Dr. Harriett Grundy

to

Mr. Brendan Truly Repellent

on Saturday, the thirteenth of October

at four o'clock

Baronial Baroque Hotel

New York City

and afterwards at a reception

R.s.v.p.
29 Alimentary Canal
New York, NY 10014

A couple giving its own wedding modestly goes into the passive tense when issuing formal invitations.

29 Alimentary Canal
New York, New York   10014

Dear Sally and Jack,

Brendan and I are getting married on Saturday, the second of June, at two o'clock here in our roof garden. We very much want you to come and stay afterwards to help us celebrate

Fondly yours,
Harriett

An informal wedding invitation is just as proper as a formal one provided that the informality is achieved honestly, with a letter, rather than by messing up the formal form (omitting honorifics, adding hearts and flowers, using nauseating phrases referring to the couple's sentiments for each other, adding other unattractive or embarrassing "personal" touches) or by using faked engraving.

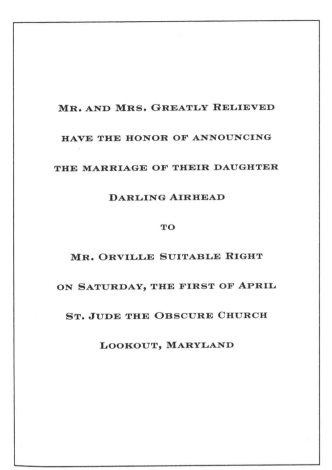

MR. AND MRS. GREATLY RELIEVED

HAVE THE HONOR OF ANNOUNCING

THE MARRIAGE OF THEIR DAUGHTER

DARLING AIRHEAD

TO

MR. ORVILLE SUITABLE RIGHT

ON SATURDAY, THE FIRST OF APRIL

ST. JUDE THE OBSCURE CHURCH

LOOKOUT, MARYLAND

Although mean-spirited people try to claim that a wedding announcement is really a request for a wedding present from those who have not attended the wedding, this is an improper thought. A wedding announcement is the announcement that a wedding has taken place. The response to it should be a letter of congratulations.

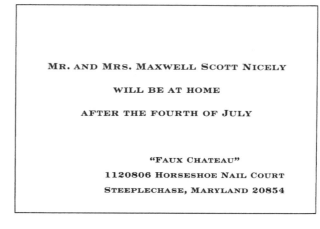

MR. AND MRS. MAXWELL SCOTT NICELY

WILL BE AT HOME

AFTER THE FOURTH OF JULY

"FAUX CHATEAU"
1120806 HORSESHOE NAIL COURT
STEEPLECHASE, MARYLAND 20854

Ms. Heather Brittany Right-Megabyte

Mr. Daniel Service McGee

29 Alimentary Canal
Apartment 2-B
After the tenth of August   New York, New York 10014

One bride has decided to shock her mother by taking her husband's name, while other has seized the opportunity to add her mother's surname to her father's. Etiquette prudently keeps out of the way when these emotionally charged decisions are made, only asking that brides let their friends know what they wish to be called. The traditional at-home card, just the right size to tuck into an address book, nicely serves this purpose.

Mr. and Mrs. Samuel McGee

request the pleasure of your company

at a reception

in the honor of

Ms. Heather Brittany Right-Megabyte and Mr. Daniel McGee

on Saturday, the fifteenth of July

at eight o'clock

The Marge Club

Lake Lebarge, Alaska

Please reply
1 Marge Drive
Lake Lebarge, Alaska   78877

The solution to the bridegroom's parents' grumbling that not enough of their friends were able to attend the wedding is the delayed reception to honor the newly married couple, rather than a road-show repeat of the wedding itself.

CHAPTER SEVEN

The Presents

"WE'VE BEEN LIVING TOGETHER for ages, so we already have everything we need." "We've both been married before, so we have two of everything." "We want to save our guests the trouble of wondering what we want."

Are those the statements of people who would truly rather not receive any presents?

Oh, perhaps. Every once in a while Miss Manners actually does hear from someone who is genuinely embarrassed at the idea that inviting intimates to a celebration generally brings forth tangible offerings.

More often, she hears such remarks from people who not only do not object to receiving presents but are way ahead of the potential givers in thoughts about how best to please the recipients. If they can't actually surprise themselves, they at least want to do everything else connected with giving the presents they will receive. Except pay for them.

How, they inquire, can they ask guests to get together and sponsor, for example, the wedding itself or the wedding trip? Or donate cash? Such a useful present and so easy to wrap.

If you will allow Miss Manners to mix in some ranting about the vulgarity of this approach, she promises to help make presents do what they are supposed to do, which is to please. The fact is that much of present-giving has become a burden in both directions, which is one reason (the other reasons being greed on the one hand and laziness on the other) that it has deteriorated into the mechanical transfer of money or selection from the recipient's shopping list.

Miss Manners acknowledges that there are many for whom the traditional household presents are not right. She is not as unsympathetic as she pretends with the exasperation of those who deplore the waste of money on unwanted goods. But first we must change attitudes, then we can see about changing the goods.

It is necessary for the preservation of civility to maintain the idea that generosity is—well, generosity. You are not supposed to seem to count on receiving presents—and presents for second weddings are not even traditional. Nor are presents supposed to be compensation to the celebrants for the expenses of hospitality.

It should be remembered that guests are guests. Should they happen to be moved to give something they think might be enjoyed, there should be a pretense that they have been successful. You have to seem pleased and grateful.

Attempting to crush out of these well-wishers any impulse to exercise their own thoughts or taste is a mistake. (Miss Manners won't even allow nice people to put "No gifts," or that painful pun about wanting the guests' "presence, not presents," on their invitations.) Rather, thoughtfulness should be encouraged.

People who claim to have "everything" have not, it seems, done all the shopping they plan to do for the rest of their lives. They merely mean that they have the staples that once characterized wedding presents. If this isn't obvious to their friends, they may—but only if asked—say modestly, "Oh, we really have all the basic household things," leaving unsaid but obvious the idea that little luxuries would be appreciated.

If the guest cares about the people concerned, he or she should be willing to try to find something suitable and pleasing. (Those who don't care enough should decline the invitation and be done with it.) Occasionally people are bound to guess wrong, which is why it is a good idea to make the place of purchase obvious and not inquire after items that may have been discreetly exchanged.

A household where there is enough flatware and appliances can usually use an extra picture frame or vase; most people welcome a case of champagne; many are known to have an appetite for art or music. Miss Manners does not presume to know the tastes of your friends better than you. She is only suggesting that expanding the idea of what makes a suitable wedding or anniversary present is better than killing the practice of generosity.

THE COMPLAINT DEPARTMENT

DEAR MISS MANNERS:

I am puzzled and hurt, having just received a reproachful thank-you note from my stepsister. I chose a generous wedding gift that I thought she and her fiancé would enjoy and sent it with a card wishing them happiness. Her note informs me that they liked my gift, even if it wasn't on their bridal registry list.

I didn't realize that the bridal registry list had become the absolute ironclad means of choosing wedding gifts and that imagination was no longer appreciated. What should I do the next time my stepsister and I meet? I don't want to allude to this incident, but I'm very much afraid she will.

GENTLE READER:

It is indeed a topsy-turvy world where a guest is deemed thoughtless for making an effort to think of something that would be pleasing and a letter of thanks chides the giver. This drives Miss Manners to despair, although she agrees that it is not worth a family quarrel. If your stepsister mentions it, you might allow yourself merely to murmur sincerely, "My intention was to please you."

DEAR MISS MANNERS:

We received an extravagant gift from my husband's childhood neighbors of a set of expensive porcelain dishes. The more I think about it, the more angry I become. I was hoping that my husband and I would be able to pick out our own china pattern, which I believe is a very personal choice. Also, we are going to be moving around and don't even have a need for something like this until we are settled in a permanent home location. What do I do about this gift that I didn't want, ask, or register for?

GENTLE READER:

Have a tantrum about it. How dare those people give you a lavish present not of your own choosing?

Now pull yourself together, please. What would you do if you had a real problem? Miss Manners will tell you exactly what you must do:

1. Write a lavish letter of thanks, as if you were grateful, which indeed you should be, and skip the parts about your dissatisfaction and indignation.
2. Return, sell, or donate the china, or give it to someone whom it will not infuriate.

The Money Angle

DEAR MISS MANNERS:

Is there a "proper" amount for a wedding gift? I have heard more and more people say that their gift must cover the cost of their dinner. Is this not just "paying admission" for attending the affair? My 25-year-old daughter is beginning to be invited to weddings of peers and cannot afford to cover the cost of her meal.

GENTLE READER:

That this idea is widespread does not rescue it from being astonishingly crass, for exactly the reasons you mention.

Etiquette recognizes no such rule, Miss Manners assures you. It assumes, perhaps naively, that wedding guests are invited solely for their emotional value, and that wedding presents are selected by the guests from within their particular financial means, solely to please the recipients.

DEAR MISS MANNERS:

I am attending a wedding in a couple of weeks. There was no gift registry mentioned or included in the invitation. The couple is rich, has lived together for years, etc. What do I give them for a wedding gift? I was thinking just a cash amount.

GENTLE READER:

Although she despises registries, Miss Manners thought the justification was to avoid giving people what they already have. And you indicate that these people already have money. Perhaps they also have the good taste not to ask for presents, making them a great rarity these days. Miss Manners is afraid that you will have to exercise some thought to determine what might please these people. That is what is meant when presents are spoken of and appreciated as being thoughtful.

DEAR MISS MANNERS:

At the ripe young age of 49, I am getting married this fall for the first time. My husband-to-be and I both own our homes and have accumulated everything necessary for each of us to live comfortably on our own. As an example, together we have five sets of dishes and 20 sets of towels! So we are faced with an interesting dilemma about guests and their gifts.

We do not need any toasters or other things that a much younger couple needs to set up housekeeping. So how do we politely tell them that the best gift for a mature couple like us is, well, cash? Is there verbiage that can be used on our invitations about gifts for someone in our situation?

GENTLE READER:

What makes you think that younger couples don't need money? Or, for that matter, that your wedding guests know you so little, and are so unwilling to give you any thought, that they will all buy you—here we go again—toasters?

But none of that matters, because there is no polite way to panhandle your wedding guests. You have informed Miss Manners that you are well off to the extent of owning two houses and a great many household goods. So why are you thinking of begging from your wedding guests?

DEAR MISS MANNERS:

What would be the tactful way to say "no presents but a money tree"?

GENTLE READER:

"Never mind all that junk—just gimme your wallet."

⁓The Philanthropic Registry⁓

DEAR MISS MANNERS:

My same-sex partner and I are planning a June wedding. Though we already consider ourselves ten years married following a religious ceremony, and our eight-year-old daughter certainly considers us married, many of our heterosexual friends and family want to witness this wedding. We are happy to go the traditional route with church wedding and reception, but we really don't need or want any more toasters. Is it acceptable to suggest a donation to the Freedom to Marry Coalition instead of gifts?

GENTLE READER:

Just how many toasters do you have? Never mind. Even people who mean well are subject to the rule against dwelling on the giving potential of their guests, Miss Manners is afraid. How they spend their money is up to them, not you.

~Whether to Send Presents~

Dear Miss Manners:

The daughter of a friend of mine announced her engagement, and today we received an invitation to the engagement party that included a request for gifts (monetary preferable).

Does any gift we give cover the gift for the wedding? When their other daughter married, we found ourselves being invited to an engagement party, a bridal shower, and eventually, the wedding. All these invitations mentioned bringing a gift. That seems somewhat excessive and a little greedy to me.

Gentle Reader:

Somewhat? And you haven't yet received the housewarming and baby shower invitations and invoices.

Engagement presents are unnecessary, but your friends are frankly stating that their events are all fund-raisers. Unless you think them worth the money, Miss Manners recommends declining.

Dear Miss Manners:

Is it acceptable for an adult to attend a wedding and not bring a gift? I feel that it is not, but my fiancé says that you will say it is perfectly acceptable.

Gentle Reader:

Oh, he does, does he? Funny, Miss Manners doesn't remember him from the Etiquette Council.

Having strenuously maintained that there is no social form, invitation, or announcement that translates as "Present due," Miss Manners might seem trapped into agreeing with your fiancé. Fortunately, she is wilier than that. If you do not feel sufficiently pleased by someone's marriage to be moved to try to contribute to that person's happiness, you don't belong at the wedding.

However, Miss Manners trusts that you do not mean the verb "bring" literally. Wedding presents—properly sent to the bride's home before the wedding, or to the couple's home afterward—are a nuisance when brought to the event, where no one has time to deal with them and there is a danger of their being lost, the cards disappearing, or, Miss Manners regrets to say, the packages being stolen.

DEAR MISS MANNERS:

When attending a wedding abroad, what is considered proper for gift-giving, taking into account the guest's traveling expense to be in attendance? Can the guest's presence be considered as a gift?

GENTLE READER:

Miss Manners is curious as to what you think your presence is worth. More than an electric can opener, but less than a tea service? Guests do not get expense accounts for attending weddings that they can then apply against the debt of a wedding present.

When to Send Presents

DEAR MISS MANNERS:

My son was in a wedding for his friend and told me that he hadn't even thought about the gift yet, since he had up to a year after the wedding to send it. I guess my shock was apparent, because he proceeded to tell me that this was the new social rule for gift-giving. He said that everyone his age knows that, and that the rules as I once knew them had changed.

GENTLE READER:

You almost caught Miss Manners there. If she hadn't been paying strict attention, she might have acquiesced in your son's assertion that this was a new rule and obliged you by sliding into the things-are-deteriorating mode.

The fact is that this is a very old rule. That it happens to be more sensible than ever, in a time when marriages themselves may not last a year, is coincidental. Any time from the announcement of the engagement until the end of the first year of marriage is considered appropriate for sending a wedding present.

⌒When to Open Presents⌒

DEAR MISS MANNERS:

At the first family wedding I have been to in years I asked my sister (mother of the bride), when the presents were going to be opened and placed for viewing. I was informed that "We don't do that anymore; the bride and groom open them the next day."

Is this new? When I was growing up, at all weddings and showers, the gifts were opened and placed for others to see.

I realize that there is no obligation to display the gifts, but I have always thought it was a courtesy, because others might enjoy seeing everything.

GENTLE READER:

It is true that etiquette did used to sanction the display of wedding presents, although not, as you seem to have experienced, with the children's birthday party/shower routine of opening them in front of the guests. Nor would they have been opening them "the next day," when the couple would be off to enjoy their first sanctioned privacy, not hanging around with nothing better to do.

The presents would be opened as each arrived—and the letters of thanks sent immediately. When the bride's parents were likely to be receiving, and perhaps even holding the wedding at home, presents were displayed on tables covered by white damask cloths, with or, more discreetly, without, the cards of the donors.

Miss Manners does not doubt that it is also true that guests relished inspecting them, but not because they found it heart-warming. You know they must have been checking to see how much was spent, and whether, in comparison, they spent too much or too little on the presents they sent. As this is not a particularly seemly activity, etiquette was already condemning the practice decades ago. Miss Manners considers it a custom justly killed.

⌒*Are They Returnable?*⌒

DEAR MISS MANNERS:

What does one say to a friend who offers to sell one back one's wedding present? I gave her the gift some time before the wedding, which I was unable to attend. After the wedding she approached me, said that she was unable to use my gift, and offered to sell it back to me. Suggestions for a civilized response would be appreciated.

GENTLE READER:

"This came with my good wishes. I don't know what you think they are worth."

DEAR MISS MANNERS:

For the past few years I have worked part-time in the customer service/returns department of a nationwide retailer with a large bridal and gift registry department. Unbelievably, many of the couples who register for gifts register for some of the most expensive dinnerware, cookware, vacuum cleaners, and bedding the store offers, even though they don't like the items and have no intention of keeping them. Their intention instead is to return the gift items for the full retail price, then purchase what they really want and pocket the difference. This practice is openly encouraged by many of the mothers of the brides and is blatantly confessed to by the brides-to-be as they await their cash rewards during the return process.

Many of these brides-to-be roll up to the customer service counter with multiple carts containing thousands of dollars worth of merchandise to return after each wedding shower and the wedding. They want to execute a quick return so that the items appear unpurchased on the registry, thus allowing other guests to purchase these same items for the next shower. They then repeat this process for any remaining showers and then for the wedding.

I have seen brides return multiples of the same items over the course of the engagement and wedding, totaling up to $6,000 per each return, explaining that they just want the cash. Also, we are required to open every item returned to ensure that there is no breakage, that it's the correct item as specified on the box, etc. In doing so, I have retrieved countless cards and notes from the giver of these gifts only to have the bride exclaim that she's glad I looked as she would never have known that card/note was in there! (This begs the question of who were you going to thank for the gift if you didn't open the giver's card to learn who had given it?)

I am sure that most people would never think of the above-mentioned practice when selecting and giving a gift. More than likely they would be disappointed to know that their gift was part of a revolving, cash-generating plan, which certainly takes the joy out of sharing in the couple's "biggest day of their lives."

GENTLE READER:

Thank you for the best argument yet against registries. Never mind that it ruined Miss Manners' day.

⟶ Are They Re-claimable? ⟶

DEAR MISS MANNERS:

My boss's daughter was getting married. I sent her a very expensive gift, but a few days before the wedding I was fired for no reason. The daughter kept the gift rather than return it to me. Was this proper, or should she have returned it?

GENTLE READER:

Only if she fired the bridegroom would she have been required to return it. Or if he fired her.

Whatever your motivation, Miss Manners is afraid that your offering still counts as a wedding present, not a gesture to ingratiate yourself with your boss. Thus the only rule that applies is that presents must be returned if the wedding—not your career—is cancelled.

TROUBLESHOOTING

DEAR MISS MANNERS:

As a bride-to-be, I have become involved in several online message boards that discuss wedding planning. One touchy topic is that of gifts. According to the ladies I chat with, and most etiquette guides I have read, a couple is not supposed to expect wedding gifts from their guests, which also explains why one should not mention gifts or include registry information on or in their wedding invitations. This I definitely understand.

But while the couple is not to expect wedding gifts, doesn't etiquette also dictate to wedding guests themselves that they are obligated to send a gift when they plan on attending a wedding? I've encountered a number of brides on the message boards who write that they feel slighted when they have planned their wedding for sometimes a year or more, taking great care to make their guests as comfortable and accommodated as possible and to follow the standards of etiquette, but still a number of guests neglect to send a wedding gift.

Almost always the other ladies will chastise the bride and call her selfish for expecting gifts. This is where I disagree. While there are many etiquette guidelines brides must follow, I feel there are also etiquette guidelines that guests must follow, and that includes sending a wedding gift! As a wedding guest, I would feel extremely rude and embarrassed to attend a wedding without sending a gift. So *are* wedding guests obligated to send a wedding gift? And how is a bride supposed to feel when someone doesn't send one?

GENTLE READER:

Obligated is a strong word, but yes, generally a wedding guest is expected to send a wedding gift if he/she is attending the wedding. The pretense of giving spontaneously and seeming surprised and pleased to receive are what make the practice civilized.

How the bride is supposed to feel about guests who do not give presents, we do not presume to dictate. Going public by posting it on blogs and message boards, however, takes it into the realm of the rude.

DEAR MISS MANNERS:

The last time I was a bridesmaid, the bride approached me after the wedding and asked me if I would write e-mail messages invoicing guests who had not given her presents. She added, "And you can start with yourself."

The groom had misplaced the card and check I had given them (she had indicated that she preferred gifts of money). After I advised her to find it, I politely declined to invoice anybody. My check was deposited within a couple days; I received a terse e-mail saying, "Thanks for the check. Sorry."

When I got married this past June, some of our guests gave us gifts, some didn't. This had nothing to do with how happy I was with the people who attended and wished us well. Having had such a wonderful time, it's become even more inexplicable to me that some people get so hung up on the gifts. And writing my thank-you letters the following week was fun: It let me relive the wedding all over again and express my appreciation for all the friendships I've benefited from.

GENTLE READER:

How wonderful that you are so overcome with appreciation of your friends that you seemingly forget to put in a much-deserved dig about your appalling one. We might not be so forgiving.

DEAR MISS MANNERS:

What did engaged couples do before it became commonplace to register for wedding gifts? Did they settle for mismatched place settings and china, or items that, while well intentioned, did not fit with their decor or taste?

I understand registering takes the surprise out of giving, but it also lets the giver know that they are giving something that will be useful to the newly wedded couple. Surely people of today understand that no gift is necessary, but that gift registration is something akin to a Christmas wish list? When I plan my own wedding, I do not wish to cause offense to anyone. Yet I am also aware that this practice was commonplace long before I arrived on this earth.

GENTLE READER:

They had rooms full of toasters and used them for furniture.

Just kidding. The practice that was commonplace long before you arrived on this earth (depending, of course, on when that was) was for relatives and friends discreetly to communicate the couple's tastes in china and the like—when asked. The department store registry, which came along in the 1920s, was still intended to be mentioned only when asked.

Now, in the days since your earthly arrival, it is unfortunately commonplace to skip all of this discretion and just put in your order. It is sweet of you to think of it as a Christmas wish list whose only offense would be ruining the surprise (we are beginning to suspect that your arrival may have been more recent than we thought); the rudeness comes more from its advertising and expectations than from the actual deed.

DEAR MISS MANNERS:

When our wedding guests ask us directly where we are registered, how can we best respond??

We registered as a concession. Friends insisted that not to register is the equivalent of asking for monetary gifts. This appalled us. Family members insisted we register to help them better express their joy to us. So as a courtesy, and hoping to avoid appearing to be money-grubbers, we conceded and registered.

We wish that guests who truly want to get gifts would ask a family member (instead of us) about the registry, or express themselves with a gift they've chosen, but we know from experience that this will not always be the case.

I want to say something that conveys that we appreciate the gesture but that gifts aren't necessary. (It's our understanding that gifts are, by their nature, never necessary, but this might be a minority opinion.) But we fear that any response that downplays or discourages gifts will prolong the discussion, and we won't be excused until we name a registry.

GENTLE READER:

We are only too familiar with the idea that guests will be befuddled if you are not telling them what to buy for you. But the notion that it is less rude to tell them how to spend their money than to demand that they hand it over directly is peculiar (not to mention unattractive) logic.

Our long-term hope is to empower gracious brides like you to trust their better instincts and reject such bad advice, but since you have already succumbed, we will endow you instead with poor short-term memory.

When guests ask where you are registered, put on your best dumb and dreamy bride face and say, "Oh I can't remember. My friends/family recommended one of their favorite places and I can't for the life of me think of the name. Emma/Mom will know," and change the subject.

DEAR MISS MANNERS:

I am in the very early stages of planning my wedding, and I believe that the current practice of couples scouring discount and department stores with a scanner, labeling everything they might possibly want so people may get it for them, is unbelievably crass.

There was a time when a wedding registry had the purpose of letting people know what china or silver pattern the couple preferred, so that guests who so chose could buy a single place setting with the comforting knowledge that others would be buying the same matching pattern. I would like to return to this practice, and only select a china, silver, and crystal pattern, and let others who do not want to buy these items choose something on their own.

My fear is that when guests go to the store that I have listed as the store where I am registered, the current practice of registering will cause them to believe that the only gifts I want are china, silver, or crystal. This is certainly not the case, and I would be happy with whatever gift they felt was appropriate (or no gift at all, if they so choose). Should I attempt to convey my philosophy of registering in a separate card, or just let them think what they will and see what happens?

GENTLE READER:

You had us until "the store that I have listed." The key is all in the advertising—or lack thereof. If you don't tell your guests where they should buy their gifts for you, they won't assume that that is their only choice.

We're afraid that you must pretend harder that you would be happy with or without whatever gift your guests deem appropriate and only give out your pattern preferences when pressed (or better, when friends and family are pressed).

DEAR MISS MANNERS:

Apparently, a service now exists that allows a couple to "register" for their honeymoon, rather than for a china or silver pattern. I have always carefully instructed our daughter, who is being married next year, that a wedding is not a fund-raiser—but as she points out, correctly, most guests will give gifts. So, she would like to know what the difference is between a guest looking to see the loving couple's preference of china pattern, or their preference of honeymoon locale? I have to admit that she has me stumped. I desperately would like to know whether or not there is, indeed, a difference.

GENTLE READER:

What exactly would her guests be paying for at this honeymoon locale? A night in the hotel room? A gift is supposed to be a tangible item, not a lifestyle choice. Finding out a china pattern preference is quite different from financing a vacation. After all, what would the bride do if she wanted to return it?

DEAR MISS MANNERS:

1. We are making Herculean efforts to downsize before we marry. Previously acquired wedding china, silver, etc., comes to the merger. Our simple wedding is morphing into a huge affair; he wants church, immediate family and friends, and I am indulging him.

   Many prosperous friends and colleagues inquire as to the gift registry: we need neither gifts nor money. His extensive network of "best friends" has indulged him in prior weddings. I am sure they could use a break. Is "no gifts pretty please" on the invitation inappropriate?

2. I suggested a donation to one's favorite charity instead of a wedding gift. Better yet, donations to MY favorite charities. He says this is especially tasteless and self-serving.

3. It seems that captive audiences, such as weddings provide, are becoming a forum for expression. At a recent wedding reception I received a card with the address of a charity and an announcement that the happy hetero couple supported gay rights "so everyone can have the right to marry." Okay, it's a wedding-related topic, indulge them. I am also seeing acknowledgments of deceased loved ones in the wedding programs lately.

If this is the trend I want to give lip service to MY favorite cause. As a widow, I dedicated my life to heart disease. The bride's side of the church knows this and would indulge me. Since the wedding is becoming a show I may as well exploit the situation.

GENTLE READER:

1. "Pretty please" doesn't make an unnecessary plea palatable. Leave it alone.
2. If you didn't keep writing MY, YOU would have a much better case for not being self-serving.
3. Your charitable sentiments are being upstaged by your desire to exploit—not the situation, but your own guests. This is neither a gracious indulgence nor a suitable punishment for your new husband's having too many best friends—or previous weddings.

DEAR MISS MANNERS:

I would like to offer a different perspective on your response relative to couples who request donations to charity rather than wedding gifts. I think their elders misunderstand their point of view. Many of our wonderful young generation see the world differently. While the older generation sees a tasteful vase, they see the pollution to the environment, near-slave labor, and depletion of the Earth's resources that went into making it. Perhaps they have no desire to surround themselves with things, however sentimental or tasteful, and prefer a more simple life, happy in the satisfaction to contributing to the sustainability of the Earth.

In today's world we are being buried in things. With the affordability of everything, it is easy to give in abundance. As a result, our lives are being consumed with managing all of our stuff.

I'd prefer to give young couples the benefit of the doubt. Virtually no one can abide by a "no gifts, please" request, so they have offered an alternative for those that simply must give something.

GENTLE READER:

You must be pleased by economic slumps. But no matter how much you try to shame us with visions of a kinder, more environmentally conscious and material-free generation, it does not take away from the fact that this couple is asking their wedding guests to pay for these values. If this couple truly doesn't care about material things, then they can simply return or donate the gifts to their charity of choice.

DEAR MISS MANNERS:

We received a mailed invitation to a wedding. We were planning on giving a gift. However, the invitation said that in lieu of gifts, the couple enclosed with the invitation a self-addressed, stamped envelope to their bank with one of their bank deposit slips so that guests would send checks to their account so they could get a home mortgage.

Is it still okay to send a gift, rather than a check to their bank? Or is the latter a new accepted etiquette?

GENTLE READER:

Perhaps you could really confuse them, and for your own amusement (or ours) send a present to the bank, since that is the address they provided. Yes, it is okay to ignore their appalling request and send them a present instead. Although the bank might appreciate it and even need it more.

DEAR MISS MANNERS:

My husband and I have been married for a year, and a few friends and in-laws constantly bring up the fact that they have not sent us a present. Generally we say something like, "Oh, we were just so happy to have you with us on our wedding day that we didn't expect anything else."

The person bringing up the topic then makes a show, promising to send something soon. However, at the next family or social event we find ourselves being drawn into the same awkward exchange with them. I have even been berated by a close in-law because the price of our china recently increased slightly. It seems she was all set to buy something, but then noticed the price had gone up and asked me to look into it.

I truly am not concerned about who did or didn't send us gifts.

I would be happy simply to have the subject drop. Might this stop as people observe the "one year limit" for giving gifts? Or is there a polite and correct way for me to put an end to this topic before we reach our next anniversary? I am tempted to send these individuals a thank-you note for thinking about getting us a gift just to be done with it.

GENTLE READER:

That would confuse them and shut them up, but we're afraid we cannot condone thanking guests for gifts not given—as much as they are asking for it. Unfortunately, you must simply continue demurring, and if your in-law asks again about the price of china, assure her that she shouldn't go to the trouble of giving it.

GIVING AND RECEIVING THANKS

⌒ *Is Thanking Passé?* ⌒

DEAR MISS MANNERS:

Three months ago I attended a wedding for a niece of mine and I have not received a thank-you for the gift I gave them. I was told by the mother of the bride that it is not necessary to send thank-you notes anymore. I have never heard of such a rude thing before.

GENTLE READER:

A fatal problem with amateur etiquette advice-givers (especially those who should have recused themselves from the situation out of a glaring conflict of interest) is that they do only half the job.

If the writing of thank-you letters is to be declared defunct, then the giving of presents must also be declared defunct. You cannot have generosity without gratitude. Miss Manners suggests you stop giving these people presents, and that you stop taking etiquette advice from them.

Should We Abolish It?

DEAR MISS MANNERS:

My wife and I attended the wedding of a close friend's son and dutifully selected a gift from their registration list. While wrapping it, I suggested that we include a note saying "We know you like the gift, so there is no need to write us a thank-you note. Please enjoy."

This sentiment appealed to me because I hate writing thank-you notes. We knew they would like the gift—they picked it out. Why not save them a little time as a sort of second gift? My wife was not, however, at all supportive of this plan and it ended there. Later, the bride wrote us a very gracious thank-you note.

Although I admit the idea doesn't feel quite right, if one applies the Golden Rule, it works. I would've appreciated receiving similar notes with our wedding gifts. And as more and more couples virtually select their own wedding gifts, maybe this is an idea whose time has come? I'm wrong, I suppose, but technically, why?

GENTLE READER:

Because you are hoping to subvert an important and time-honored ritual, even though Miss Manners admits that it has already been nearly drained of meaning.

That presents have come to be thought of as payment for hospitality is a repulsive notion that means that we are selling one another our social company. But if couples frankly started offering tickets for sale to watch them being married, Miss Manners doubts that they would have many takers. Once the sentiment is removed, people would realize that better entertainment, and probably better meals, are available elsewhere.

The sentiment in regard to presents comes from the thoughtfulness and generosity of the giver. As you have noted, gift registries kill the thoughtfulness part. You propose to kill the acknowledgment that there is still generosity involved.

Miss Manners cannot really blame you for thinking that there isn't much left to kill. But while even a part of it is still alive, she hopes that people will want to restore meaning to this ancient ritual, instead of just doing one another's shopping. Either that or dispose of present-giving entirely. When that happens, you will be thankful to hear that you will no longer have to express thankfulness.

⌒⌒ Dividing the Task ⌒⌒

DEAR MISS MANNERS:

When my great-nephew married a precious little blonde, they had several showers plus wedding presents from many people. The bride asked (or told) the groom to send thank-you notes to his side, and she would send them to her side. (Frankly, I have never heard of the bride not sending all of the thank-you notes.)

The groom never sent a thank-you note to anyone. There are many hurt feelings, and even after all this time it is still being talked about. I am sure neither the bride nor her mother is aware of this.

Who do you think is at fault—the groom who never was good at thank-you notes, the bride for not following up to make sure it was taken care of, or the mother of the bride for not overseeing this as she did everything else? The mother of the groom cannot be faulted, because she tried many times to get him to write the notes.

GENTLE READER:

At first, Miss Manners thought that only extreme family loyalty could leave a question in your mind about whose fault this shocking omission was.

After all, your great-nephew not only failed to write the notes that were expected of him, but led his wife to believe that he had done them. Apparently he still hasn't confessed. Do you not wonder why, when the matter was first mentioned, the gentleman did not say, "I'm no good at writing letters," and offer instead to perform some task that his bride preferred to avoid?

But when Miss Manners looked at your suspects, her own suspicions arose. Is there a bit of a sniff in your declaration that you never heard of a bridegroom's writing letters? It is, in fact, not uncommon. About two generations ago many couples abandoned the strict allocation by gender of household tasks and started sorting them by turns or by individual preference.

That you ignored the obvious and went so far as to suggest not just the bride but also her mother as candidates for blame is what made Miss Manners think there might be more here than the natural inclination to believe that there is no place for one's own family to marry except down.

She suspects a case of Female Fault—the sort of reasoning that has a wife forgiving her adulterous husband and casting all blame on the nearest (to the husband) female. Indeed, generations of ladies used to be admonished that they were responsible for making the other gender behave. If you think you might harbor such notions, Miss Manners begs you to banish them. They are neither fair nor seemly.

⟨The Wrong Division⟩

DEAR MISS MANNERS:

Since the majority of the '60s generation, especially brides, are slow with thank-you notes for gifts, could a self-addressed, stamped envelope with note paper be enclosed in the gift box? Brides enclose similar envelopes for R.s.v.p.s.

GENTLE READER:

Miss Manners sees that you are generously willing to forgo the give-and-take of present-giving by assigning the guest both the task of giving the present and thanking him- or herself for having done so. This doesn't seem quite fair. Perhaps such a bride ought to be allowed to buy herself a present and then thank herself or not as she prefers.

⌒ Deputizing the Task ⌒

DEAR MISS MANNERS:

I attended a grand wedding in my daughter's husband's family and sent them a pair of silver candlesticks. After quite some time, I received a thank-you note.

But the odd thing was that the note was not in the bride's handwriting but in her mother's! I know her handwriting well and so does my daughter. There is no mistaking it. The note was written in the first person—"I," not "they"—throughout. Such as "Bob and I really love the silver candlesticks, and they look so nice in our new home," signed with the daughter's new name.

Miss Manners, is this now an acceptable way of thanking someone for a wedding gift? To me, it almost borders on forgery. Nor does it do the daughter any favor, as she certainly isn't teaching her daughter the values of responsibility or honesty, do you think?

GENTLE READER:

It seems to Miss Manners that your friend has long since taught her daughter something about responsibility: namely, that she can get her mother to do her job.

DEAR MISS MANNERS:

I am a little disturbed about a new trend among some of my friends and colleagues—a new duty for bridesmaids, especially maids and matrons of honor: Many of my friends claim that one of the bridesmaids' duties is to write thank-you notes for the bride as this takes a lot of responsibility off of an otherwise stressed and busy woman who has so many wedding details to attend to.

Did I miss something? I was a bridesmaid five times and never

129 PRIMROSE PATH
BROOKDALE, CONNECTICUT

Dear Aunt Stacey and Uncle Trevor,

Darling Airhead gasped when we opened your box and saw the amazing brass elephant. What a unique idea. We both feel very comfortable with elephants and Darling is trying to decide whether it should be on the coffee table or on top of the bookcase. We hope you will come and see it — and us — once we get settled in our apartment. We're looking forward to seeing you at the wedding. Darling joins me in thanking you for such a handsome and generous present.

Darling sends her love with mine,

Orville

It doesn't matter whether the bride or the bridegroom writes the letters of thanks for wedding presents provided that these go out immediately after the arrival of each present and are not in the handwriting of the bride's mother. An expression of enthusiasm for the specific present is required, whether or not it is felt.

offered to do this! I am quite happy that no one offered to do so for me when I was a bride, because I find the new tradition a bit tacky. Although the bridesmaids are being thoughtful and doing something for the bride, I feel that the bride herself should take the time to write her own thank-you notes as a sign of her appreciation for the gifts. I personally do not want to receive a thank-you letter from someone other than the gift recipient.

After all, no one says the bride has to handle all of this responsibility solo. I did enlist some help—from my groom, since he also received and benefited from the gifts. Please let me know if I am correct in being disturbed by this latest trend.

GENTLE READER:

While they are at it, why don't the bridesmaids save the bride the trouble of writing little love notes to the bridegroom? Or take over the job of keeping him feeling loved while she is so busy?

The trend you mention—Miss Manners prefers that you not dignify this revolting change by calling it a "tradition"—is a steady increase in using bridesmaids as servants who needn't be paid and wedding guests as taxpayers who needn't be personally thanked.

⌒ The Form Letter of Thanks ⌒

DEAR MISS MANNERS:

At an extremely extravagant wedding I attended there was a printed card at every place setting at the dinner table stating, "Thank you very much for sharing this special day with us, and thank you for your gift."

Am I behind the times? I am twenty-seven and have been to many weddings, but never came across this. I thought a thank-you note was to be very personal, handwritten, and was to state the gift received.

GENTLE READER:

Personal? Do you think of the relationship between bridal couple and their guests as personal, rather than commercial?

Evidently these people think otherwise. They have provided an all-purpose, standardized receipt, which is not going to thrill those who had hoped to hear that whatever they had selected actually touched and pleased the couple. But Miss Manners can imagine that their method would be of advantage to those who had not selected a present and who can now forget about doing so, although honor would then require them to leave the card on the table.

~Donated Thanks~

DEAR MISS MANNERS:

A relative of mine recently got married. On the back of their wedding program they stated that "in lieu of thank-you notes for all the gifts you have given, we are going to use that money to donate to a local charity." Most of my family was speechless. Is this some newfangled way of getting out of responsibility?

GENTLE READER:

Yes. At least Miss Manners was not previously aware of people stooping quite so low as to suggest that expressing gratitude for the generosity of their relatives and friends was a waste of money when they could be putting poor children through college for the number of cents a stamp costs.

Yet the pious invocation of "charity" as an excuse for bad behavior has grown startlingly in the last few years. Embarrassing and dunning friends is supposed to be whitewashed by the claim that "it's for a good cause." As if decent human consideration of others were not a good cause.

Miss Manners can only sigh sadly over what a waste of money it was to give this couple wedding presents.

~Overdue Thanks~

DEAR MISS MANNERS:

Having been advised by a new bride that, according to Miss Manners, she had a year to get out her thank-you notes, I'd like you to clarify that time frame. I do not think a year is correct, but it seems to be a widespread notion.

GENTLE READER:

This is a fiction perpetrated by brides with writer's cramp. No, they do not have a year in which to answer. Miss Manners gives them about twenty minutes after the arrival of each present; more lenient souls admit the possibility of its taking up to two weeks. The highly rude notion that one can wait a year to express thanks seems to have originated from a perhaps willful misinterpretation of a correct rule: One can send a wedding present within a year after the marriage. But once received, a gift must be acknowledged immediately. And please tell that bride that Miss Manners is contacting her lawyer about a case of slander.

DEAR MISS MANNERS:

I never sent thank-you cards after I was married over two and a half years ago. After about a year had passed and I had not sent them, I was just embarrassed to.

But since then, thinking about how I did not send them makes me nauseous. I feel like a horrible, horrible person. I have to say this is the most terrible thing I have done (or not done). Is there any way to make it right? I'm torn between sending people apology notes, but I am afraid of what people will think, especially if they never realized they didn't get a thank-you note from us. Will they assume theirs got lost in the mail? Please, please help. Thank you.

GENTLE READER:

You are very good at groveling, Miss Manners is pleased to observe. That is what is needed. Something along the lines of "I have been criminally remiss in thanking you for your great generosity, and can only hope that you will be kind enough to forgive me . . ." along with an account of how much you have been enjoying using the particular present all this time.

⁓ Thanking for Money ⁓

DEAR MISS MANNERS:

Over half of the wedding gifts we received were gifts of money. How would one go about writing a thank-you card to someone for such a gift without sounding crude?

GENTLE READER:

However useful and welcome money may be, it is, Miss Manners would like to point out, a crude present. For one thing, the recipient knows exactly what it cost. The most graceful way to disguise this in your thanks is to select a real present on that person's behalf—that is, to tell the donor what you have bought or plan to buy with the money. The rest of the thanks can then apply to the present, as if the giver had selected it.

⟨Extracting Thanks⟩

DEAR MISS MANNERS:

I left a wedding gift in the form of a check at a wedding I attended several months ago. I had met the bride once before, years ago, but had never met the groom; thus far, I have not received any acknowledgment that my gift was received. It was cashed a month after the wedding, but I would like to know that it was received by the proper party. Is there any specific, correct waiting time before making inquiries? I could call the bride's parents, but do not want to embarrass them or their daughter unless necessary.

GENTLE READER:

You know, and Miss Manners knows, that what bothers you is not the presumption that the check was stolen and cashed with a forged signature but the likelihood that these ingrates took your money and never bothered to thank you for it.

To give a present to someone who doesn't even acknowledge it is galling. You shouldn't be ashamed to admit it—to admit it to Miss Manners, that is. You can't admit it to the ingrates or their relatives, because that would be a social declaration of war.

This brings us back to your claim that you are merely afraid that your present went astray. Indeed, that is the excuse used to point out that a present was never acknowledged. Miss Manners doesn't know why she forced your real feelings out of you, except as ammunition against the rude, who are given to claiming, on no evidence whatsoever, that "no one cares about receiving thank-you notes anymore."

In the case of a bought present, one voices doubts about the store where it was purchased, or the mail or delivery service, so as to avoid accusing the recipient. With checks it is harder, because you have evidence from your own bank that the check was received. By all means, question the parents (who seem to be the people you actually know) as to whether this is, indeed, their daughter's handwriting, with which you are not familiar. Let them figure out why you are not familiar with their daughter's handwriting, so they can pass the embarrassment on where it belongs.

TROUBLESHOOTING

DEAR MISS MANNERS:

My maid of honor was my sister, Luann, who has multiple sclerosis and is in a wheelchair. She performed all of the MOH duties perfectly, and nobody ever had any "problem" with her being in the wedding except one friend of the family, "Susan," who gave an audible gasp and began whispering when Luann came down the aisle.

At the reception, she came up to me and told me, within earshot of Luann, how "brave" I was having "a cripple" in my wedding, and then asked some very personal questions about my sister (like how she uses the restroom).

She then sat next to Luann and began talking and cooing at her like an infant and even tried to spoon-feed her some cake before my mother took her away. Susan made a nasty comment to my mother about how she was trying to "help" and then sulked and threw angry looks at my family for the rest of the wedding.

The only thank-you card I have left to write is the one to Susan. I just cannot bear to write it. I'd rather send the gift back. I never want to speak to or see her again. Just this once, can I forgo this thank-you note?

GENTLE READER:

We are afraid not. What you are thanking her for after all is her present, not her demeanor. And you cannot directly redress her behavior, however much it may be deserved.

You have our sympathies, and just this once we will allow you to forgo the format of a properly written thank-you letter, which never begins with the actual words "thank you"; this practice relies on the generous pretense that there might be other reasons to correspond with the gift-giver than being honor-bound to express gratitude. With this woman that is not the case. A curt "Thank you for the [whatever]" will do.

DEAR MISS MANNERS:

I received this "pre-printed" thank-you note for a wedding gift:

In the gifts around our home, we see the smiling faces of our brothers, sisters, and good friends. We hear their laughter and feel their embraces. Thank you for the lovely gift and the memories you helped create.

Our names were scratched at the top, but even the signature was printed. I was horrified. Is this a new trend?

GENTLE READER:

If it is a trend—never a justification for bad behavior—it is indeed horrifying, but also incredibly creepy. Who wants to see smiling faces, hear laughter, and feel embraces from inanimate objects? Did your friends register for a horror movie? Unfortunately, there is no proper response to this thoughtlessness, but should you ever want to visit these people's house, you might not want to be left alone in their living room.

DEAR MISS MANNERS:

What is the rule on thank-yous for wedding presents these days? If you were present at the opening of the present and they thanked you personally, does the recipient then not need to send a written thank-you? What if you were present during the opening of presents, but the couple did not get to your present before they got tired and quit opening?

GENTLE READER:

For small presents given in person, spoken thanks are enough, but serious presents still require letters—and all wedding presents are considered serious.

While you may feel slighted that the couple got tired before opening yours, we're guessing that it was much appreciated by the other guests, who were probably equally tired. You are owed a written thank-you letter only from the couple, however.

DEAR MISS MANNERS:

When I was helping my husband clean his car about a week ago I found, in the trunk, all of the thank-you notes from our wedding! Within a month of our wedding, I had written thank-you notes to everyone who sent a gift. I gave them to him and asked him to take them to the post office.

We have been married for almost a year and they are still in his trunk! I was livid, and he doesn't understand why. I tried to explain to him that it was horribly gauche to not acknowledge the gifts we received. It turns out that he has never written a thank-you note in his life and just doesn't get why it is so important.

I have seen many, but not all, of the people who gave us gifts, and none of them ever told me that they didn't get a thank-you note. Miss Manners, I am so very embarrassed! Since we are only two months away from our one year anniversary, would it be wrong to mail the thank-you notes? Could I open them, write an apology for the tardiness, and put them in a new envelope?

GENTLE READER:

Wait! Don't open them! There is a chance that the look of the envelopes, or the denomination of the stamps, will support your groveling cover letter about your horror at having just found these.

You needn't say why, as long as you pour on your horror and shame. The temptation to blame your husband will be huge (especially since he won't even acknowledge the gravity of the situation), but your marriage will be the better for it if you present a unified front. There will be a time when you will need his loyalty in return, and then, if you must, you can cash in.

Until then, encourage him to execute tasks in your domestic routine that he finds more pressing—while you maintain a firm hold on writing and mailing letters.

CHAPTER EIGHT

The Wedding

W HEN TELEVISION SHOWS make a special effort to boost their
ratings, they stage a wedding. The entertainment industry
knows how powerfully moving it is to watch two people undertake the
most formal and solemn commitment of their lives in a time-honored
ritual of the society—even when this is being done by fictional characters and portrayed by those who have made a notorious number of such
commitments before.

Why don't real people get that?

Why, instead of drawing on the power of the ritual, do officiants as
well as bridal couples now use the wedding ceremony to summarize the
love story, roll the credits, and supply biographical material? Why do
they undercut the formality with colloquial chatter and kill the solemnity with jokes? Why do they think that it is fitting to go public with the
kind of love patter that should be whispered in private?

Miss Manners understands tweaking the standard services a bit
to make them fit. It is generally recognized that "man and wife" is an
unfortunately unparallel phrase and that "to obey" is a vow best omitted

because it is destined to be broken. Wording will also have to be adjusted for weddings that involve same-sex couples or different religions.

But although she has taken a stand against the show business wedding, Miss Manners cannot understand why anyone would want to trash a classic script in favor of the sort of material that the entertainment industry stuffs into press packets.

Yes, the officiant and the couple might get a few charitable laughs for their amateur theatrics. For that, they sacrifice the homage that any serious wedding ceremony elicits: proud smiles, misty eyes, and long-married couples reaching out for each other's hands.

THE DAY BEFORE

At last, the wedding festivities begin. The bride, after months spent tracking down her dream dress, is wearing jeans and a T-shirt. Her mother is nowhere to be seen. The bridegroom is openly pitted against his affianced. Some of her bridesmaids are on his side, and all of them are running around shouting gleefully.

The wedding march is not being played. Softball is being played.

To the exasperated father who wanted to know when field day became a wedding ritual, Miss Manners can offer only the gentle assurance that it is not obligatory to hold one or to attend. The proper wedding minimum is about three hours, consisting of a ceremony immediately followed by a celebration. It is usual to hold something smaller the night before, and possible—but certainly not necessary—to stage a three- or four-day festival of sports, spas, dinners, brunches, tours, parties and, if the bride or bridegroom is royal, a parade through the streets for cheering subjects.

For most local guests, a wedding ceremony followed by a reception, which may or may not take the form of a meal, is quite enough. They have homes to go to before and after, and should not be made to long for them. For others, nothing may ever be enough, but the wedding hosts should not be made to long for their departure.

DEAR MISS MANNERS:

My sister is having a full wedding (the couple has lived together for a few years) and all of the immediate family is traveling from out of town. Most are returning immediately after the wedding, and my sister is upset that no one is staying over an extra day to watch her open her gifts. Is this a new tradition—watching the bride open gifts?

GENTLE READER:

How old is this bride? She seems to be confusing the tradition of the single-digit birthday party with her wedding. Watching people open presents, unless they are the joking offerings of a girlish shower or rare adult birthday party, is not a grown-up occupation.

The new tradition here, if you want to call it that, is the marathon wedding. Next-day parties featuring the bridal couple did not appear until everyone was willing to admit that the newlyweds had no particular desire to be alone together.

A guest's obligation, when attending a wedding, is still only for the ceremony and the celebration immediately following. If others want to hang around longer out of sentiment, curiosity about the wedding presents, or cheaper air fares, it is optional to plan events to entertain them. But guests are not obliged to stay and witness the marriage unfold.

THE NIGHT BEFORE

What are you supposed to do the night before the wedding?

Oh, stop giggling. Nowadays, people don't even do that the night of the wedding, judging from the number of weary wedding guests who beg Miss Manners to suspend the rule about staying at the wedding reception until the bridal couple leaves. Today's bridal couples aren't going anywhere while they still have anyone else left around to entertain them.

The problem of the night before the wedding is quite a different one.

Then everyone wants to party. People who came in from out of town don't want to watch movies in the hotel; they want to see who got invited and who got left out. The bridesmaids want to show everyone how good they can look when they choose their own clothes instead of that awful dress the bride chose, and they want to look over the groomsmen, who want to look over the bridesmaids.

Reunited classmates want to find out about the jobs their classmates got. Previously united relatives want to see how badly their replacements have aged. The bride's parents need a break with drinks. Even the bride is torn between the desire not to have bags under her eyes the next day and the feeling that it's stupid to do nothing, especially if there is anyone in town who might otherwise be involved in a form of entertainment that does not feature her at its center.

This is clearly not a time to improvise. The principals are so etiquette-logged by this time that they can't cross the street without trying to look up the correct order. There are so many relatives and friends available that to choose a few would inevitably insult others. So proper people look to tradition to tell them what to do.

Then they have a problem. It happens that there are at least three traditions for the same night, most involving the same people at differ-ent events. For example, there is the tradition of the bachelor party, and a more recent matching event in which the bride and bridesmaids, in the noble name of equality, endeavor to out-vulgar the bridegroom and groomsmen.

Then there is the very old custom of the bride's parents' dinner, in which people who are already at the social and financial breaking point are forced to give a major dinner party the night before a major event for which they can't figure out how to use the same flowers. And there is the more recent tradition by which the bridegroom's parents give that dinner, which presents them with an opportunity to get even with the bride's family for allotting their side so few invitations to the wedding.

The idea of both parental dinners is twofold: To make sure that the wedding party attends the rehearsal by tying up their evening and to make sure the wedding comes off by tying up the bridal couple's evening.

Miss Manners attributes the continuing popularity of separate last-night-out parties for the bridegroom and bride to the evening's stunning potential for outright disaster. One might presume that such a freedom-frolic would lose its zest for couples who have long been keeping house together, but perhaps its likelihood for creating a public cause of complaint between the couple actually adds some needed zest to the wedding itself. In contrast, the bride's parents' dinner would probably only strain the sanity of that couple and their relations with the new in-laws, which is why it has been pretty much dropped. For years the bridegroom's family got off free financially, on the idea that their son would take over the sole support of the bride forever, but not even the bride believes that anymore.

An increasing sense that it is only fair for both families to be involved has made the bridegroom's parents' dinner the most usual pre-wedding-night custom now. It is the one that has Miss Manners' vote, since she is squeamish about attending weddings of families in the state of open hostility likely to result from the other options.

She cautions the bridegroom's parents to remember that they must be just as fastidious about the dinner as if they had been undergoing the rigor that has been driving their counterparts nuts. They must include the spouses and para-spouses of the wedding party, and remember to invite hardship cases—elderly relatives, people who have traveled for months to get there—unless other social provision for these people has been made. It is, everyone should remember, a time to be socially generous to those with whom you are about to become cemented, like it or not.

THE CEREMONY

⌐ Taking Sides ⌐

DEAR MISS MANNERS:

I am in a bind over an invitation to the wedding of two friends. I met the bride and groom at the same party, therefore I know both of them equally and for the same amount of time. When I

This is the basic plan for standing at the altar, with bridesmaids and ushers fetchingly grouped in the background. However, it is charming as well as proper to gather the couple's other parents and such children as might have arrived in the marriage by proper or other means.

am asked at the wedding on which side I would like to sit, what side should I choose?

GENTLE READER:

The side with fewer people on it. While the custom is to seat the bride's side to the left and the bridegroom's to the right (the reverse for Jewish weddings), Miss Manners reminds you that it is not a soccer game with fans rooting for other sides.

DEAR MISS MANNERS:

When the bride's family and friends (as with the groom's) sit on the same side of the aisle as the bride and attendants, who stand, they cannot see the bride's face during the ceremony. All we can see is her back—as lovely as it may be! Nor can we hear her vows well.

I think the bride's and groom's family and friends should switch sides so that the faces of the bride and groom can be seen

The Recessional

This bridegroom is happy not only because he is in love but also because he was not required to conscript extra ushers so that the recessional would look like a mass wedding. The flower girl was told to sit quietly with her parents after the processional, but her jumping back in, drunk with attention, has been greeted with fond amusement by the guests. Being more mature than she, they realize that a wedding is not entertainment and therefore have refrained from applauding during or after the ceremony.

by those most important to them, and their words can be clearly heard. Even the bride's and groom's parents cannot see the faces of their children during the ceremony with the traditional seating arrangement.

Since I have three boys ages 9-16, my chances at effecting this change at one of their weddings are pretty small—if I'm still around when they decide to tie the knot! So I thought I should start with the popular front.

GENTLE READER:

Your chances are excellent if you have a confidential talk with your sons' ushers. Reversing the sides is fine with Miss Manners, and no one else can remember which side is which.

DEAR MISS MANNERS:

My son is marrying, and his father and I are divorced. I now have a female life partner (for 10 years); he (son's father) has not remarried. What are the rules about where we are seated at the wedding and the reception/dinner?

GENTLE READER:

Miss Manners' new rule is that parents and their attachments should be seated wherever they may be expected to have a reasonably pleasant and civilized time. Whether that is near or far in your particular case, you know better than she.

⌒ Gawking ⌒

DEAR MISS MANNERS:

During a wedding, when the bride is marching down the aisle, is it okay for all the pews of guests to turn around and gawk as she proceeds down the aisle? I seem to think it is just fine to watch her as she passes, but feel somewhat out of place since everyone else is rubbernecking. What is appropriate?

GENTLE READER:

Rubbernecking. Standing for the bride's entrance is a bit much in Miss Manners' opinion, but ignoring it would be cruel.

THE RECEPTION

The two styles of menus for wedding guests are Dainty and Heartburn. Dainty, which can be little more than finger sandwiches, wedding cake, and champagne or punch, is a bit more chic and a whole lot cheaper.

Nevertheless, Miss Manners does not advise administering this to families coming from one of the many traditions that consider that a wedding doesn't constitute a real union unless the guests reel away holding their bloated tummies.

In making such choices, the time of day is what counts. Are these people going to be starving? A morning or noon wedding, which is the most formal, is followed by a wedding breakfast, which, in the inscrutable vocabulary of etiquette, means a luncheon. An afternoon wedding requires teatime fare. In recent years, the standard American wedding has been held in the evening, which requires a full dinner and does not allow ladies the pleasure of wearing hats.

DEAR MISS MANNERS:

My fiancé and I have been saving and would like our wedding and reception to be a celebration, with as many of our family and friends as we can afford to host in attendance. We sat down with our budget and found that while we can afford to serve hors d'oeuvres, cocktails, and cake, we cannot afford to serve a full dinner.

Is it acceptable to hold an evening wedding ceremony (around 7 p.m.) followed by a reception at which only cake, hors d'oeuvres, and cocktails are served? We planned to note on the invitations that the ceremony would be followed by a cake reception so that none of our guests would come expecting a full meal. Most will be from out of town, so they would probably have to go out to a restaurant for dinner before the ceremony.

Is our frugal approach to the reception refreshments within the bounds of acceptable etiquette, or are we on the verge of committing a social *faux pas*?

GENTLE READER:

Your guests will be committing many. They will be rushing their waiters, showing up late for the ceremony, and—warning or no warning—whispering to one another, "Can we sneak out and get a hamburger?" Miss Manners has never understood the preference for evening weddings when daytime ones are more sophisticated, but marrying during the dinner hour and not providing dinner is unfair to your guests.

⌒ The Long Wait ⌒

DEAR MISS MANNERS:

We waited for two hours at one wedding reception, and the bride and groom showed up as we were leaving. They were joyriding in their rented limousine. At another we waited an hour and a half while pictures were taken. My mother (who was once kept waiting three hours at a wedding reception) told me that in her day photos were taken a week in advance so that delays were avoided. We can't figure out what has changed.

GENTLE READER:

What has changed is the concept that guests are guests. These people seem to think of them more as a background crowd with nothing better to do than to stand around until there is something to watch. The first couple preferred to entertain themselves, rather than their guests, and the second wedding was aimed at posterity, rather than at those in attendance. That their victims don't retaliate by simply going home when they are ignored is, Miss Manners believes, a miracle of manners.

⸺ The Receiving Line ⸺

DEAR MISS MANNERS:

My fiancé and I are hosting our own wedding. We are both young and on good terms with our families, but we are doing all the planning, inviting, and paying. Many of the guests will be friends of ours and strangers to our parents. Nevertheless, we would like to preserve the nice Jewish custom in which the bridal couple does not appear before the guests until the wedding ceremony itself, and we would like to leave before the end of the party. This would put our parents in the position of greeting and sending off our guests. Is this appropriate etiquette? If so, how should the situation be handled? Or does our position as hosts require that we be present from beginning to end?

GENTLE READER:

You are in luck, Miss Manners is happy to tell you: Your wishes exactly coincide with correct wedding etiquette, which is different from host etiquette at normal parties.

The Receiving Line ~ *Informal Wedding*

Proper Remarks ~ (L to R)

[*To bride's mother*] "What a lovely wedding." [*To bridegroom's mother*] "What a lovely wedding." [*To bride*] "I wish you great happiness. You're such a beautiful bride!" [*To bridegroom*] "Congratulations! You're a lucky man." [*To matron of honor*] "What a beautiful wedding. And you look so lovely."

All responses to remarks above are, "Thank you—I'm so glad you could be here."

Guests are not received before a wedding ceremony, but at the beginning of the reception, even if it is in a different location. By that time, you will be a married couple, able to take your place in line with your parents.

You are supposed to leave the reception before the guests, a privilege granted only to bridal couples and presidents. Off you go, in a shower of—well, seldom rice these days, but rose petals or bubbles—leaving your parents to see off guests whom they now know.

The Receiving Line's Order

DEAR MISS MANNERS:

My husband and I are giving my stepson a small wedding reception soon and need your advice on receiving-line etiquette. Both the bride's parents and the groom's parents are divorced and are either remarried or seriously involved with another. The reception is small, only fifty to seventy-five people. It is formal, with candlelight dining. My husband is paying for most of the expenses. The bride's mother is also contributing. The bride's father and the groom's mother are not contributing to the occasion. In what order should the receiving line be?

GENTLE READER:

In order of the size of their financial contributions, Miss Manners supposes you expect her to say. Deadbeats need not apply.

Well, money has nothing whatever to do with it. The custom is for either the mothers of the couple, or their mothers and fathers, to receive with the bridal couple. If you and the bridegroom's mother get along well, you might join them as a hostess, but Miss Manners hopes you will not make an issue of it. There are too many extraneous people here, some of them not even related, and they will all be screaming to be treated "fairly."

However, you asked only about the order. If you want to have a receiving line nearly as long as the guest list, Miss Manners will put her feelings aside and give you an order:

1. The bride's mother
2. The bridegroom's father
3. You
4. The bride's mother's husband
5. The bridegroom's mother
6. The bride's father
7. The bride's stepmother
8. The bride's stepfather

And oh, yes—then the bride, bridegroom, and bridesmaids. Except for the bridegroom, gentlemen (fathers and groomsmen) may be excused from receiving-line duty if they insist.

Note that this is not "order of importance." The traditional idea is to mix up the two families (bride's mother, bridegroom's father, bridegroom's mother, bride's father). Miss Manners has merely added the rule, when families are mixed enough already, of avoiding juxtaposing people who used to be married to each other, or to each other's spouses. It makes far too interesting a spectacle for the guests.

DEAR MISS MANNERS:

My daughter is getting married next summer. Her father and I divorced 10 years ago and have very little contact. He married his mistress. They have invited her parents to the wedding. As the mother of the bride and hostess of this event, how do I greet these people?

"Nice to meet you"? No. "Thanks for coming"? No. I am not happy to meet them nor will I be happy they came. My daughter does not have a relationship with these people.

GENTLE READER:

Oddly enough, "Nice to meet you" is never the correct remark to make for a first encounter. It is true that the French always declare themselves enchanted, but we wary Americans consider this judgment premature. "How do you do?" is the correct greeting, and Miss Manners promises you that to say it, you do not need to care how they do.

⌒ The Case Against Receiving Lines ⌒

DEAR MISS MANNERS:

I feel that a receiving line is unnecessary—that mingling and greeting the guests individually at the reception is more personal. Several of my co-workers believe that the traditional receiving line is mandatory for the 250 guests who will be attending our wedding.

GENTLE READER:

Let us say that you got Miss Manners to agree with you. "All right," she would declare, "no receiving line, provided you guarantee that the key figures of the wedding will all greet every single one of those two hundred and fifty guests personally, making absolutely sure not to miss any."

How would this be managed? Well, the bride, bridegroom, and at least some of the parents, as hosts, would all have to stand by the door to be sure to get everyone entering. *Poof!* You have reinvented the receiving line. Now perhaps you can tell Miss Manners why the very name of such a practical and hospitable institution frightens people.

DEAR MISS MANNERS:

Whatever happened to the receiving line at wedding receptions? It seems as if the current trend is to "announce" the wedding party as they arrive at the reception. Having stood in a few receiving lines myself, I understand how tedious they can be, but how else does one greet one's guests? If one is a guest at such a wedding, when is the proper time to approach the bridal couple to offer good wishes, or the parents to thank them for their hospitality?

GENTLE READER:

Here is what happened to receiving lines: People who spend fortunes on showy weddings, complete with fancy clothes and decorations, decide that a receiving line is "too formal." What exactly they think is a more formal occasion than a wedding, Miss Manners cannot say.

Instead, they decide, they will just move around the reception, saying hello to everyone there. Only they don't. They get caught up chatting, dancing, eating, and being photographed, and leave it to their hapless guests to catch them when they can.

⟶ *The Menu* ⟶

DEAR MISS MANNERS:

My fiancé is Italian and I am Yugoslavian. He would like Italian food served at our reception. I do not want to make my side of the family feel left out by serving Italian dishes only, nor do I want a mishmash of international courses or dishes representing both sides. In fact, I do not want to make an ethnic statement at all with the food. I simply want something neutral (roast beef, for example) that just feeds everyone.

My fiancé will not agree to this compromise and claims his side will be offended. My family is willing to go with the Italian food, but I am not. This will only serve to have the meal slant the wedding to one culture.

GENTLE READER:

In the New World we don't consider eclectic menus to be "an international mishmash," but rather the interesting use of different traditions. This is especially appropriate when it is likely to flatter and please the guests, not to mention the bridegroom.

It has not escaped Miss Manners' attention that you are marrying into a family of Italian origin, as he is into a family of Yugoslavian origin. Casting out both traditions for the sake of fairness is a bad way to start a marriage. Hardly better is the notion that everything must be exactly equal. If both families felt strongly, you should try to please both in the menu. But if your family doesn't care, what possible reason is there not to please his?

DEAR MISS MANNERS:

We are planning a wedding dinner for fifty guests. The caterers offer three entrée choices, with selections to be made in advance. This plan would entail response cards listing choices, a seating chart, place cards, etc. It seems to me that we, as hosts, should simply decide on a single entrée as we would if the dinner were at our home.

GENTLE READER:

Miss Manners shares whatever exasperation you may feel that people cannot simply sit down nowadays and eat—or not eat—whatever is put in front of them. They have to whine about it. There were always restrictions because of religion or allergies, long before people began scrutinizing their plates for moral or nutritional implications, but polite people accepted graciously what was offered, eating what they could and ignoring the rest.

Home entertaining has now had to alter slightly as a result of the society's preoccupation with what it eats—or food fussing, to use the technical term. A good host is by no means obliged to provide different meals-on-order for everyone, but does attempt to have a wide-ranging menu that will give at least some sustenance to everyone. Try to do the same for the wedding dinner. Miss Manners finds the project of having guests order in advance not only ridiculous and cumbersome but ultimately futile, as no two or three choices could possibly accommodate all the variations now in common practice.

⟋The Bar⟍

DEAR MISS MANNERS:

Do you think it is appropriate to have a full or partial cash bar at a wedding reception? Some co-workers and I were wondering if it would be rude to ask your guests to pay for a drink, or whether today's economy warrants such actions.

GENTLE READER:

Miss Manners is going to take to drink herself if she keeps having to listen to that argument. No, you cannot use the economy as an excuse for the extreme rudeness of charging your own guests for their refreshment.

Have you never heard of the blesséd poor who share what little they have, while vile and greedy people who begrudge sharing are accursed? If you can't afford liquor at your wedding reception, serve tea or punch. If you can't afford that, serve water. But serve it graciously.

DEAR MISS MANNERS:

What's your beef with a cash bar at wedding receptions? Weddings are incredibly expensive, and a couple starting out shouldn't have to go in the hole for thousands of dollars just to throw a reception where Miss Manners and a bunch of other deadbeats can have unlimited liquor. I thought you were a classy broad!

If we should encounter one another at a wedding reception then your first drink will be on me and you can hustle the rest yourself! I DARE YOU TO PRINT THIS!

GENTLE READER:

Suppose you go first and explain why anyone would want to stage a thousands-of-dollars event for people whom they think of as deadbeats, and why other people would want to attend the wedding of those who thought that of them. This will give Miss Manners a moment to think of a tactful way of saying that she does not care to drink with you.

⁓ The Discriminatory Bar ⁓

DEAR MISS MANNERS:

A friend told me that at her wedding reception she plans on having champagne for the wedding party only. I think it is rude and ill-mannered not to include everyone. I have suggested that since they cannot afford champagne for everyone, they shouldn't have it just for some. Instead, they should just have it for themselves after the reception is over. She says this has been done at other weddings (which should not justify it as being proper).

GENTLE READER:

It sure doesn't. The perversions of hospitality being practiced at modern weddings would make your hair curl, Miss Manners trusts. However, this has got to be high among them. If one cannot afford something special for one's guests, one does not consume that very thing in front of them. Nor does one invite certain people and then demonstrate to them that they are second-class guests.

Did the bridegroom have a part in this idea? If not, Miss Manners worries about him. If so, she only worries about their children.

⌒In Which the Bride and the Bartender Fight over the Tips⌒

DEAR MISS MANNERS:

At a wedding reception where there is an open bar, there is a large brandy snifter, vase, glass jar, whatever on the bar. Who is the money which is left by the guests meant for? I say it is a tip for the bartender. My daughter says the money is for the bride and groom. Please advise as to who is correct.

GENTLE READER:

Nobody. Everybody here is so incorrect that Miss Manners feels like offering you all the change in the bottom of her purse just to go away. There is no correct use of a large brandy snifter on the bar at a wedding reception except for the convenience of a guest requesting brandy; the vase should be used for flowers, and the glass jar should have been thrown away once the maraschino cherries were used up. At a private function, it is not customary to tip the bartender, much less the bride.

⌒The Seating Plans⌒

DEAR MISS MANNERS:

Why do brides take it upon themselves to arrange seating charts like a fourth-grade teacher? Since their guests are presumed to be adults, can't they make their own decisions about whom to eat with?

I attended a cousin's wedding halfway across the country. A sizable contingent of my family was going, and since I am fond of them and do not often have the chance to see them, the opportunity seemed worth the airfare and hassles of travel.

But we were assigned tables for dinner, and while most of my family sat at one table across the room, I ate with eight total strangers. (Since I am perceived as single, the invitation was for me only, and I did not bring my significant other.) While these people were all very pleasant, I would have preferred to spend time with my family.

Shortly after, I attended the wedding of a college friend where the guests fell into two categories: dear friends I haven't seen in some time, and people I had hoped never to see again in my life. Again we were assigned tables, and you can guess where I was assigned. Granted that the meals only last an hour or so. But when you've traveled a great distance to see people you haven't seen in years, time is more valuable.

GENTLE READER:

The reason that adults can't find their own seats at a wedding is that they turn childish and start turning over chairs to save seats, arguing about where they want to be, feeling no responsibility for wallflowers, and so on. For a formal meal, seating should be worked out in advance.

But these brides were operating on the assumption that the only social desire of single people is to meet other single people. While weddings are traditional sources of other weddings, such is not always the case. Weddings also function as family reunions, and this should be taken into account. Alternating family seating groups with ones including strangers likely to be of interest romantically or socially is a sensible compromise.

⟨ The Favors ⟩

DEAR MISS MANNERS:

I have been having a hard time picking out wedding favors within our budget that will make it further than the garbage can once our guests return home. We have allotted one to two dollars per guest. Our gift budget does not lack as a result of money being improperly allocated; we have needed to find many ways to cut corners.

My fiancé and I have thought to instead donate the money to

an organization which does research on the terminal illness to which we lost his mother a couple of years ago. Do you think that our guests would appreciate the sentiment, or be miffed that they were not given individual gifts? Would we be better off giving each guest some cookies or candies?

GENTLE READER:

Who told you that you had to give out wedding favors? Etiquette has never thought of weddings as comparable to children's birthday parties, where the guests might need consolation for not being the center of attention.

Donating money for medical research is a fine idea if you can manage it, and Miss Manners commends you. But it has nothing to do with your wedding guests. It cannot be construed as any sort of favor to them. You owe them only the hospitality of the occasion. Drawing attention to your having considered, and then decided against, giving them little presents will not strike them as charming.

The Toasts

DEAR MISS MANNERS:

When our daughter got married, a strain developed between the groom's parents and ourselves. They chose not to speak at the rehearsal dinner or the wedding. I'm sure no one has to speak about their son or daughter, but isn't it strange?

GENTLE READER:

As these people are now your daughter's parents-in-law, Miss Manners urges you to put the omission down to an oversight or stage fright and relieve that strain. Only if you promise to do so will she tell you, for the record, that yes, if the bridegroom's parents give the rehearsal dinner, his father (or mother) should welcome the guests with the first toast, to be returned by the bride's father, after which anybody who is so moved, sober, or brief may offer one. At the wedding reception the best man offers the first toast, and others may follow, including the bridegroom, to offer toasts to his bride and to her parents.

DEAR MISS MANNERS:

My girlfriend has honored me with the task of being her matron of honor at her wedding. She is a dear friend and I want to be a part of her special day.

However, since becoming engaged, her fiancé has become increasingly controlling. He has "forbidden" her from traveling without him even if it's to visit her family. He refuses to even "allow" her to spend the night before the wedding in a suite with her wedding party, instead insisting that she sleep with him! Her parents haven't been huge fans of her fiancé either, but in the end just want her to be happy . . . and he seems to make her happy, I guess.

I have to give a toast at the wedding. I have nothing particularly nice to say about the groom, but don't want to make an awkward speech that totally ignores him. I'm waiting for the right words to come to me, but I'm just not coming up with anything. What do I say?

GENTLE READER:

The matron of honor is not required to endorse the bridegroom. Miss Manners suggests that you let the best man do that, if he is so inclined.

Even if you thought the gentleman to be the catch of the century, your toast should be more of an appreciation of the bride, along with your wishes for the couple's happiness. Your public compliment to him, which you can surely say sincerely, is "You're a very lucky man."

⌒⁓ The Music ⁓⌒

DEAR MISS MANNERS:

When attending a wedding reception and sitting with friends or family one may not have seen for some time, it would be most enjoyable to concentrate more on companionship than on the loud band. As the volume goes up louder and louder, it becomes impossible to hear what the person next to you is saying. One must leave the table and find a quieter spot to catch up. Would it be rude to ask that the volume not be so loud? Or is this standard at wedding receptions? Very inconsiderate.

GENTLE READER:

Yes, it is—inconsiderate, standard, and loud. But before you take that as Miss Manners' encouragement to stop the wedding by saying, "Will you kids please quiet down; some of us are trying to talk!" she must ask how you plan to make your request. You cannot, of course, disturb the wedding, and you cannot step in and manage it. What you can do is to take one of the hosts aside—make that the parent with whom you are connected—and ask plaintively, "Is there somewhere the guests at my table can go to talk? We don't want to bother anyone, but we can't hear ourselves over the music."

⁓ *The Dances* ⁓

DEAR MISS MANNERS:

I am curious about the tradition of wedding dances. What is appropriate for an evening wedding with a band or DJ? We have the happy couple's First Dance. Then there is the Father/Daughter Dance, followed by the Mother/Son. By now all the guests at the reception are happily chatting amongst themselves, no longer paying attention, and we segue into the Son and Mother-in-law, etc. How long should the dances be, and how many should there be?

GENTLE READER:

The idea is for the bridal couple to open the dancing, not to give a private dance featuring their relatives, while the guests' function is to stand around admiring them.

Or not. No wonder couples confess to nervousness about the simple act of dancing with each other. Getting married is not a sufficient qualification to stage a dance performance before an audience.

Miss Manners gathers that you have heard about those lists in which the order of dancing is specified for a long line of relatives and attendants, regardless of whether or not they are on speaking terms. Such overplanning arises from the suspicion that the gentlemen of the wedding party are innocent of the requirement to dance with the principal ladies instead of following only their personal preferences.

The idea is for the parents to dance with the couple and one another, and by the way, it would be nice if the gentlemen asked Granny to dance, too. And for the guests to be treated as guests. Guests should not be kept waiting, even the full length of one dance. Halfway through the bridal couple's dance, the bride's father cuts in to dance with his daughter and the bereft bridegroom turns to his mother (this can also be done with the respective in-laws first). At this point, the bridesmaids and groomsmen should take to the dance floor and encourage the other guests to follow.

Presumably, the bridal couple's enjoyment is in gazing at each other, not in being gazed at.

DEAR MISS MANNERS:

During the planning of my daughter's wedding, I frequented a forum where planning a wedding is discussed. Although I found several topics a bit disturbing, the one that bothers me the most is what is referred to as a "dollar dance."

I'd never heard of it before. It seems the guests pay to dance with the bride. Many posters found the idea tacky and offensive, as did I. Some said it was tradition in their part of the country or in their culture. Some said it's just a dollar and will help pay for the honeymoon. I never joined in on that particular subject, but I was wondering, what do you make of this?

GENTLE READER:

You must have stumbled on a site for taxi dancers, but the poor things are being given shocking advice.

Miss Manners does not doubt that money is to be had by offering the bride for short rentals, but it is a distasteful way to begin a marriage.

DEAR MISS MANNERS:

As someone in the wedding party, how can I avoid participating in the dollar dance without seeming sullen or judgmental? I know that I can't say anything to her about it; I just want to seem supportive and game without being an accomplice to their money-grubbing behavior.

GENTLE READER:

You could occupy yourself by being an exceptionally thoughtful bridesmaid, asking any gentlemen who seem isolated to dance with you. Or by powdering your nose.

If you are caught and queried, however, Miss Manners suggests your saying charmingly, "Oh, I think he is priceless—and certainly beyond my reach."

PROCEDURE FOR WEDDING GUESTS

1. It goes without saying (ha) that all guests will have replied to the wedding invitation the moment it arrived, using the same style (third person or informal letter) in which it was written, and on behalf only of those to whom the invitation is addressed. Now they must fulfill a pledge to show up, dressed according to the formality of the occasion (neither in white, red, nor, except for gentlemen's evening clothes, black), rather than defying it in the name of comfort or personal style.

2. They will have been moved to send (but never bring) wedding presents, bearing in mind that it is not necessary to give more than a

note of congratulation to an acquaintance whose wedding they do not care to attend. While it is desirable to please the couple, neither is it necessary to comply with any rude attempts to direct what the guests are to buy, donate, or contribute.

3. At the reception, they must head for the receiving line immediately upon arrival. Only after telling the bride's and bridegroom's mothers and any fathers present that it was a beautiful wedding, the bride that she is beautiful and that they wish her the best, the bridegroom that they congratulate him, and the bridesmaids that they look beautiful, may they head for the bar. They are expected to socialize with other guests, but not to use the occasion to inquire into these people's prospects of being married.

~"And Guest"~

DEAR MISS MANNERS:

I am a divorced woman. When I am invited to a wedding, birthday, or any other special occasion, it is addressed to me "and guest."

Is it customary for the guest to pay some of the expenses, such as for his dinner or for the gift? I assume that since he is my guest, I do not expect him to pay for anything. However, what if he asks or wants to contribute? In the card, if I am paying for the monetary gift that is enclosed, do I sign my name only, or do I write his name too, although he made no contribution? Does he also write in the guest book? Since I am inviting him to go to the party with me, is it customary for me to pick him up, since I'm going there anyway?

GENTLE READER:

You are asking for rules on a practice that Miss Manners considers wrong. Inquiring of one's friends, "Who is that charming man you've been seeing?" so as to invite him by name is one thing; giving one's guests two slots each, the other to be filled however that person wishes, is another. The result is that occasions that should be celebrated by one's intimates are half populated by strangers.

Now Miss Manners will pull herself together and address the reality of the situation. Yes, the gentleman is your guest and should not be asked to pay anything, or to buy a present for a stranger. Who drives whom is a matter of convenience. As he did attend, his name should appear with yours in the guest book. That at least gives his hosts a chance to find out afterward who was there.

⁓ Fielding Questions ⁓

DEAR MISS MANNERS:

I have just received the joyous news that my younger brother is to be married in a little over a year. While I share his excitement, I am already dreading the wedding day for one reason: I am gay.

In and of itself, this should not cause such strong anxiety. However, I anticipate seeing many of my more distant relatives who are unaware of my sexual orientation. I expect them to start asking me (and my immediate family) questions about my plans for marriage, as I am nine years older than my brother.

Because I am open at almost any other social function, I would probably just tell them the truth and add that I have been living happily with a wonderful man for several years, dismissing any distress at that response as the inquirer's problem. At my brother's wedding, however, I feel that such honesty would detract attention from my brother's special day and place it unwillingly on me.

I don't want to offend my relatives, as such questions are neither prying nor insensitive and are politely meant to engage me in friendly conversation. Yet I would like to discourage such conversation from the beginning. To complicate matters, I expect that my lover will also be invited to the wedding, as my other immediate family members welcome him as a member of our family.

GENTLE READER:

Miss Manners appreciates your delicacy in not wanting to make your brother's wedding into a coming-out party for yourself. She also would like to note that "When are you going to get married?" is about the most unpleasant conversation opener there is, for anyone of whom it might be asked, at a wedding or anywhere else.

But she notices that the wedding is a year off. Surely your family will have some opportunity to be in touch, informally, during that time, with the relatives who will be attending. They could easily slip in a pre-introduction to your lover and mention how happy they are to have him in the family. Although Miss Manners does not believe in announcing anything about one's sex life, your living arrangement is properly of interest to those who care about you.

Badly Behaved Guests

DEAR MISS MANNERS:

When my wife and I get invited to the wedding of a son or daughter of our friends, we usually don't go to the church part but always go to the wedding reception. We make sure to talk to the bride and groom and always bring a gift.

The reason that we don't go to the church is because I'm not a religious person, my wife is not a member of a major religion, and this is known to our friends. But a number of people not involved in the weddings have let their displeasure be known to us in no uncertain terms. Are we obligated to go to the church if we want to exercise our desire to go to the reception? Are we inconsiderate, and does this give them the right to be rude to us?

GENTLE READER:

Miss Manners does not recall "the right to be rude" as being in the Bill of Rights and grants it to no one. But she can certainly see how you and your wife tempted these people beyond endurance.

Attending a wedding ceremony is not an expression of one's own religion or an endorsement of anyone else's. It is participation in a ceremonial milestone in the lives of people who are important to you in a way that merely attending their social events is not. What you and your wife have done in following your idiosyncratic reasoning unrelated to the understanding and customs of the society, is to establish the idea that you attend parties but not more serious events.

DEAR MISS MANNERS:

During our wedding reception a number of friends mentioned to us that the wife of one of my best friends was passing out bright (orange with black print) flyers for her new house-cleaning business. (Our wedding colors were orchid and black.) At the time I did not know what to say or do, so we did nothing. Should I have said something to her at the time? Is it too late to say something now? Was this proper?

GENTLE READER:

Please don't give Miss Manners false clues, however entertaining. For one awful moment, she thought your objection might be that the flyers clashed with your color scheme.

It would have been preferable to stop this outrage when it occurred, although Miss Manners sympathizes with your paralysis at the idea of reprimanding a wedding guest. You could have sent an usher to collect the flyers and hand them back to the offender with the explanation, "This is not a business occasion."

Now it seems pointless to make a fuss, unless you plan to take the unwise step of inviting this person to another party. In that case you could say, when you issue the invitation, "This will be a social occasion at which we prefer that business not be conducted." Better yet, you can have great fun turning the wedding anecdote into the kind of you'll-never-believe-this story that gets funnier, Miss Manners promises you, as time goes by.

DEAR MISS MANNERS:

We hope you can tell us what would be the proper etiquette technique when there are plenty of leftovers from the sweet table at a wedding reception. I say to eat what you want and take home any leftovers, knowing that it would be a waste of food if it's not eaten. My family says to eat what you want and leave the leftovers alone, or bring home any leftover pastries only if they are served at each table and the bride and groom don't mind that you take them.

GENTLE READER:

What did you have in mind here? Tapping the bridal couple on the shoulders during their last dance and asking them if you could run off with their food?

Miss Manners gathers that your plans involve more than taking home two bites of wedding cake to put under your pillow so that you can dream of your future spouse. Is going off with two or three layers of uneaten cake and the pastry platter more like what you were considering?

It is kind of you to worry about food waste, but that happens to be the hosts' problem. Perhaps they have plans for it. Perhaps, unless you plan to outlast them, not everyone will be finished eating by the time you decide that there is enough to sustain you later. Miss Manners has defended the practice of the so-called doggie bag at restaurants, but this case is different; there, the diner has purchased the food. Guests are offered refreshment at an event, not a share of the investment for future use.

DEAR MISS MANNERS:

As a bridesmaid in the wedding of my dear friend I was so happy to be a part of their special day. But after the wedding at the hotel bar I drank too much and participated in some inappropriate behavior with one of the bride's cousins in front of members of her family. I do not remember anything that transpired, and I am mortified. When I realized she was upset and "disappointed" I accepted responsibility and apologized. Can I ever regain her respect? How do I interact with her and her family now that I have made a fool of myself?

GENTLE READER:

It's a good thing you accepted responsibility, since everyone saw you. Makes it hard to blame it on poor staff work. But evidently your apology was insufficient. Perhaps it was of the level that would befit a one-time lapse at an ordinary party. For a wedding, you need something more.

Miss Manners suggests confiding in your friend that you are not just humiliated but terrified that you might have a serious drinking problem and have foresworn liquor (at least in her and her family's presence). She will be forced to switch from indignation to sympathy, which is at least a step back to friendship.

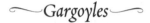

Gargoyles

DEAR MISS MANNERS:

My stepson is going to be married this spring. My husband's two ex-wives will be there. Am I required to speak or be civil to these gargoyles? The wedding is going to be a small home wedding, so there will be no graceful way of avoiding the two.

GENTLE READER:

Absolutely, Miss Manners requires that you be civil and speak to all the guests at the wedding. Unless, of course, your object is to inform everyone present that your husband is in the unfortunate habit of marrying nothing but gargoyles.

DEAR MISS MANNERS:

My stepdaughter will marry soon, and several immediate family members have asked me to keep the bride's mother—my wife—under control at the wedding. At my stepson's wedding, when my stepdaughter introduced a friend to her father with "Dad, I'd like you to meet Jane Doe; Jane, this is my father," my (sober) wife said in a loud voice, "He's just the sperm donor!"

In addition to uttering such a rude statement, I believed it poorly reflected the truth. The father of my stepchildren is an upstanding man and met his support obligations resulting from the divorce. He has maintained a good relationship with his children and with me. What do I say to my wife to try to avoid a repeat performance?

GENTLE READER:

"I hope you won't put me in a position where I will have to defend him in public."

TROUBLESHOOTING

DEAR MISS MANNERS:

My fiancé and I grew up 5,000 miles apart. It would be too expensive for us to pay for everyone to fly in to one central location for a wedding, and we need to know if etiquette allows for a wedding in one location and the reception in a completely different location (5,000 miles difference) and on different dates. I do not want anyone to feel slighted by not being invited, but we would feel horrible inviting people to an event that they would require a plane ticket for when we are not in a financial situation to pay for the tickets.

GENTLE READER:

There are many solutions to your problem, but somehow yours seems to be the least convenient, most expensive, and most baffling. Half get to witness the occasion, but go away hungry. Half are well fed, but emotionally empty since they didn't get to witness the very event they are celebrating. And for those who choose to get the complete experience, you haven't saved them money at all.

Your desire to pay for your guests' travel expenses is extremely generous, but it is neither expected nor necessary. Either choose one of the locations (traditionally the bride's) for both or hold it in the middle and let your guests decide whether or not they can afford the trip. If you would like to have an additional party (perhaps after the honeymoon) in the hometown of the other family for those who missed it, that would be acceptable and help assuage your sweet but misplaced guilt.

DEAR MISS MANNERS:

My fiancé and I are busily planning a smallish wedding and are expecting to have a handful (6 or 7) of younger guests with us. The children range in age from four to about 11. We are wondering if it's okay to have a kid's table at the reception?

It seems that the kids would enjoy each other's company more than boring adults, and having a break from the children might allow the parents to enjoy the reception more. We're having a plated dinner and have arranged for a special kids' meal to be served to the children (so there's no need for Mom or Dad to dish up plates).

We were going to make arrangements for a child minder (*not a guest*—a paid person) to sit at that table with the kids just in case someone decides to stab someone else with a fork, or whatever other hijinks a table of young children might get into. We were also planning on having some activities/toys/games on hand for the children to play with if the reception gets boring for them. Is this idea okay? Is it horribly rude to ask parents to sit away from their offspring? Is there a better way to handle this?

GENTLE READER:

On the contrary. It is thoughtful. But you might find that your grown-up guests will be clamoring to sit there, too. From what we've heard, what goes on at the children's table is exactly what adult guests keep trying to get away with: insulting one another, playing with their (electronic) toys, swapping seats, and demanding special foods. So leave a few extra seats available at the table.

DEAR MISS MANNERS:

Is it rude to leave a wedding before the bride? If yes, should a person not attend an evening wedding because the late hour does not agree with them? Does the excuse one has for leaving early make a difference—for example, a young resident doctor who has just completed an 18 hour shift versus a couple who just doesn't like to stay up late? Do the same rules apply to daytime weddings? Does it matter if the bride seems to hang around forever and never changes into a smashingly smart going-away outfit, serving as a clue for the guests that they are free to leave?

It seems as if the only entertainment provided for guests at weddings is dancing (often to music that thoughtlessly does not appeal to guests of all ages) and catching up with friends and family (which is made difficult by the previously mentioned music). The entertainment is supposedly provided for the benefit of the guests—if they receive no pleasure from it, why can't they leave?

My mother insists it is a supreme insult to the host and hostess to come and eat the food and then skedaddle—if too many people do it, the room is empty and loses the festive atmosphere. Your answer will help us at our next day, post-wedding ritual: drinking tea and tsk-tsking the details of the event.

GENTLE READER:

Let us help you with the essential question here: Is it rude to leave before the bride (joined presumably by the bridegroom, whom you don't mention, but whose absence at this juncture would provide much to your tsk-tsking the next day)? When weddings lasted a reasonable length of time and the smartly dressed couple did actually leave before their guests, it would have been rude to leave before them. As you point out, however, nowadays it is a challenge to outlast them. A good time to make a getaway is after the cake has been cut and served (and allowed a reasonable amount of time to be eaten). But if you want to earn the right to your tsk-tsking (and not become the subject of it yourself), you'll keep your sleeping habits and entertainment preferences quiet.

DEAR MISS MANNERS:

After the wedding of two dear friends of mine, there came a rather amazing moment when the bride and groom started cleaning up the joint while the guests were still enjoying the reception. This was a matter of dumb necessity, I gather: The hall had to be cleared out by a certain time, and the newlyweds wouldn't dare ask the guests to wash dishes and stack chairs, so they just started doing it themselves with a handful of guests immediately pitching in.

It was a frustrating situation, because on the one hand, one can't sit idly by, eating cake while others are busy cleaning. But on the other hand, one wants to stick up for one's rights as a guest and not let oneself be shanghaied into an impromptu work detail.

I could sense that the guests were unanimously thinking as I was: "The bride and groom should obviously not have to clean up on their wedding day ... surely, somebody else should be doing this ... but does that somebody have to be *me*?!" I did my part, and it certainly didn't kill me, but I'm wondering what the rules of etiquette dictate?

GENTLE READER:

Did the bride at least get to stop at midnight when her clothes turned back into rags and the mice took over? You and the other mice did the only thing you could, since clearly the couple must have had no other choice but to do what they did. It seems a bit unseemly, therefore, to dwell on your selfless act by citing your social status as a guest. Clearly, in this case, you have been outranked.

With Apologies and Best Wishes to the Bride . . .

DEAR MISS MANNERS:

As a bride-to-be, I've noticed a little bit of something resembling Open Season on Brides, even in your own lovely work. Brides all over are being chastised as being selfish, petty, insensitive, etc., these days.

In response, I'd like to make a few suggestions to the friends and family, and friends-and-family-in-law, of the bride-to-be:

- **Out-of-towners:** No, I did not schedule my wedding on your birthday or anniversary just to annoy you. I picked the date because it was the only day available in my church in the next calendar year. If you can't come, I'm sorry. If you do come, please don't complain to me about your accommodations, the food at the reception, or how much all this nonsense is costing you. I already know how much it costs. I'm helping to pay for it.
- **Close friends:** Don't ask me, "Why wasn't I asked to be a bridesmaid?" Please be careful not to rewrap and give me the gift I gave you for your wedding.

- **Attendants:** If you can't afford the expense, tell me when I ask you to be an attendant. Then I can offer to pay, or you can bow out gracefully. If you want some say in how the dresses look, keep your eyes peeled and help me shop. Please keep in mind that I'm dealing with a group of women of very different tastes and sizes and I'd like to please you all as much as possible. When invited to "preview" a dress before the decision, either go and look at it and give me your opinion, or don't complain about the choice made. Please don't fuss about the relative size or attractiveness of the other ladies or the groomsmen. They're also our friends.
- **Groomsmen and best man:** I spent months planning for this day. I would appreciate it if you would deliver the groom to the church on time, not noticeably suffering from the effects of too much alcohol.
- **In-towners:** If you can stand the thought, offer to put up some out-of-towners. You will claim my undying devotion. Offers to drive these people to the reception, to the airport, or wherever will also be greatly appreciated. Some day I may be able to return the favor for your child.
- **Family:** Talk about the "other" family quietly, preferably somewhere else, after the reception.
- **Everyone:** Please answer my invitation promptly. And don't do it with a phone call, either. If you don't want to get me a present or throw me a party, fine. There's no obligation. Just don't try to explain it to me. Please don't criticize my choice of china, crystal or silver—or husband. Don't ask me how much anything, or all of it, costs. Make an effort to socialize with anyone who looks lonely at the reception. Don't ask if you can bring a friend!

    If you could make an attempt to do the above, I'd appreciate it more than all the presents or parties in the world. And please—no more spoiled-bride anecdotes. I may snap and run after you, screaming, waving my Bridal Organizer.

GENTLE READER:

Miss Manners will thank you for this excellent lesson just as soon as she can control the blush suffusing her delicate cheeks. For, indeed, you are quite right that Miss Manners has allowed herself to become snappish during wedding season, when she has been overexposed to brides whose credo is After All It's My Day. Any sensible person who hears someone speaking in an imperious tone of "her day" would be wise to consider that it therefore isn't going to be anyone else's day, and to leave her to enjoy it alone.

To brides such as yourself, who try to plan a pleasant day for everyone, only to suffer the sort of treatment you describe, Miss Manners offers her apologies, sympathies, and pledge of assistance.

Index

Page numbers in *italics* refer to illustrations.

Academy Awards influence, 87
accommodations, 108, 143
afternoon weddings, 93, 258
alcoholic beverages, 3, 8, 108, 266–68
Anglo-American wedding format, 24
announcements, 108
    engagement, 34, 45–47, 170
    wedding, 176–78, 193–97
annulments, 17
applause, 94–95
assignment cards, 189
at-home cards, 194–95
attendance at weddings, 12
attendants, xii, 25, 123–33, 286
attire:
    for bridegrooms, *104*
    for brides, xiii, 73, 105
    for bridesmaids, 7, 12–13, *88*
    Queen Victoria's, 87
    for stepparents, 113–14
    for wedding guests, 73, 205, 274

baby showers, 54, 55
babysitters, 159–60, 162

bachelorette parties, 50, 204, 254, 255
bachelor parties, 112, 254, 255
bars, 266–67, 268
bartenders, 268
best man, 23, 25, 112, 124, 125–26, 270–71, 286
best person, 26
birth mothers, 109–10
boutonnieres, 112
bridal bouquets, 106, 112, 122, 153
bridal industry, xi, 3, 29–30, 31
bridal registries, 12, 22, 52, 64, 76, 171, 188, 220, 222, 227–28, 230–33, 234, 238
bridal showers, 8, 11, 50, 51, 54–57, 61–64, 113–14, 188, 204
bridegrooms, 13–14
    attire for, *104*
    family welcoming of, 107
    father of, 112–13, 117, 124
    honeymoons and, 121–22
    mother of, 111–13, 140–41
    reception performance of, 98
    thank-you letters and, 239–40
    wedding rings and, 15, 122

289

bridegroom's parents' dinner, 254–55
brides:
    advice to, 11–14
    attire for, xiii, 73, 105
    father of, 14, 107–9, 114, 115, 116–17,
      121, 183–84
    "giving away," 25, 115–16, 118
    mother of, 89, 107–8, 117–18, 121,
      124–25, 139–40
bridesmaids, 8, 12–13, 23, 129–30, 254
    abuse of, 9–10, 31, 32, 68, 128–29, 230
    attire for, 7, 12–13, 88
    duties of, 126
    expenses and, 8, 128–29
    financing dresses for, 85–86
    grounds for firing, 130–32
    at "personalized" weddings, 70
    pregnant, 126–27
    showers hosted by, 54
    tattoos on, 127
    thank-you letters and, 241–43
bridesmaids' luncheon, 55
bride's parents' dinner, 254–55
buffet-style meals, 19

calligraphy, 179, 191
cancellation notices, 95, 96
cash bars, 266–67
cash contributions, see donations, cash, as
    present; fund-raiser weddings
caterers, 185, 203, 265
Catholic Church, 93, 105
cell phones, 97
ceremonies, xii, 16
    altar grouping at, 256
    civil, 21, 143–44, 195–96
    as extravaganzas, 2
    formal church, 26
    religious differences and, 105
    seating arrangements at, 109, 255–57
champagne, 267
charitable donations, 83–84, 223, 234–36,
    244, 269–70
child-care facilities, 160
children:
    babysitters for, 159–60, 162
    engagements and, 35, 48

    as members of the wedding, 133, 149–50
    out of wedlock, 149
    parties for, 161
    at receptions, 282
    as wedding guests, 92, 118, 157–63
children's wedding party, 161
church weddings:
    facing the congregation at, 94
    hats worn at, 93
    mother of the bride and, 124–25
    open invitations to, 146–47
    same-sex couples and, 59, 223
    seating at, 109, 113
civil ceremonies, 21, 143–44, 195–96
commemorative platters, 120
congratulations, letters of, 195, 197, 199,
    274–75
corsages, 113, 114
country club receptions, 205
co-workers, 163–66, 172

dancing, 283
    "dollar dances," 273–74
    order of at receptions, 114, 117, 272–73
dates, setting, for weddings, 96–97
day before weddings, 252–53
destination weddings, 104–5, 107, 154–55
diamonds, 49
dinners:
    parental, 254–55
    rehearsal, 140, 270
    wedding, 75, 203, 257–58, 265–66,
      268–69
distant venues for weddings, 95–96, 201,
    281–82
divorce, 8, 21, 95
DJs, 120, 272
"dollar dances," 273–74
donations:
    cash, as present, 2, 3, 74, 75–76,
      78–80, 222–23
    charitable, 83–84, 223, 234–36, 244,
      269–70
    of food, 86, 189
    toward home purchase, 75, 79–80, 236
    toward honeymoons, 31, 75, 134, 199,
      273

in lieu of presents, 84–85, 122–23, 176, 230, 245–47
   suggested in invitations, 75, 76, 176
double showers, 55–56
"dress denim," 205

elopement, 5, 15–19, 29
e-mail invitations, 26, 170
engagement rings, 34, 37, 39, 40, 42–45, 46, 49–50
engagements, 33–65
   announcements of, 34, 45–47, 170
   bridal showers and, 8, 11, 50, 51, 54–57, 61–64, 113–14, 188, 204
   children and, 35, 48
   congratulations and, 47
   fiancé(e) defined, 34–35
   length of, 35–36, 66
   parental permission and, 40–42
   parties, 50–53, 74
   prenuptial contracts and, 57–59
   presents and, 46–47, 51–53, 60–61, 224
   proposals of marriage and, 11, 33–34, 36–40
   reactions to, 47–50
   same-sex couples and, 47–48
   soliciting cash and, 62–63
   thank-you letters and, 64–65
   troubleshooting and, 59–65
engraved invitations, 20, 179, 208–17
envelopes, 190–91, 207
   self-addressed, 64–65, 206, 240–41
etiquette misconceptions, 1–3
evening weddings, 259
expenses:
   bridesmaids and, 8, 128–29
   estimating, 11–12
   for guests' travel, 201, 281–82
   parental contributions to, 5–6, 7–8, 23, 67, 68–69, 71, 119, 121
   planning and, 119–23
   travel, 201, 281–82
   useless wedding paraphernalia and, 119–20

family harmony, 30–31
family-only weddings, 50, 51

fantasies, secret, and weddings, 67
father of the bride, 14, 107–9, 114, 115, 116–17, 183–84
father of the bridegroom, 117, 124
fiancé(e)s, 34–35, 45
filming of weddings, 89
financial frankness and weddings, 76–87
florists, 90
flower girls, 133
flowers, 7, 108, 120
food donations, 86, 189
foreign countries, weddings in, 225
Freedom to Marry Coalition, 223
fund-raiser weddings, 74–76, 224, 233
fuss, avoiding, and weddings, 16

garter, retrieving of the, 105–6
gay relatives and friends, 151–52, 276–77
   see also same-sex couples
gender roles, 23–25, 240
gift displays and weddings, 226
"giving away" the bride, 25, 115–16, 118
general principles of weddings, 1–32, 285–87
goody bags, 3
grandparents, 116, 151–52
greediness, 76–77
groomsmen, 8, 12–13, 15, 23, 112, 254, 286
guest books, 64
guest lists, 106, 112, 137–69
   auxiliary guests and, 152–66
   newly recognized relatives and, 141–42
   problematic candidates and, 139–43
   problematic cases and, 150–52
   problematic invitations, 143–50
   singles and, 156–57
   troubleshooting and, 166–69
   wedding size and, 137–38
guests, 2–3, 8, 68
   abuse of, 10–11
   attire for, 73, 205, 274
   bad behavior and, 277–81
   couples as, 152–55
   estimating expenses and, 11–12
   financial frankness and, 77

guests (*continued*)
    honeymoon donations by, 31, 75, 134,
        199, 273
    obligations of, 229–30, 253
    and presents, *see* presents
    substitutes for, 168–69
    uninvited, 147–48, 166–68
    wedding attire for, 73, 205, 274

handwritten invitations, 20, 179, 214
hats, 93
home purchase donations, 75, 79–80,
    236
honeymoon registries, 63, 233–34
honeymoons, 31, 105
    donations toward, 31, 75, 134, 199,
        273
    as family vacation, 121–22
honorifics, 182–83
host-yourself invitations, 178–79

informal weddings, 251–52
invitations, xii, 14, 23, 25, 71, 286
    accepting, 197–98
    addressing of, 191–92
    assembly of, 190–92
    assignment cards and, 189
    to co-workers, 163–66, 172
    deceased parents and, 182
    declining, 186–88, 198–200
    donations suggested in, 75, 76, 176
    e-mail, 26, 174, 204, 206
    engraved vs. handwritten, 20, 179,
        208–17
    envelopes for, 190–91, 192, 206, 207
    examples of engraved and handwrit-
        ten, *208–17*
    failure to respond to, 185, 186–87,
        203–4
    far-flung, 143
    to former lovers, 142–43, 199–201
    "and guest" designations, 31, 32, 153–
        55, 275–76
    honorifics and, 182–83
    "host-yourself," 178–79
    informal, 179–80
    invalidation of, 148–50

    mailing of, 192
    naming the hosts on, 180–81
    to newly recognized relatives, 141–42
    "no gifts please" on, 61, 219, 235
    to old friends, 150–51
    open, 146–47
    planning and, 106–7, 108
    problematic, 143–50
    "for professional reasons," 164–65
    reception-not-included, 27
    registry cards and, 188
    reneging on, 202
    response cards and, 185–88, 205–7
    same-sex couples and, 143–44
    to second weddings, 145–46
    self-addressed fill-in cards and, 3
    stay-away, 145
    traditional, 6, 181
    troubleshooting and, 203–7
    unborn babies and, 157–58
    verbal, 69
    Web sites and, 12, 170–72, 173–74

"Jack and Jill" parties, 74
Jewish weddings, 256, 260

limousines, 13

maids of honor, 23, 54–55, 123–25, 204,
    241, 247
marriage licenses, 112
master of ceremonies, 71, 88, 120
matron of honor, 123–25, 241, 271
menus, 12, 68, 258–59, 264–66
ministers, 29, 48, 94
Miss Manners on Weddings (Martin), xi
money bags, 74, 79, 80–81
money trees, 62, 223
mosques, 94
mother of the bride, 89, 117–18
    at church weddings, 124–25
    relatives and friends of, 139–40
mother of the bridegroom:
    disapproving, 111–12
    friends and relatives of, 140–41
music, 108, 120, 271–72
"My Day," weddings as, 66–73, 287

name changes, 194–95
neighbors, 152
newspaper announcements, 46
night before the wedding, 253–55

officiants, 88, 112, 122, 251, 252
open-ended relationships, 34–35

paper (and electronic) work, 170–207,
    208–17
paraphernalia, useless, for weddings,
    119–20
parental dinners, 254–55
parents:
    bridegroom's parents' duties, 112–13
    bride's parents' duties, 107–8, 121
    deceased, 182
    divorced, 68, 112–13, 114, 180, 181,
        257–58, 261, 263
    elopement and, 5, 15–19, 29
    as financial backers, 5–6, 7–8, 23, 67,
        68–69, 71, 119, 121
    multiple, 181–82
    at receptions, 272–73
    sex change of, 183–84
    unmarried, 108–9
    wedding plans and, 23, 24–25, 30–32
parents-in-law, 29
parties, 11
    bachelor, 112, 254, 255
    bachelorette, 50, 204, 254, 255
    for children, 161
    engagement, 50–53, 74
    "Jack and Jill," 74
    post-honeymoon, 141, 145
    pre-wedding, 50–55, 254–55
party favors, 3, 269–70
pastors, 94
performing at one's own wedding, 98
"personalization," xi–xii, 4, 69–71
pets at weddings, 155–56
photography and photographers, 29, 114,
    120, 260
    "candid pictures" and, 4
place card holders, 119
planning, 99–136
    attendants and, 123–33

expenses and, 119–23
    family considerations and, 107–18
    proper procedure and, 103–6
    troubleshooting and, 134–36
    upside-down, 106–7
post-honeymoon parties, 141, 145
prenuptial contracts, 57–59
presents, xiii, 2, 3, 12, 218–50
    as admission tickets, 89, 221–22
    cake in lieu of, 86–87
    cash donations as, 2, 3, 74, 75–76,
        78–80, 222–23
    ceremonial opening of, 63–64
    charitable donations as, 83–84, 223,
        234–36, 244, 269–70
    destination weddings and, 107
    donations in lieu of, 84–85, 122–23,
        176, 230, 245–47
    donations toward home purchase as,
        75, 79–80, 236
    donations toward honeymoon as, 31,
        75, 134, 199, 273
    engagements and, 46–47, 51–53,
        60–61, 224
    guests' obligations and, 229–30
    for host and hostess, 52–53
    household items as, 219–21
    inappropriate behavior and, 71–72
    listing desirable items and, 4
    "no gifts, please," 61, 219, 235
    non-givers of, 81–83
    registries for, see bridal registries; hon-
        eymoon registries
    returnability of, 227–28
    second weddings and, 22, 219
    for showers, 54, 55–57
    thank-you letters for, xiii, 13, 64–65,
        108, 119, 195, 226, 230, 237–50, 242
    troubleshooting and, 229–37
    unacknowledged, 237, 246–47
    when to open, 226, 253
    when to send, 225–26
previous marriages, offspring from,
    91–92
programs, printed, 90
proposals of marriage, 11, 33–34, 36–40
    by women, 39–40

receiving lines, 110, 111, 117, 120, 126, 140, 260–61, *261*, 275
    protests against, 263–64
    order of, 261–63
receptions, xii, 18–19, 27, 88, 105
    boycotting, 111–12
    bridegroom performance at, 98
    cash bars at, 266–67
    children's table at, 282
    cleaning up after, 284
    at country clubs, 205
    dance order at, 114, 117, 272–73
    delayed bridal couples and, 259–60
    after elopements, 16, 18
    leftover food at, 278–79
    menus for, 258–59
    money bags at, 79, 80–81
    money gifts for, 75
    music at, 120, 271–72
    open bars at, 268
    seating arrangements at, 109, 257–58
    toasting at, 108, 110, 117, 125–26, 270–71
    when to leave, 261, 283–84
recessionals, 13, *257*
re-enacted weddings, 20–21
registries, *see* bridal registries; honeymoon registries
registry cards, 188
rehearsal dinners, 140, 270
rehearsals, 108, 254
response cards, 185–88
ring bearers, 118, 126, 133
rings:
    engagement, 34, 37, 39, 40, 42–45, 46, 49–50
    wedding, 15, 122, 126
rituals, 16
rubbernecking, 258
same-sex couples:
    acknowledging announcements of, 195–97
    as guests, 151-52, 276–77
    guests' attitudes toward, 47–48, 59–60, 143–44
    presentation of, 23

soliciting donations for, 223,
    wording changes to ceremonies of, 252,

save-the-date cards, 119, 148–49, 170, 174–75
"scripted" weddings, 90–91
seating arrangements, 109, 255–58, 268–69
second spouses, 7
second weddings, 21–23, 44, 118, 125, 145–46, 219
show business weddings, 87–98, 173–74, 252
showers:
    baby, 54, 55
    bridal, 8, 11, 50, 51, 54–57, 61–64, 113–14, 188, 204
"sponsored" weddings, 77–78
stepparents, 113–17, 183, 184, 280–81
synagogues, 94

tattoos, 127
thank-you letters, xiii, 13, 64–65, 108, 119, 195, 226, 230, 237–50, *242*
"theme" weddings, 12, 69, 71, 73
tissue paper, 190
toasts, 108, 110, 117, 125–26, 270–71
tradition, 4
    discarding, 27
    gender roles and, 23–25, 240
    "giving away" the bride, 25, 115–16, 118
    invitations and, 6, 181
    money bags and, 80–81
    night before the wedding, 254
    proposals of marriage and, 37–39
    retrieving of the garter and, 105–6
    seating arrangements and, 255–57
transportation, 108
travel agents, 90
travel expenses, 201, 281–82
troubleshooting, 97–98, 281–84
    engagements and, 59–65
    fund-raiser weddings and, 85–86
    general principles and, 28–32

guest lists and, 166–69
invitations and, 203–7
"My Day" weddings and, 72–73
planning and, 134–36
presents and, 229–37
show business weddings and, 97–98
thank-you letters and, 247–50

Unity Candle, 27
ushers, 118, 125, 133, 257

video cameras, 97–98
videography, 13, 71, 92, 120
virtual showers, 54–55

Web sites, 12, 78–79, 170–72, 173–74
wedding announcements, 176–78,
    193–97
wedding breakfasts, 258
wedding cakes, 86, 120, 283
wedding dinners, 75, 203, 257–58, 265–
    66, 268–69
wedding dresses, xiii, 15, 105
"Wedding Fatigue," 14–15, 171
wedding planners, professional, 2, 7, 69
wedding planning, online, 229
wedding rings, 15, 122, 126
welcome baskets, 3, 119
widows and widowers, 125, 142

7/22